The Compl

Green Building and Remodeling Your Home

Everything You Need to Know Explained Simply

Martha Maeda

THE COMPLETE GUIDE TO GREEN BUILDING AND REMODELING YOUR HOME: EVERYTHING YOU NEED TO KNOW EXPLAINED SIMPLY

Copyright © 2011 Atlantic Publishing Group, Inc.

1405 SW 6th Avenue • Ocala, Florida 34471 • Phone: 800-814-1132 • Fax: 352-622-1875

Website: www.atlantic-pub.com • E-mail: sales@atlantic-pub.com

SAN Number: 268-1250

Library of Congress Cataloging-in-Publication Data

Maeda, Martha, 1953-
  The complete guide to green building & remodeling your home : everything you need to know explained simply / by Martha Maeda.
     p. cm.
  Includes bibliographical references.
  ISBN-13: 978-1-60138-364-8 (alk. paper)
  ISBN-10: 1-60138-364-9 (alk. paper)
  1. House construction. 2. Dwellings--Remodeling. 3. Ecological houses. I. Title.
  TH4860.M34 2011
  690--dc22
                         2011011088

PROJECT MANAGER: Amy Moczynski
INTERIOR LAYOUT: Antoinette D'Amore • addesign@videotron.ca
PROOFREADER: Andrell Bower • bowera@gmail.com
COVER DESIGN: Meg Buchner • meg@megbuchner.com
BACK COVER DESIGN: Jackie Miller • millerjackiej@gmail.com

Printed in the United States

Printed on Recycled Paper

690.

Chapter 10: Green Interior Design 239

Chapter 11: Green Renovation for Existing Homes 251

Chapter 12: Certification and Financing 273

Conclusion

Appendix A: Load Analysis Worksheet for Solar or Wind Electricity System

Appendix B: Acronyms Used in the Book

Appendix C: Helpful Websites

Appendix D: Green Building Glossary

Bibliography

Author Biography

Index

Introduction

The modern concept of "green building" has its roots in the environmentalism movement of the 1960s and the oil shortages of the 1970s, when energy efficiency became a priority. During the 1970s, many federal, state, and local energy codes and regulations were enacted to encourage building energy-efficient homes and commercial buildings. Green building became its own industry during the 1990s. The American Institute of Architects (AIA) formed the Committee on the Environment in 1989 and published the Environmental Resource Guide in 1992. The first local green building program was introduced in Austin, Texas in 1992, offering rebates, technical assistance, and free publicity to developers who incorporate "green" features into homes and other structures. In 1998, the U.S. Green Building Council (USGBC) launched its Leadership in Energy and Environmental Design (LEED) program to certify green buildings. In 2004, the Green Building Initiative introduced the Green Globes™ certification program in the United States. Green building is expected to become a $135 billion industry by 2015.

A green home conserves energy and water, minimizes waste, and provides a wholesome living environment for its occupants. This can be accomplished, on a small or large scale, through a variety of design and building practices, selecting building materials and technologies, and implementing "green" habits. The scope of your green project will be defined by the available financial and physical resources and by your priorities. If you are not building a new home or planning a major renovation, there are many ways

to make your house greener, including upgrading your air conditioning system, switching to energy-efficient light bulbs, installing a solar energy system, and using native plants for landscaping.

This book introduces the principles of green home building and design. You will learn about energy efficiency, passive heating and cooling, alternative energy systems, natural lighting, nontoxic building materials, and water conservation. You will also learn how to select "green" contractors and other professionals, the legal aspects of green building contracts, and how to get financing for a green home project. Chapter 9 includes an overview of green building materials and tells you where to find green products for the interior of your home. The final chapter discusses how you and your family can live a greener lifestyle and lay the foundation for a green future.

Green building is a complex science, and a book like this cannot cover every topic in detail. Throughout the book and in the appendices, you will be directed to resources where you can find additional information. Several federal agencies and organizations including the Environmental Protection Agency (EPA) and the U.S. Green Building Council (USGBC) offer online guides for green building. You can also learn a great deal from the green building professionals such as architects, landscapers, and solar contractors who will be working with you on your project.

Building green is not a technique; it is a philosophy. Whether you are concerned about the environment on a global scale or simply trying to build the best possible home for your family and yourself, you are thinking green. A green home has very low energy bills, is built to last for decades without needing expensive repairs and replacement parts, and is a healthy, safe, and comfortable place to live. If everyone built green, there would be a significant worldwide reduction in greenhouse gas emissions, the rate of deforestation, and the loss of biodiversity. As you read this book, you will find your horizons expanding, and you will begin to think about your life in a new way. Have a pleasant and enjoyable journey!

What is Green?

The basic theory of green building is very simple: any building construction should be done in a way that supports the natural cycle of life and its systems. Although it is almost impossible for human beings to live and work without having some negative effects on the environment, green building strives to minimize that impact as much as possible by using processes, designs, and products that do not deplete resources, disturb ecosystems, or disrupt natural life rhythms. Some green building practices seek to have a positive impact on the environment by contributing to regenerating resources. Green design is sensitive not only to the environment, but to the life rhythms of the people who will live or work in a building. It aims to maximize comfort and provide sunlight, fresh air, and protection from pollution and noise.

The concept is simple, but the practice of green building can become complicated. Green building encompasses three objectives: energy efficiency, conserving resources, and creating a healthy indoor environment for the building occupants. In practice, these objectives sometimes counteract

each other; for example, a highly energy-efficient air conditioning system might contain components that cannot be recycled when the system ceases to function. Some trade-offs are inevitable in selecting materials and technologies for a green project. The choices that must be made are unique to each green building project because they are determined by many factors, including climate and geographical location, the physical characteristics of the building site, local availability of building materials and trained professionals, the needs of the building occupants, and the personality and financial resources of the builder.

Green Building Basics

Energy efficiency: A well-designed green home uses as little energy as possible to maintain the comfort of its occupants. Renewable energy is used whenever possible. Energy efficiency not only saves on utility bills, but it also reduces greenhouse gas emissions and air pollution because less fossil fuel is burned.

Conservation of resources: Conventional construction consumes large amounts of water, wood, cement, metal, and plastics. Using alternative building materials made of recycled or renewable content, and more durable components that do not have to be replaced, reduces waste. Green homes use fixtures and appliances such as low-flow showerheads, faucets, and toilets and ENERGY STAR dishwashers and washing machines to conserve water. Low-volume irrigation systems, rainwater collection systems, wastewater treatment systems, and hot water recirculation systems also save water. Traditional suburban lawns consume excessive amounts of precious water and fertilizer and displace native species. "Green" landscaping preserves habitat, incorporates native plants, and uses less water.

Durability: Many conventional homes are built with products that will not last a long time, such as shingle roofs that must be replaced every 12 to 25 years. Faulty construction and inattention to detail lead to moisture leaks that cause premature deterioration of walls and sidings. Green homes are built to last and are easy to maintain and repair.

Indoor air quality: The air inside a home often contains spores and allergens from mold and mildew caused by water leaks and poorly designed heating and air conditioning systems; dust and particles from air ducts; polluted air drawn into the house from outside or from a garage or basement; and toxic chemicals given off by

paints, adhesives, and cleaning products. Toxins including lead, radon, asbestos, and pesticides also contribute to poor indoor air quality. Green building uses nontoxic, low-emitting products, creates an airtight barrier between the interior of a building and the outdoors, and closely monitors the design and performance of ventilation, heating, and cooling systems.

Green building is also called "sustainable building" and "high-performance building" because it aims to be as efficient as possible from design until the building is demolished (in green building, the term is deconstructed) and its remnants are disposed of. Sustainability and high performance translate into lower costs, with the result that some green building practices are now becoming standard for conventional builders.

Conventional building design typically considers only the environmental impact of the finished structure. Green building takes a much wider view and calculates the effect every activity associated with a building has on the environment. Green building considers the impact of new land development on the community, the energy and resources used to manufacture and transport building materials to the site, energy and water use in the building, disposal of waste products, how the building materials and components can be eventually salvaged and reused, and even the pollution generated when occupants of the house drive to work, school, and shopping.

Green Building Concepts

Green building is not just a technique; it is guided by a philosophy that defines the green aspects of a building during design, construction, occupation of the building, and ultimately its deconstruction. The terminology used in green building may seem unfamiliar if you have never been involved in a green building project before. Here are some of the basic concepts of green building:

Sustainability

A primary goal of green building is **sustainability** — using available resources in a way that does not deplete them for future generations and allows their use to continue indefinitely. Green building uses processes,

designs, and products that do not deplete natural resources and, in some cases, that actively contribute to regenerating resources. A sustainable building minimizes its water and energy use, improves the quality of life for its occupants and the community, cuts down on waste, and does not contribute significantly to the depletion of natural resources throughout the entire life of the building.

The terms "sustainable building" and "green building" are often used interchangeably. Sometimes "green building" is used to refer to buildings constructed for environmental reasons, and "sustainable building" to refer to those that are constructed to conserve costs and energy.

Energy efficiency

Energy-efficient design uses the least possible amount of energy to get the desired result. For example, south-facing windows that allow sunlight to warm the interior of a building but prevent heat from escaping will reduce the need for heating in the winter. Natural air circulation helps to cool a building in summer.

A building can be made more energy efficient by using insulation to help maintain the temperature inside the building: sealing cracks and air leaks and using materials that do not conduct heat and cold for window frames. In hot climates, materials that reflect or re-emit absorbed heat are used on roofs and exteriors to keep the interior of buildings cooler.

The amount of energy needed to heat or cool a building can be reduced by using a geothermal system and by installing devices that transfer heat or cold from outgoing air to incoming air.

An energy-efficient product or appliance uses less energy than a conventional product but provides the same service. For example, energy-efficient window air conditioners use about 10 percent less energy than conventional air conditioners but still provide the same quality and level of cooling.

ENERGY STAR®

Products that earn the ENERGY STAR® rating prevent greenhouse gas emissions by meeting strict energy efficiency guidelines set by the U.S. Environmental Protection Agency and the U.S. Department of Energy.

ENERGY STAR, a joint program of the U.S. Environmental Protection Agency and the U.S. Department of Energy, assigns energy performance ratings to buildings and appliances. A building or an appliance that meets EPA energy efficiency requirements is given an ENERGY STAR rating to let consumers know that they are saving resources when they purchase it.

Renewable resources

A **renewable resource** can be replenished naturally at a rate that is greater than the rate at which it is consumed. Wind and solar power are considered renewable sources of energy because wind and sunshine are abundant and natural, and energy from these sources is easily accessible and has the potential to be replenished at a faster rate than it is consumed. Bamboo is considered a renewable building material because it grows rapidly; it reaches a mature height of 75 feet in two months, and its cultivation does not require using pesticides.

Environmentally friendly/ eco-friendly materials and practices

The terms environmentally friendly and eco-friendly refer to products, materials, buildings, and practices that cause little or no harm to the environment and only minimally interfere with natural ecosystems. Straw bales, which are blocks of wheat, rice, oats, and other grain stalks, are an ex-

ample of an eco-friendly building material because these natural materials from leftover agriculture do not require using non-renewable resources for production. Building materials made with recycled content or waste products, such as concrete made with fly ash from coal-fired power plants, and materials that are completely recyclable or biodegradable when they are no longer needed are considered eco-friendly.

Ecological design

Ecologically designed waterfront apartments.

Ecological design uses systems compatible with nature and modeled on natural systems to synergize with the surrounding environment and minimize damage to the landscape. Most conventional buildings are modeled after machines rather than nature and are designed to conform to industrial processes. Ecological design is sometimes referred to as "green design."

Ecological design faces a number of problems, including a dearth of knowledge about how to apply ecology to design. Ecologists understand ecology in different ways; some focus on energy usage while others focus on management processes. Building professionals typically have only a shallow understanding of ecology and follow a long tradition of machine-oriented design. Many natural processes, such as the growth of trees and the decomposition of materials, occur over periods of time that exceed a human lifespan, while man-made processes occur rapidly and at will.

Embodied energy

Raw natural resources, such as limestone, clay, iron ore, sand, gypsum, wood fiber, resins, coal, and petroleum products, are used in building a home. Energy in the form of electricity, diesel fuel, gasoline, wood, coal, or nuclear power is used to manufacture finished products out of these raw materials and construct a house. The cumulative impact of using all these natural resources and energy is not immediately apparent. Embodied energy refers to the total amount of energy expended in acquiring and pro-

cessing raw materials, transporting them to the building site, and installing them in a building. Products with greater embodied energy typically have a greater environmental impact because of emissions from the fossil fuels used to process and transport them. A highly durable product, though, has less environmental impact when you consider that it can remain in use for longer periods than another less durable material with less embodied energy. Also, some products have a much lower embodied energy when they are recycled, which makes them more environmentally sound than a product with less embodied energy that cannot be recycled. Scientific studies of embodied energy have produced databases and software programs that calculate the embodied energy of individual materials and entire buildings. It is sometimes difficult to compare the embodied energy of two similar building materials because there is no accepted worldwide standard or method, but embodied energy should never be ignored when selecting materials for building.

Life cycle

The life cycle of a product, building, or material encompasses every phase of its existence, from its initial creation to its destruction. In green building, cost and sustainability are calculated over the life cycle of a building or material, not just when it is built or purchased. The life cycle of wood floors would include harvesting wood from a forest, manufacturing the wood into a usable product, transportation to the job site, installation, use and maintenance of the product, and ultimately, the disposal of the product when the building is demolished or the flooring is replaced.

Recyclable materials

Recyclable materials are made of various kinds of metal, plastics, glass, paper, or fibers that can be broken down and reused to manufacture a new product — ideally a new version of the same material. Recycling eliminates using energy and resources to create brand new materials and prevents tons of waste from going into landfills. Asphalt is one of the most recyclable construction materials available. Many forms of paper, metal, plastic, and glass are also easily recycled. Whether a material can be recycled is an important factor in determining the greenness of a particular building material.

Reclaimed materials

Reclaimed materials include discarded materials that can be salvaged and used in a new way. Wood from old furniture and buildings can be reused to create new furniture and buildings. Reclaimed materials differ from recycled materials in that they have not been re-processed and made into a new product, but can be used in their original form for another purpose.

House built from pieces of a highway

Big Dig House, SsD
(www.ssdarchitecture.com/works/residential/big-dig-house)

When a portion of Highway I-93 was dismantled for Boston's Big Dig project, civil engineer Paul Pedini thought the steel and concrete should be recycled instead of being thrown away. The result was the 4,300-square foot Big Dig House in Lexington, Massachusetts. The home was constructed using 600,000 pounds of steel and concrete from the highway plus some new materials. The floors and roof are made of concrete slabs, each about 40 feet long and weighing up to 25 tons. The engineering and design firm Single Speed Design saved time and money by using most of the salvaged materials from the Big Dig in the condition in which they were found. The frame was erected in about three days. The materials are capable of carrying much higher loads than an average building, which allowed for an extensive roof garden watered with captured rainwater. Windows placed high in the walls allow light to enter deep into the interior, and strategic overhangs shade the windows from intense summer sunlight. The exterior is covered with cedar siding and glass that leaves the steel tubes and beams exposed. The house cost $645,000 to build and saved $20,000 in demolition and dumping costs. As a prototype, the house demonstrates how obsolete roadways could be dismantled and used to construct schools and other public buildings.

Closed loop material cycle

Closed-loop material cycle (CLMC) refers to a construction project employing materials and building elements that can later be recovered and infinitely recycled through natural or industrial processes. Today, much of the debris from demolished buildings ends up in landfills, even though it contains some elements that could potentially be reused. One goal of the

green building movement is to develop building materials that can be completely recycled when the building reaches the end of its life.

Deconstructability

The concept of deconstructability is taking hold not only in the building industry, but also in auto and electronics manufacturing. In deconstructability, the goal is to make a product using components that can be removed and reused when the product becomes broken or obsolete. Instead of exploding an unwanted structure or smashing it with a wrecking ball, the building is dismantled piece by piece, and its components are salvaged for reuse in another building or recycled into another product.

Collaborative design

In conventional building, the architect creates a design and then contractors, plumbers, and electricians follow the plans. In green building, the construction team is part of the design process and everyone affected by the project has input from the beginning. All team members combine their expertise to design systems that interact. This maximizes design efficiency and also prevents delays and extra expense when changes have to be made during construction.

Misconceptions About Green Building

The green building industry has expanded and received considerable attention in the media. Though studies have confirmed that green building is environmentally sound and financially viable, critics continue to voice misgivings. Some of the critics' concerns are legitimate, but a number of misconceptions continue to influence the attitude of the public. Some common misconceptions are:

Green building is for environmentalists.

Though environmentalists are advocates for green building, many of the benefits of green building appeal to everyone. Who would not be interested in saving money on utility bills and in living in a low-maintenance home

where the air is free of toxins, allergens, and dust? In most communities, a green home brings a higher price on the real estate market.

Green building costs more.

In conventional building, costs are calculated in terms of initial (upfront) investment in materials and construction. Green building considers the life cycle of each product, material, and process that goes into the building's construction and operation. Although some green materials do cost more than conventional items — for instance, natural wool carpeting is more expensive than conventional synthetic carpeting — the cost of many green building materials is comparable to the cost of conventional materials. Manufacturers of building materials are responding to the demand for environmentally responsible products by bringing down their cost.

A green project design considers the long-term budget for operating and maintaining a building, as well as the initial cost of construction. Today, the initial cost of construction materials, permits, certification, and consultation is slightly more expensive for a green building than for a conventional building. However, using sustainable and durable building materials decreases maintenance costs over the lifetime of the home and will probably pay for the larger initial investment many times over. Over the lifetime of a building, the savings realized by installing rainwater systems and energy-efficient systems such as solar panels or wind turbines outweigh the costs of implementing them.

Vendors of green building products typically quote a **payback period** — the number of months or years it will take for the savings realized by the product to pay for its initial cost. The payback period for many green technologies, such as solar panels, insulation upgrades, and energy-efficient air conditioners, is shortened substantially by federal and state tax deductions.

Green building is too involved.

Green building can seem intimidating to someone who is unfamiliar with it. Green building designs, terminology, and ways of thinking about material usage deviate sharply from concepts of conventional building. In fact, the basic principle of green building is simple: seek a cleaner and more

energy-efficient environment both inside and outside the building. Architects, consultants, and contractors who specialize in green building can help you learn about the process.

If a building cannot conserve energy, it cannot be green.

Energy conservation is only one aspect of being green. If budget restrictions inhibit installing energy saving systems such as solar or wind power, there are many other things builders can do to make a home greener. For example, installing bamboo flooring or formaldehyde-free countertops is considered a green practice but has little to do with energy conservation.

Green buildings are always made from recycled material.

Greenness is not determined solely by the extent to which recycled materials are used. Not all building materials are recyclable, and using only material that has been recycled for a building would be almost impossible. Green building involves many factors, such as orienting your house to best use of solar energy and considering the sustainability of the overall building design. In cases where the recycling process requires a lot of energy or transporting materials over long distances, using a new building material may prove to be greener than using a recycled one.

Green buildings are ugly.

Many people believe that green buildings look ultra-modern, plain, and futuristic, but green buildings can also mirror conventional building designs. Architects and engineers can tailor a building design to meet just about any expectation. Green building features such as natural wool carpets, polished concrete floors, and recycled glass are beautiful in themselves.

There is nothing wrong with conventional building materials and processes.

Many conventional building components have harmful environmental and health effects. Commonly used paints contain high levels of volatile organic compounds (VOCs) that are given off into the air for months and even years. Most trim moldings and wood floors are coated with a chemi-

cal sealant that is hazardous to health. Vinyl tiles can emit harmful dioxins long after they are installed, and some conventional countertops, wood products, and carpets are soaked in formaldehyde, a chemical proven to be hazardous to the environment, people, and animals.

The Evolution of Green Building

Anasazi Indian dwellings in Bandelier National monument.

Some green building practices are thousands of years old. Ancient builders used natural building materials to create comfortable and energy-efficient structures that were adapted to local climates. The Anasazi Indians, who inhabited what is now Arizona, Utah, Colorado, and New Mexico about 2,000 years ago, positioned their homes and villages to optimize natural light and heat from the sun. Their homes were built in tightly knit communities so that resources could be shared. The Anasazi captured rainwater and built using resources found in the immediate area, such as mud, earth bricks, sand, and wood. Ancient Romans positioned their bathhouse windows to face the sun and benefit from its warmth, and the Greeks positioned their dwellings to absorb the sun's warmth. Many of these characteristics have become principles of modern green building: design that makes the most of natural light and warmth; using local building materials; and community planning that minimizes environmental impact.

Rise of environmentalism

Human beings have negatively affected the environment for thousands of years as they cleared forests for agriculture, abandoned arable land after all the nutrients had been leached out of it, overhunted and overgrazed, started forest fires, and in some cases built large cities that depleted water supplies. The Industrial Revolution, which began with the establishment

of the first large factories during the second half of the 18th century, rapidly accelerated the impact of human activity. For a century and a half, the opportunity for growth seemed limitless as one new technology led to another, transportation became more efficient, buildings became taller, and cities grew larger. There was a general attitude that wilderness existed to be conquered and developed and that progress could be measured by growth in the number of cities and factories.

During the second half of the 19th century, social activists in the United States and Europe began to agitate against unhealthy working and living conditions in cities and industrial areas, and laws were passed to protect workers and to ensure clean drinking water and adequate sanitation. In the United States where timber barons had made fortunes cutting down large tracts of forest and selling the wood, a few conservationists began to speak out about the need to preserve wilderness areas. Ralph Waldo Emerson and Henry David Thoreau wrote about the appreciation of nature. In 1851, a California businessman named George Gale inadvertently drew international media attention to the issue of conservation when he cut down a 2,500-year-old sequoia tree known as "Mother of the Forest" in order to display a section of its bark in a traveling sideshow. The ensuing public outrage resulted in the establishment of the first federal state park in Yosemite Valley in 1864, followed by Yellowstone National Park eight years later. In 1892, Henry Senger, Warren Olney, and John Muir established the Sierra Club to promote the preservation of wilderness areas. Today, the Sierra Club strives, "to practice and promote the responsible use of the earth's ecosystems and resources."

The Forest Reserve Act of 1891 established a U.S. Forest Service and gave the president authority to designate forested public lands as protected areas. During his term in office, Theodore Roosevelt increased federal land reserves to almost 200 million acres and established federal control over the building of dams and irrigation projects. In 1916, The National Park Service Organic Act established a National Park Service in the United States.

Growth of Energy Consumption in the United States

The introduction of affordable automobiles and electric power caused energy use in the United States to jump from 100 million Btu per person at end of 19th century to 214 million Btu per person in 1949. A Btu (British thermal unit) is the amount of heat required to raise 1 pound of water 1 degree Fahrenheit at one atmosphere pressure, equal to 251.997 calories.

Energy consumption increased steadily to a peak of 359 million BTU per person in 1978 and 1979. In 2009, the U.S. consumed 308 million Btu of energy per person, 44 percent above the 1949 rate. In 2009, total U.S. energy consumption was 94,578,267 billion Btu; 7,743,759 billion Btu of that was from renewable energy sources.

During the era of prosperity that followed the Great Depression and World War II, suburbs and urban sprawl arose around U.S. cities. Fertilizers and pesticides came into widespread use, and air conditioning made it possible to live and work comfortably even in hot and humid climates. However, there were alarming signs of an environmental crisis. A suffocating blanket of smog covered Los Angeles (1954); in 1952 a "London fog" killed 4,000 people in four days; in 1948 an atmospheric inversion in which high temperatures in the upper atmosphere prevented cooler, polluted air on the ground from circulating temporarily raised the death rate in Donora, Pennsylvania, by 400 percent; in 1953, smog killed between 170 and 260 people in New York. In response, the National Air Pollution Control Administration (NAPCA) was established in 1955 under the Department of Health, Education, and Welfare (HEW). A predecessor to the Department of the Interior's Water Quality Administration (FWQA) was established in 1948 to deal with severe water pollution problems including untreated sewage and industrial waste, dying rivers and lakes, and scalding water poured directly into streams and rivers.

Environmentalists began to predict a global disaster unless public attitudes toward natural resources changed. In *A Sand County Almanac*, published posthumously in 1949, ecologist Aldo Leopold suggested that human beings have an ethical responsibility to live in harmony with the natural

world. *Silent Spring*, published by Rachel Carson in 1962, carefully documented the dangers of the pesticide DDT and led to its use being banned in the United States in 1972. This book made the public aware that toxins and pesticides are health hazards.

In 1969, biologist Paul Ehrlich published *The Population Bomb*, which discussed the effects an expanding population has on the environment. The same year, a group of scientists published *The Limits to Growth*, which discussed the effects of human activity on the environment. In May 1969, Secretary General U. Thant of the United Nations declared that the Earth had only ten years to avert environmental disaster; the next month, he placed most of the responsibility for this catastrophe on the United States.

EPA building in Washington D.C.

In 1970, President Nixon signed The National Environmental Policy Act (NEPA) establishing a Council on Environmental Quality (CEQ) and requiring federal agencies to prepare Environmental Impact Statements for any major project that might potentially have environmental consequences. Later that year, the Environmental Protection Agency (**www.epa.gov**) was established to police air, water, and solid waste pollution.

"A thing is right when it tends to preserve the integrity, stability, and beauty of the biotic community. It is wrong when it tends otherwise."

Aldo Leopold, *A Sand County Almanac*

Energy Crisis of the 1970s

The United States experienced a wake-up call when worldwide oil shortages led to two energy crises during the 1970s. Suddenly it became apparent that the United States would be competing with other large economies for a limited and dwindling resource. In October 1976, physicist Amory Lovins published an article in the journal *Foreign Affairs* called "Energy Strategy: The Road Not Taken." Until then, energy conservation had not been considered as a serious strategy for reducing fossil fuel consumption. Government policymakers began to make energy conservation a priority.

In 1978, Congress passed the National Energy Act (NEA) to reorganize a disjointed national energy policy. The NEA created energy efficiency and conservation programs, alternative fuel programs, tax incentives, and regulatory and market-based initiatives. Many of the regulatory initiatives have since been abandoned, but the NEA included important components that became the basis for today's clean energy incentives. Part of the NEA, the Public Utility Regulatory Policy Act (PURPA), mandated local utilities to pay their customers for excess electricity generated by their solar and wind systems.

In the late 1970s, President Jimmy Carter announced a plan to conserve energy and pursue renewable energy sources such as solar power. The U.S. government became increasingly involved in the green building and energy conservation movement, motivated by the compelling need to reduce dependence on fossil fuels and the carbon emissions resulting from their use.

Emergence of Green Building Guidelines and Regulations

Any product or building can claim to be "green," but as the movement for sustainable building began to expand during the 1980s, it became clear that official standards are needed to certify that a building is truly energy-efficient and environmentally sound. The first certification system, the Building Research Establishment's Environmental Assessment Method (BREEAM), was established in 1990 in the United Kingdom to measure

the sustainability of new commercial buildings. The Leadership in Energy and Environmental Design (LEED) program was introduced in the U.S. in 1994 by the U.S. Green Building Council.

In 2004, the Green Building Initiative (GBI) introduced the Canadian Green Globes rating system to the United States. In 2005, the American National Standards accredited GBI as a standards developer. LEED and Green Globes certifications are both currently used in the United States.

In 2005, the National Association of Home Builders (NAHB) published the *NAHB Model Green Home Building Guidelines*. The *Guidelines* are voluntary. They cover six areas including lot preparation and design; resource efficiency; energy efficiency; water efficiency and conservation; occupancy comfort and indoor environmental quality; and operation, maintenance, and homeowner education, and can be customized to reflect local geographic and climate conditions. The NAHB National Green Building Program (NAHB Green) (**www.nahbgreen.org**) launched in 2008 includes an online scoring tool and a wealth of educational tools and resources for homebuilders and homebuyers. In addition, many city building codes incorporate sustainable building standards, and there are more than 50 state and city green home building initiatives in the United States.

Other building certification programs include CASBEE (Comprehensive Assessment System for Built Environment Efficiency, Japan), Green Star (Australia), BREEAM Gulf, and Evaluation Standard for Green Building (China).

Conclusion

Green building is a simple concept, but its implementation often involves complex trade-offs to achieve several objectives. A green home project strives for energy efficiency, durability, reduction of waste, an excellent indoor environment, and minimal impact on the environment. This is accomplished using a variety of building materials, technologies, and building practices. Every green building project is unique because the design and choice of materials are determined by the physical characteristics of the

individual site, local availability of materials and expertise, and the needs of the building owner.

Many green building practices are becoming standard for all construction and are now part of state and local building codes. Federal, state, and local governments have invested substantially in promoting green building because of its potential to reduce the demand for energy. The green building industry is expanding rapidly, and manufacturers are responding to the demand by increasing production and lowering the costs of green products, and revolutionary new products are regularly introduced to the market. Conventional builders are rapidly adapting to these new products and technologies.

Why Build Green?

he reasons for building a green home or making your home greener are compelling. Many green homeowners are concerned about the environment and are deeply committed to reducing their personal consumption of precious natural resources. Even if you are not an environmentalist, building green makes sense. Many elements of green building design can be implemented for little or no extra cost compared to conventional building techniques. A green home realizes substantial savings on energy bills and maintenance. Green building is becoming increasingly popular and, depending on the area where the home is located, a green home sells up to 25 percent more than a conventional home. In many areas, tax credits and financial incentives are available to homeowners who build green homes or add energy-efficient upgrades. As of September 2010, green building legislation and initiatives were present in 12 federal agencies, 33 states, and in 384 localities.

Everyone has heard horror stories about Chinese drywall and toxic mold making homes uninhabitable, but many common building materials and household furnishings release harmful chemicals into the air, and moisture

from poorly designed and maintained heating and air conditioning systems often results in the growth of mold and mildew. A green home design ensures that you and your family breathe clean air and are not exposed to harmful toxins. McGraw-Hill Construction's report, *Green Outlook 2011: Green Trends Driving Growth*, found that green buildings represent 25 percent of all new construction activity, and predicted that green building (residential and commercial combined) will become a $135 billion market by 2015. This chapter reviews some of the reasons for this rapid growth.

Global Concerns

World population mushroomed from about 500 million in 1550 to 2 billion in 1930, 3 billion in 1960, and 6.6 billion in 2007. By 2025, it is projected to reach 8.5 billion. An ecological footprint is the amount of land needed to provide the resources that support a specific population or a human activity. The average **ecological footprint** of a North American (the amount of land needed to provide water, food, fiber, waste assimilation, and disposal) is about 12 acres. Five times the surface area of the Earth would be needed to give every person in the world the lifestyle of a North American. In order to provide basic necessities for all the world's population, people living in highly developed nations will have to reduce their individual consumption of natural resources.

Consumption and waste in the U.S.:

- About 8 percent of energy used in the United States goes to heating, pumping, and treating water, according to the EPA. Implementing alternative, greener, and more sustainable systems to treat, pump, and heat water alone could have a significant impact on energy consumption.

- Debris and waste from the construction and demolition of buildings equals approximately 160 million tons per year. The construction, demolition, renovation, and use of buildings generate about two-thirds of all non-industrial solid waste in the United States.

- In the United States, impervious surfaces, such as roofs and paved parking lots, that prevent rainwater and melted snow from soaking into the ground make up an area nearly as big as the state of Ohio. Thirty-five percent of rainwater runoff is due

to roofs of offices, homes, stores, and patios, according to the EPA. The result of excessive runoff is flooding, erosion, and water contamination from pesticides and other chemicals.

• On average, more than 250 million tons of garbage and waste, including construction waste, is generated in the United States each year. Most of this goes to landfills and is not recyclable.

Greenhouse gases

Greenhouse gases are chemical compounds that trap heat in the Earth's atmosphere by absorbing the energy radiated when sunlight striking the earth's surface is reflected back into space. Some greenhouse gases including carbon dioxide, water vapor, nitrous oxide, and methane, occur naturally and are emitted by both by natural processes and human activity. Others, such as hydrofluorocarbons, perfluorocarbons, and sulfur hexafluoride, are synthetic greenhouse gases emitted from a variety of industrial processes. These are sometimes referred to as High Global Warming Potential gases ("High GWP gases").

If some greenhouse gases did not exist, the Earth would be very cold. Without them, temperatures on the Earth's surface would be about 60 degrees F lower than they are now, and life as we know it would not be possible. Over time, if atmospheric concentrations of greenhouse gases remained relatively stable, the temperature of the Earth's surface would stay roughly constant. Scientific evidence indicates, however, that human activity during the past century has exponentially increased the presence of greenhouse gases in the atmosphere, contributing to a rise in global average temperature and related climate change. Most of these greenhouse gases, primarily carbon dioxide and methane, have been emitted through the burning of fossil fuels.

Most people are aware that carbon dioxide emissions from automobiles, airplanes, and trains have a serious negative effect on our environment, but few realize the extent of the environmental damage caused by buildings. In 2007, buildings were responsible for 38.9 percent of total carbon dioxide emissions in the United States. Commercial buildings contrib-

uted 18 percent, and residences contributed 20.8 percent of total carbon dioxide emissions.

Green building seeks to harvest energy in a responsible manner and create sustainable products without emitting harmful greenhouse gases or other byproducts. At the end of their life cycle, sustainable products can be recycled and used to manufacture new versions of themselves.

> ## Calculate greenhouse gas emissions for your household
>
> The online Environmental Protection Agency (EPA) Household Emissions Calculator (www.epa.gov/climatechange/emissions/ind_calculator.html) estimates your personal or family's greenhouse gas emissions. It suggests what you can do to reduce your greenhouse gas emissions, energy use, and waste disposal costs and calculates how much you can save (in dollars and emissions). You will need your most recent electricity and fuel bills.

Fossil fuels

Many traditional building practices consume resources that are finite, such as coal and oil. Coal, which provides more than a quarter of the world's energy, was formed as accumulated plant remains deposited 360 to 286 million years ago during the Carboniferous Period were buried and subjected to intense heat and pressure. Oil generates 40 percent of the world's commercial energy. Oil and natural gas formed when the remains of marine organisms that lived around 300 million years ago were trapped under sediments on the ocean floor and subjected to similar heat and pressure. Fuels that formed over hundreds of millions of years cannot be replenished

Coal Plant

once they are used up. Scientists estimate that the world's coal reserves will be depleted in 155 years. Over the past 50 years, rapid population growth and industrial expansion has caused a seven-fold increase in the global demand for oil. The demand for oil is generally expected to continue growing at

an average annual rate of 1 to 2 percent. The world has already consumed almost half the total amount of conventional oil that most experts estimate will ever be available. It is generally predicted that world oil production will begin to decline by 2020, and even the most conservative scientists believe the decline will begin before 2030.

Many people are concerned about human dependence on fossil fuels, not only because they are nonrenewable, but also because the extracting, transporting, and consuming these fuels create environmental hazards and requires using energy. Competition for access to these resources causes wars and political strife. Extracting oil and natural gas from the ground often results in environmental devastation for people living in the immediate area and releases toxins into the ground and water table. Oil refineries also produce solid waste such as wastewater sludge, which can contain high levels of toxic materials. According to the EPA, constructing large oil-fired power plants has a negative impact on surrounding animal and plant habitats. Coal mining is hazardous, and every year coal miners are injured or lose their lives in mining accidents. There are ethical questions surrounding the equitable distribution of fossil fuels, and the United States' and other developed economies' excessively using resources taken from countries where human rights and the well-being of less-privileged classes are not adequately protected.

Traditional buildings not only use energy generated by burning fossil fuels, but also incorporate materials that are either made of petroleum products or that are manufactured using energy from fossil fuels. Green building practices reduce or eliminate dependence on energy from fossil fuels and use building components made from renewable and recyclable materials.

Global warming and climate change

Global warming is the slow rise of the Earth's average surface, air, and water temperatures. Although global warming has been naturally occurring for thousands of years, it has increased at an alarming rate over the last 100 years. It is now universally accepted that human activities such as burning fossil fuels, which releases greenhouse gases into the atmosphere, manufacturing, cutting down forests, and interfering with waterways have hastened the process. The National Oceanic and Atmospheric Administra-

tion's (NOAA) *State of the Climate Report* and the National Aeronautics and Space Administration's (NASA) *Surface Temperature Analysis* indicate that the average temperature of the Earth's surface has increased by about 1.2 degrees F to 1.4 degrees F since 1900. The resulting changes to our ecosystems threaten our world food supply and the continued existence of many species of organisms. According to scientists, unless we cut greenhouse gas emissions in half by 2050, there will be a global food shortage and many species of plant and animal life will become extinct.

Evidence such as the following indicates global warming is a significant threat:

- The rapid melting of glaciers due to rising temperatures is causing a decrease in populations of animals such as polar bears that depend on these glaciers for food, water, and survival. According to "Global Warming Fast Facts" by National Geographic, Glacier National Park in Montana now has only 20 percent of the glaciers it had 100 years ago.

- An increase in the occurrence and intensity of natural disasters, including wildfires and hurricanes, in recent years may be attributed to changes in temperature that create idiosyncratic weather patterns.

- According to a September 2008 study published by the Proceedings of the National Academy of Sciences, rising sea temperatures have a devastating effect on coral reefs. Coral reef destruction and die-off increased tremendously in 1998, possibly because of harsh weather conditions prompted by rising core temperatures. This included El Niño, a strong, warm ocean current that was very powerful in 1997 to 1998 and was responsible for droughts and higher temperatures in the Pacific, Mexico, and Central America during those years.

Opposition to the concept of global warming

Although there is scientific evidence of accelerated global warming and its potentially disastrous effects on human life and the environment, significant numbers of people still do not believe global warming poses a threat to human life and to the environment. Some of the arguments against the existence of a global warming threat include:

- The urge to reduce consumption goes against the natural development of the human race and the rate at which it is growing and modernizing.

- Global warming is taking place, but it is a natural, nonthreatening event that has been occurring for thousands of years and poses no significant risk to human, plant, and animal life.

- There is little evidence to support the theory that rising temperatures have contributed to severe weather conditions such as hurricanes.

- Even if temperatures do rise, human beings will adjust. There is no evidence to support the theory that increased temperatures will lead to a higher mortality rate.

A December 2009 finding released by the EPA officially recognized that certain greenhouse gases such as carbon dioxide lead to serious short- and long-term illness, including respiratory problems and cancer, and are hazardous to people's health.

Reaction to Global Warming Heats Up

The Kyoto Protocol, a document initially introduced and adopted in Kyoto, Japan, in 1997, seeks to minimize global warming by imposing regulations on greenhouse gas emissions and fossil fuel burning. Nearly 40 countries have signed the protocol and have committed to addressing global warming.

The U.N. Environment Programme (UNEP) recognizes that reducing carbon emissions and energy use in commercial buildings is the fastest and cheapest way to cut back global greenhouse gas emissions and slow climate change. Federal and local governments in many countries offer tax incentives, grants, and low-interest loans to encourage green building.

The time is quickly approaching when green building will be the global standard for construction.

Your Carbon Footprint

The goal of green and sustainable building is to minimize your carbon footprint. Your carbon footprint is a calculation of the amount of carbon dioxide and other greenhouse gases the choices you make every day generate. You can minimize your carbon footprint by adopting green building practices, using renewable energy in your home, and building with green materials that do not deplete natural and nonrenewable resources. You can calculate your carbon footprint using the Nature Conservancy Carbon Footprint Calculator. (www.nature.org/initiatives/climatechange/calculator/?gclid=ClmTnI_er6UCFU1m7Aodn0bEbQ)

Energy Savings and Return on Investment

The average household spends at least $2,000 a year on energy bills — over half of which goes to heating and cooling. Construction costs for a green home may be about 3 percent higher than for a similar conventional home, but the lower energy bills will make up for that in just a few years. The savings will be even greater as energy costs continue to rise.

Some green building components, such as photovoltaic or wind energy systems, require a significant initial investment that might not pay for itself for two or more decades; tax credits and renewable energy initiatives in many areas help to offset these higher costs. Even if your green home does not incorporate an alternative energy system, substantial energy savings are realized simply through its design and construction. Properly insulating the slab, walls, and roof; using passive heating and cooling techniques; and an energy-efficient heating, cooling, and ventilation system shave hundreds of dollars off your annual energy bills.

The popularity of green building varies from one part of the country to another, but the demand for environmentally friendly and energy-efficient homes is increasing. Depending on the area where your home is located, it could sell for as much as 25 percent more than a comparable conventional home.

According to a report published in *The Appraisal Journal*, the resale value of an energy-efficient home increases by $10 to $25 for every $1 reduction in annual utility bills. EPA/DOE studies indicate that the value of a home increases from $11 to $25 for every $1 reduction in annual utility bills. If you save $100 a month on your electric bill, your home's value could increase by an estimated $18,000 based on the assumption that its value increases $15 for every $1 of annual energy savings. Research by the American Solar Energy Society shows that solar electric systems in California, in particular, increase a home's value and that the increase is often equal to, or more than, the solar system's initial cost. Installing a photovoltaic (PV) system with solar panels that generate electricity for a home adds more to the resale value of a home than upgrading the kitchen or adding a swimming pool.

The ROI Tables on the website of the GreenandSave.com Optimization Service Group, and energy designer and consultant (**www.greenand-save.com/master_roi_table.html**), give detailed estimates of the return on investment (ROI) and payback time for individual green components and upgrades. The company's founder, Charlie Szoradi, reports that utility bills for his green-renovated 1950s four-bedroom home are less than $60 per month, compared to $600 per month for similar homes in his neighborhood.

Indoor Environmental Quality (IEQ) and Health

Excellent indoor environmental quality (IEQ) is one of the primary objectives of green home building. The occupants of a green home should live in a comfortable environment with plenty of natural light, breathe clean air, and never come into contact with toxins, allergens, carcinogens, or harmful chemicals.

Indoor air pollution is among the top five environmental health risks. According to a study by the commonwealth of Massachusetts, indoor air contaminants are responsible for or aggravate half of all illnesses. A national survey conducted by the American Lung Association and released in May 1999 concluded that North Americans spend an average of 65 percent

of their time at home and as much as 90 percent of their time indoors. Though gaseous and particle pollutant levels inside a house are typically two to five times higher than the level of pollutants in the air outside the building, in some buildings they are as much as 100 times higher than those found outdoors. Gases and particles are released into the air by home furnishings, building materials, appliances, pesticides, cleaning products, laser printers, glues and adhesives, hobby materials, and sometimes by the soil beneath the house. Particles and gases are released by burning natural gas in appliances such as gas stoves and dryers and fuels burned in fireplaces and furnaces, as well as by activities such as cooking and smoking. Pollutants in outside air can also enter the home through open windows and vents. Moisture in walls, floors, and ceilings from water leaks and uncontrolled humidity can lead to elevated levels of allergens and mold spores and the growth of dust mites, which need moisture to survive.

> **Particulate** is a general term used for indoor air pollution that consists of various types of particles suspended in the air, such as bacteria, viruses, dust mite feces, pet dander, fungal spores, pollen, particles, and asbestos fibers. Particles such as dust, smoke, and bacteria are often no larger than .3 microns. These tiny particles can get deep into the lungs because they are not easily filtered out by your nose and throat. When inhaled, these particles can cause infectious and allergic diseases.

A person inhales approximately 15,000 quarts of air each day. Children, the elderly, and the chronically ill are especially vulnerable to the effects of indoor air pollution because they are in the home most of the time. Children breathe faster and inhale 50 percent more air per pound of body weight than adults, and pesticides and other chemicals can be more harmful to them because their bodies are still growing. Poor indoor air quality has a detrimental effect on the health of more than 15 million Americans who have asthma and 28 million who suffer from hay fever and other allergies.

Newer homes that have been well insulated and made airtight to prevent the loss of heated or cooled air exacerbate the problem because less fresh air enters the structure. Pollutants become more concentrated in the trapped air. A poorly adjusted air conditioning system in a tightly sealed house may create lower air pressure inside the house, which draws in airborne pollutants such as sewer gases, pesticide residues, and car exhaust from outside.

Bathroom exhaust fans, range hood fans, clothes driers, and central vacuum systems all forcefully expel air from the home, thus causing outside air to seep in through any available openings in building walls, ceilings, floors, doors, windows, and air circulation systems.

Symptoms related to poor indoor air quality

The Aerias AQS IAQ Resource Center website lists the following symptoms of health problems associated with indoor air pollution (www.aerias.org/DesktopDefault. aspx?tabindex=3&tabid=79):

- Headaches
- Nausea
- Runny nose
- Sneezing
- Chest congestion (wheezing, shortness of breath, tightness in the chest)
- Eye problems (dry, itching, tearing, or sore eyes, blurry vision, burning eyes, problems wearing contact lenses)
- Throat irritation, sore throat, hoarseness, dry throat
- Fatigue (unusual tiredness, sleepiness, or drowsiness)
- Chills and fever
- Muscle pain (aching muscles or joints, pain or stiffness in upper or lower back, pain or numbness in shoulder and/or neck, pain or numbness in hands or wrists)
- Neurological symptoms such as difficulty remembering, difficulty concentrating, or feeling depressed, nervous, or anxious
- Dizziness
- Dry skin
- Allergies
- Asthma
- Multiple chemical sensitivity (MCS)
- Hypersensitivity pneumonitis (an allergic inflammatory disease of the small air sacs deep in the lungs caused by hypersensitivity to mold, bacteria, or other allergen particles of small size)

Other negative effects such as cancers or reproductive problems may not manifest themselves until years later.

Outdoor air enters and leaves a house in three ways: infiltration, natural ventilation, and mechanical ventilation. In **infiltration**, uncontrolled outdoor air flows into the house through openings, joints, and cracks in walls, floors, and ceilings and around windows and doors. **Natural ventilation** allows air to move through opened windows and doors. Wind and differences between indoor and outdoor temperatures cause the air movements associated with infiltration and natural ventilation. **Mechanical ventilation** devices include both outdoor-vented exhaust fans like those used in kitchens and bathrooms, and whole-house air handling systems that remove indoor air and distribute filtered and conditioned outdoor air throughout the house. The **air exchange rate** is the rate at which outdoor air replaces indoor air. When the air exchange rate is low, pollutant levels in the house can increase.

Off-gassing

Off-gassing is the slow release of toxins, chemicals, and gases from a material. Off-gassing can cause severe allergies and respiratory problems, as well as other long-term health issues. Many paints used on interior walls continue to release chemicals long after they have dried. "New paint smell" (or the "new carpet smell" when new carpeting is installed) is actually the off-gassing of a product. Walls and siding, cabinets and furnishings, carpets, and wood and vinyl flooring can continue to release chemicals into the air for years after they have been installed.

Volatile organic compounds (VOCs)

New paint and carpet release dangerous VOCs.

Volatile organic compounds (VOCs) are natural or synthetic chemical compounds found in many conventional building materials that can off-gas easily in normal temperatures and air pressures. Some VOCs pose significant health risks, depending

on the type of VOC, level of exposure, and combination with other VOCs. The EPA regulates certain VOCs through the Clean Air Act and Clean Water Act, but many that are not regulated are found in the materials most commonly used in construction.

Follow your Nose

The best way to determine the presence of a VOC is by using your nose. The smell that accompanies new materials such as carpeting, paint, and car interiors, often referred to as "new carpet smell," "new car smell," or "new paint smell," is indicative of the presence of high levels of VOCs that may be toxic.

VOCs found in paint and carpeting, cleaning products, furniture, the toner for printers and photocopiers, and even clothes that have been dry cleaned contribute significantly to indoor air pollution. Studies from the EPA have shown that VOCs can be up to 1,000 times more concentrated indoors than outdoors because of lack of ventilation. Some of the short-term health effects of VOCs include:

- Headaches, dizziness, and nausea
- Fatigue
- Nosebleeds
- Skin irritation

Asbestos

During the late 19th century, asbestos became a popular component of building materials and many other products because of its flexibility, ability to absorb sound, and resistance to damage from heat, electricity, and chemicals. Though manufacturers became increasingly aware of the health risks associated with asbestos

Asbestos roofing is being removed from an old building.

during the 1940s and 1950s, its use did not come under the regulation of the U.S. Occupational Health and Safety Administration (OSHA) until

1972. Asbestos is now banned in 60 countries, including the United States and the members of the European Union.

If you are renovating a home constructed before 1972, you may have to remove materials containing asbestos. In addition to insulation, asbestos was also used for roof shingles, floor tiles, ceiling tiles, piping, flashing, siding, insulation around ducts, pipes and fireplaces, and in vermiculite attic insulation. When crushed, asbestos separates into millions of tiny fibers that cause serious health problems when they are inhaled. Ripping or tearing materials containing asbestos during demolition and construction can release asbestos fibers into the air. If asbestos material is undamaged and unlikely to be disturbed, the Consumer Product Safety Commission (CPSC) suggests it be left alone.

According to the EPA, asbestos causes the following health problems:

Asbestosis: Asbestosis is a lung disease that involves scarring of lung tissue caused by inhaling asbestos fibers. The scarring makes it more difficult for the lungs to absorb oxygen. There is no cure of asbestosis.

Lung cancer: Lung cancer is commonly attributed to asbestos exposure and is responsible for the largest number of deaths from exposure to asbestos. According to the Environmental Working Group — a nonprofit organization dedicated in part to exposing public health dangers — nearly 10,000 deaths a year can be attributed to asbestos, including lung cancer.

Mesothelioma: Mesothelioma is a form of cancer directly linked to asbestos exposure. The rare form of cancer is found most often in the lining of the lungs, abdomen, and heart and can take years to develop after the initial exposure to asbestos. The government is making efforts to prevent children from being exposed to asbestos in schools to decrease the likelihood they will develop a long-term illness such as mesothelioma.

Asbestos is particularly harmful to those who work in the construction industry because they are most likely to work directly with it. Symptoms of asbestos-related diseases may not appear until 15 to 30 years after exposure. The EPA regulates removing asbestos because it can be so dangerous for those who handle it. For this reason, asbestos is referred to as an occupational health hazard.

Through the Clean Air Act and the Toxic Substances Control Act, the EPA bans asbestos in many building and consumer products including the following:

- Insulations, including for boilers, hot water tanks, and pipes

- Spray-on applications "containing more than 1 percent asbestos to buildings, structures, pipes, and conduits unless the material is encapsulated with a bituminous or resinous binder during spraying and the materials are not friable after drying," according to the EPA

- Corrugated paper, rollboard, commercial paper, specialty paper, flooring felt, and any new asbestos product.

Radon

Radon is a tasteless, colorless, odorless, radioactive gas that can cause serious health problems, including lung cancer and other respiratory diseases, if inhaled in large amounts. Radon is a natural gas released by the breakdown of uranium and can be found in soil, rock, and water. Radon gas seeps into homes through cracks or seams in the foundation. It is not harmful in natural outdoor settings but can become extremely harmful in confined spaces with limited ventilation, such as buildings and homes. According to the EPA, radon is the second leading cause of lung cancer deaths in the U.S. and radon exposure accounts for more than 20,000 lung cancer deaths per year.

See page 50 for an EPA map showing areas with potential for elevated radon levels. Zone 3 areas have the lowest potential, but elevated levels of radon have been found in homes in all three zones.

Lead

Lead, a toxic metal most often found in paint, soil, and water, is poisonous in certain forms, particularly to children. In 1971, the Lead-Based Paint Poisoning Prevention Act (LBPPPA) established definitions for lead-based paint and lead poisoning and identified lead-based paint in federally funded housing as a potential hazard. The act was amended in 1973. In 1978,

the Consumer Product Safety Commission banned the residential use of lead-based paint.

Demolition, as well as other renovation activities such as sanding and cutting, can disrupt lead paints and create exposure to lead dust, which is toxic to vital organs such as the lungs, heart, and liver. Exposure can lead to lead poisoning, which can cause serious neurological issues.

Formaldehyde

Formaldehyde, a toxic chemical compound, is used to produce many materials found in the interior of buildings, such as cabinets and flooring. It is also a by-product of combustion and certain other natural processes. It is a known carcinogen and can cause respiratory, skin, and allergy problems. According to the U.S. Institute of Health, in 1987 the EPA recognized that formaldehyde could cause cancer in humans if they are exposed to it for long periods of time or in high doses. The International Agency for Research on Cancer (IARC) subsequently classified formaldehyde as a carcinogen.

The EPA further recognizes the dangers of formaldehyde in manufacturing and building materials. Formaldehyde can be found in dozens of materials used in both the home and the office, including fuel-burning appliances that are not properly vented, such as gas stoves or kerosene space heaters; adhesives used for cabinets and furniture; drapes; floor finishes; paints; and other coating products. Formaldehyde can release dangerous gases for years after it has been initially used. It is used in a variety of ways and in a number of building materials including:

- Wood cabinetry
- Plywood
- Wood paneling
- Textiles and draperies
- Concrete
- Adhesives and glues
- Pressed wood shelving and particleboard containing urea-formaldehyde (UF) resins

Other sources of formaldehyde in the home include cigarette smoking, household products, and using unvented, fuel-burning appliances, such as gas stoves or kerosene space heaters.

Ozone

On hot sunny days, ozone forms close to the ground and can flow into a house through open windows and doors. Inside the house it interacts with other household emissions to form harmful secondary compounds that are absorbed into building materials and then gradually are released into the air. One study found that products containing pine and citrus oils produced formaldehyde and ultrafine particles when elevated levels of ozone were present.

Tight envelope plus ventilation

A green home is built with a **tight envelope** — a foundation and walls that seal out radon gases — and uses both natural and mechanical ventilation to circulate fresh air through the house. If necessary, an air filtering system is used to remove particulates from the air inside the house. Exhaust fans draw off gases from cooking or fuel combustion. During renovation and construction, ductwork is sealed and steps are taken to protect building occupants from exposure to dust and toxins. Low-VOC paints and furnishings and materials that do not contain formaldehyde and other toxins are used for the interior of the home. Air conditioning systems are carefully sized and balanced to avoid excess moisture or humidity in the home, and the home occupants are careful to select nontoxic cleaning and pest control products.

Obstacles to Building Green

Some aspects of green building, such as higher initial costs for construction and materials and the additional time it may take to order and receive supplies, might discourage you from going green. The following are some factors to consider before deciding whether green building is right for you.

There may be a higher initial investment

Some green building projects will cost more initially than conventional projects. If you are building in an area where green building supplies are not readily available, you may have to increase your budget to purchase materials. Though a wind or solar energy system realizes significant savings on energy bills, the initial cost of all its components can be thousands of dollars. An experienced green builder can build a home that meets requirements for LEED certification for about 1 percent more than the cost of building a conventional home. If the builder does not have a thorough knowledge of green building, the cost could be 4 to 5 percent higher. Getting LEED certification for a home can cost between $3,000 and $7,000 in addition to construction costs. Though you can recoup the cost of many green features over time through savings on energy bills, repairs, replacement, and maintenance, you may not feel you have the financial resources now to make the initial investment.

Energy efficiency does not always increase the value of a building.

Building appraisers who provide valuation services do not always see energy efficiency as an added value to the building. The appraisal process is subjective in some ways and can vary from appraiser to appraiser. Appraisers may recognize the importance of energy efficiency but may not have the necessary tools and data to verify that their calculations are accurate. As more builders adopt green building practices, the appraisal process will become more structured, just as the process of LEED certification has done.

Lenders base their calculations on the information submitted by the appraiser. A home that costs more to build because it has green components, such as a geothermal or solar system or a durable roof, may not be appraised at its full value by a conventional appraiser, which would make it more difficult to obtain a mortgage.

Green building may require more planning.

There is no specific way to go green. You will have to consult an architect and possibly an engineer to evaluate what design strategies will work best for you and what materials you will be able to use. You may not be familiar with green manufacturers in your area or know what kinds of materials you can get to fit your budget. Green building can be like putting together the pieces of a puzzle. If this is your first experience with green building, it will probably take longer to create a plan and determine projected costs than it would for a conventional building project. Constructing a green building can take significantly longer if you are seeking LEED certification and do not familiarize yourself with the requirements prior to beginning the process.

It can be difficult to determine what is truly "green."

It can sometimes be difficult to determine which of several possible approaches is "more green." An action that satisfies one principle of green building might have negative effects that violate another principle. For example:

- When renovating an existing building, you will have to decide if it is more green to reuse the previous furniture, carpeting, and flooring — all of which have high levels of VOCs and other toxins — or to throw these materials away, which adds more waste to landfills, and purchase greener materials that will last much longer and be healthier.

- You must choose if it is better to buy bamboo flooring that must be shipped all the way from Asia using a significant amount of fuel and contributing to global warming or to purchase local wood that requires minimal transportation but has been harvested by clearing a forest.

- Is it better to throw out old household appliances that are not energy efficient and replace them with new, energy efficient models to reduce energy consumption, or is it better to keep the old, less efficient appliances and not dispose of them?

Conclusion

The three primary reasons for building green — concern for the environment, energy conservation, and good health — appeal to almost everyone. Even if financial concerns are foremost, the savings energy efficiency generates justify the additional cost of many green technologies and design features. The health risks associated with exposure to some synthetically manufactured building materials are only now being recognized. Many green building requirements are already required by local building codes, and the green building industry has expanded rapidly during the past decade. It seems clear that green building will soon become standard practice.

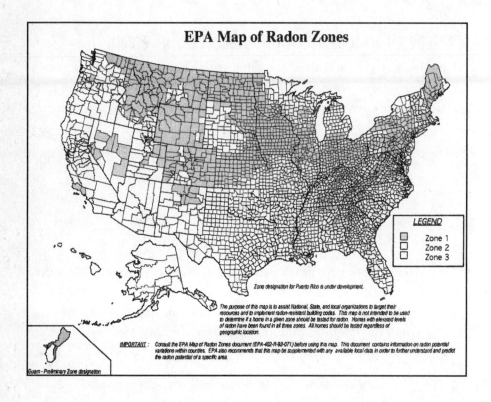

EPA Map of Radon Zones

LEGEND
Zone 1
Zone 2
Zone 3

Zone designation for Puerto Rico is under development.

The purpose of this map is to assist National, State, and local organizations to target their resources and to implement radon-resistant building codes. This map is not intended to be used to determine if a home in a given zone should be tested for radon. Homes with elevated levels of radon have been found in all three zones. All homes should be tested regardless of geographic location.

IMPORTANT : Consult the EPA Map of Radon Zones document (EPA-402-R-93-071) before using this map. This document contains information on radon potential variations within counties. EPA also recommends that this map be supplemented with any available local data in order to further understand and predict the radon potential of a specific area.

Guam - Preliminary Zone designation

Planning and Designing Your Green Home Project

For a conventional building project, an architect typically designs the building, and then a contractor is hired to construct the building according to the architect's plans. During construction, the plans are often altered to accommodate a change in building materials or correct an unforeseen design flaw, which results in delays and additional costs. Plumbers and electricians often have to work around unexpected obstructions, thus increasing their labor costs. A key element of green building is a collaborative design or high performance design process in which everyone involved in the project participates from the beginning: architects, engineers, contractors, tradesmen, and the home's future occupants. The home is designed as an entire system with components that interact with each other to realize maximum energy efficiency and economy of design.

Each green home project is uniquely tailored to suit the geographical location and physical characteristics of the building site, the needs and aspirations of the building occupants, the philosophy of the designer, local materials and services, zoning laws and requirements, and the construction budget. Even when a stock building plan is used or the home is a modular (prefabricated) home, careful attention is paid to how the building is situated on its site, and adjustments may be made to better integrate the

building with its surroundings. There may be a particular feature, such as a spectacular view or old wood salvaged from a nearby barn, that the homeowner wants to emphasize. Your budget will define the scale of your green home and the choice of technologies and materials you use.

Whether you are buying land and building a new home or adding green features to an existing home, the planning and design process is similar. A **green renovation** is a complete makeover that may involve reconstructing some or all of an existing home's architectural features; replacing old equipment, appliances, furnishings, and flooring; installing energy efficient windows and doors; repairing the walls, foundation, and roof and adding insulation; adding alternative energy sources; or changing the landscaping. A retrofit typically involves upgrading some of a home's features or systems with a greener alternative, such as a solar power system or an energy efficient air conditioner. A retrofit or renovation can be done one step at a time as funds, time, and supplies become available. Some green building objectives can be achieved simply by making slight changes to your lifestyle. Whether your project is large or small, it will be guided by the same principles of green building.

Principles of Sustainable Building
- Build in a location that will maximize conservation and minimize destruction.

A new building should be located on a site that will enable sustainability with minimal interference with the natural habitats and ecosystems that surround it. The orientation of a building on the site contributes to its sustainability. The building's orientation also determines how much its interior temperature is affected by wind and external weather conditions, and how storm water runoff is managed. Building on a site that is within an already-existing community is greener than building on previously undeveloped land. Preserving existing vegetation and using native plants for landscaping maintains a habitat for local wildlife and reduces the need for irrigation.

A rustic looking garden shed was built with timber recycled from an old barn.

- Reuse, refurbish, recycle.

Reusing materials not only conserves resources, but it also saves money. If you will be demolishing part of your structure for a remodel, try salvaging items to reuse in your new building. Broken concrete, used tile, and wood from old buildings can be used for flooring, wall facings, architectural features, and outdoor landscaping. Often you can revamp, refinish, and transform items like desks, chairs, and other furniture into completely new-looking products. An interior designer experienced in green design can suggest ways to reuse existing materials.

- Implement systems that will conserve energy and resources.

Green buildings use natural resources such as sunlight, wind, shade, and water to provide heating, cooling, electricity, and interior lighting. Large south-facing windows, light shelves, skylights, and sun tunnels direct natural light to the interior of a building. Water and energy conservation systems include dual flush and low-flow toilets, low-flow water fixtures, hot water recirculation, and heat recovery systems. Capturing and harvesting rainwater and using a gray water system reduce dependence on water from water treatment plants.

- Implement systems that decrease waste.

Simply using energy efficient light bulbs such as compact fluorescent bulbs, as well as energy-efficient appliances and machines, greatly reduce energy consumption and waste. Recycling water, reusing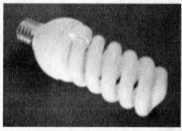
building materials, minimizing scrap and waste during construction, and capturing rainwater all reduce waste. The design of a green home should include efficient methods for disposing of household garbage — space for storing plastic and paper for recycling, and for composting vegetable waste and yard clippings. Finally, consider how various components of the home will be disposed of when the home is deconstructed.

According to the Union of Concerned Scientists, 90 billion pounds of greenhouse emissions can be prevented if every U.S. household replaces just one regular light bulb with an energy efficient light bulb.

- Use natural, sustainable, nontoxic building materials and products.

Using building materials that minimize harmful effects on the environment is perhaps the easiest, most practical, and most affordable method of going green. For example, choose bamboo flooring instead of traditional wood floors. Because bamboo grows back quickly and does not require destroying forests, the impact on the environment is minimal. Use environmentally friendly cleaning products such as phosphate-free laundry detergent. Create a healthy indoor environment by using low- or no-VOC paints or natural finishings on your walls, formaldehyde-free cabinets and natural wool carpets.

A matter of lifestyle: The New American Home

For the past 28 years, The New American Home (TNAH) has been constructed in conjunction with the NAHB International Builders' Show as a showcase for innovative building technologies and the latest building products. Every year, it shows the newest design trends, construction techniques, and materials that builders can use in any new or remodeled home. The home incorporates products donated to the project by members of NCHI, the National Council of the Housing Industry, the leading manufacturers and suppliers for the construction industry. The New American Home 2011 was a custom residence constructed for a specific buyer on three lakeside lots near downtown Orlando, Florida, and involved deconstructing two older homes.

Over the last ten years, green building has become a central theme of the New American Home. In 2000, The New American Home exceeded energy code standards by 18 percent; the 2011 home exceeded them by 70 percent. TNAH 2011 was built to attain "Emerald" status of the National Green Building Standard (NGBS, ICC 700), the highest level of energy efficiency achievable under the Standard. In addition to the most advanced green building technology and construction, it features dynamic aesthetic design, including fountains, pools, and solar elements. The home received the following green building certifications:

- National Green Building Standard, Emerald
- ENERGY STAR certification
- FGBC (Florida Green Building Coalition) Platinum certification
- Florida Yards and Neighborhoods designation
- Florida Water Star designation
- Progress Energy Home Advantage Program

The home incorporates all of the latest green features, including passive design, tankless water heaters, lighting fixtures with LEDs, zoned air conditioning, super-efficient

windows and doors, solar technology, insulation, and low-maintenance water-efficient landscaping. However, the single-family home has an area of 8,000 square feet and four refrigerators. Forty-six percent of the energy use in the home is attributed to lifestyle use. This highlights an important issue: many of the homeowners who desire and are able to afford the latest green technologies do not live energy-efficient lifestyles. All of the energy-efficient features they employ only serve to offset an excessive consumption of energy.

The underlying principles of green building — sustainability through protection of the environment and conservation of natural resources — are only partially served when individuals consume far more resources than they need. Read more about The New American Home (**www.buildersshow.com/generic.aspx?sectionID=1999**).

Establishing Priorities

A green building project begins with the building owner(s) determining the scope of the project and the green features that will be incorporated in its design. The design priorities for every project are not the same. In a hot, arid climate, the priorities would probably be minimal water usage, an energy-efficient cooling system, and using a photovoltaic system to provide electricity. In a cold, wet climate, the priorities might be passive solar heating, storm water management, and natural lighting. Some homeowners want their green home to be a prototype for sustainable construction in their area, or to demonstrate their personal commitment to conservation. If family members suffer from asthma or allergies, a clean and toxin-free indoor environment might be the first priority.

It is helpful to consult an architect or a local contractor with green building experience to learn what green features are feasible for your geographical location and your budget. He or she will be familiar with the technologies and methods used to build other green homes in your area, and may suggest ideas that you have not thought of. You will also find extensive information online, including magazine articles and reviews and photos of green homes. If possible, tour some green homes in your area, and visit showrooms and home improvement stores to see first-hand how various products and materials look and function.

Your Green Home Priorities

The answers to these questions will help you define the objectives of your green project and guide your design and construction team.

Why do you want to build a green home or make your existing home green?

List your motivations for going green, in order of importance.

Where is the building site located?

Your geographical location determines whether certain green features can be successfully implemented in your home. Also, some state and local municipalities and some utilities give tax breaks and incentives for homeowners who install energy-efficient systems and appliances.

What are your family's needs?

How many bedrooms do you need? How many baths? Will the home have a studio or an office? Do family members need space for special hobbies or activities?

What kind of interior layout would be ideal?

Consider the layout of each floor. What kind of spaces do you need? Will you be entertaining? Do children need a play area? Pay attention to acoustics and noise levels.

What kinds of energy systems will be implemented?

Energy systems using solar panels and wind turbines provide clean and renewable energy; effectively reduce your carbon footprint; significantly decrease your electricity costs; and conserve natural resources. However, these systems are not practical in every geographical location. You might not be able to power your entire home with solar or wind energy, but you can install a grid-tie system that supplements your power supply with electricity from a local utility. You can also use solar or wind energy for specific purposes such as heating air or water, or operating a water pump or outdoor lighting system.

What kinds of water, plumbing, and sewer systems will the building utilize?

Water conservation is an essential aspect of sustainable building, especially if you are seeking LEED certification. Will you be getting water from a well or from your municipality water supply? Will you have a septic tank or connect to a sewage system? Do you plan to recycle water from sinks and showers (gray water) or to collect rainwater? Local zoning laws may specify how sewage and storm water run-off must be dealt with, and special permits may be required.

What is your budget for the project?

Some green features may have to be eliminated during the design process if they are too costly or replaced with less expensive alternatives. Are you willing to pay extra for certain features?

Are you going to seek certification for your home?

If you want to seek LEED or Green Globe certification, your project team must consider LEED or Green Globe requirements at every level in order to achieve the maximum number of points. Implementing these requirements may result in additional costs apart from the application and inspection fees.

What green design criteria will you use?

Even if you are not seeking certification, LEED and Green Globe standards still provide thorough guidelines for producing a green building. If LEED or Green Globe standards will not be used, the building owner must outline detailed design criteria for the project team.

What elements will the exterior of the building include?

Are there natural views or landscape features on the site? What type of landscaping do you want? Will there be outdoor areas such as patios, playgrounds, walkways, pools, gardens, or seating areas? How will you irrigate the landscaping? Will there be a garage approached by a driveway or additional parking for guests?

How long do you intend to stay in the home?

Will this be a long-term residence, or will you be selling the house in a few years? Is this your primary residence or a vacation home? Some green features, such as solar electricity systems, take as long as a decade to pay for themselves. If you do not plan to live in the house for more than a few years, or if you live there for only part of the year, you should determine whether you will be able to recover your investment.

What is the resale value of similar green homes in your area?

In some areas, green homes sell for considerably more than comparable conventional homes; in other areas, there is little difference in the price. The market depends on the popularity of green building among local buyers. If you are financing a green project with a mortgage or a loan, know what to expect. Are you willing to pay for improvements if you cannot recover the cost when you sell your home?

Finding Green Professionals and Choosing Your Design Team

Once you have defined your aspirations for your green building project, it is time to find the green professionals who will bring them to fruition. The scope and complexity of your project will determine the kind of professional help you need and the number of people on your green building team. A solar contractor has the know-how and skills to retrofit your home with a photovoltaic energy (PV) system or a solar water heater, and a reputable air conditioning company can install an energy-efficient air conditioner and heat-exchange system, check your ductwork, and upgrade your insulation. Some companies specialize in green retrofits. For a renovation or a new home, the architect is the key figure. Your architect is your representative during the whole construction process; he or she will help you to understand green building, design a structure that meets your objectives, manage builders and contractors, and check to see that everything is being done according to specifications. It is important to choose an architect with whom you can have a strong and trusting relationship.

Role of the architect

- Designer
- Owner's representative and primary point of contact
- Project administration and management
- Bidding and contract negotiation
- Construction administration
- Research and interpretation of building codes, life safety codes, zoning laws, and environmental impact
- Budget management
- Coordinating engineers, landscape architects, interior designers, and other contractors
- Overseeing materials selection
- Acting as the owner's "eyes and ears" on the construction site
- Documentation of the project
- Assistance and representation at public hearings when required

Finding an architect

The following are some online resources you can use to find an architect.

- Find green building architects in your area by searching the online directory of American Institute of Architects (AIA) (**www.aia.org**) and the "Find A Pro" directory on the USGBC's Green Home Guide website (**http://greenhomeguide.com/findapro**).

- Search for LEED-accredited professionals through the Green Building Certification Institute's (GBCI) LEED Professional Directory (**https://ssl27.cyzap.net/gbcicertonline/ onlinedirectory**).

- Search for green professionals on the National Home Builders' Association's *Directory of Professionals with Home Building Designations* (**www.nahb.org/directory.aspx?directoryID=1415**).

- You can also search green websites, magazines, and eco-friendly blogs such as LowImpactLiving.com (**www.lowimpactliving. com/categories**) or Sustainable Sources (**http://directory. greenbuilder.com/search.gbpro**).

- Some areas have their own green professional certification programs and online directories, such as California's Build It Green (**www.builditgreen.org/en/directories/search.asp**) or the Austin Energy Green Building Professionals Directory (**www. austinenergy.com/energy%20Efficiency/Programs/Green%20 Building/Resources/usingDirectory.htm**) in Austin, Texas.

Ask friends and contacts for references, and talk to people in your area who have recently completed similar green building projects. A real estate agent or a manufacturer's representative may be able to suggest someone he or she has worked with. Every architect has unique talent and a personal style. Before deciding on an architect, examine the work of several architecture firms and conduct interviews to get an understanding of each architect's experience, philosophy, and commitment to green building. Explain your vision for your home and see how interested the architect appears to be in your project. Ask to see samples of the architect's work. If possible, visit a

building that is still under construction to see how the site is managed and organized. If you are planning to have your building certified, ask whether the architect has LEED or other certification credentials or has worked on other certified building projects. Ask for references and question them about their experiences during their building projects. Go to the architectural firm's website and read its mission statement. Most sites have photos and information about significant projects the company has done. Do an Internet search using the architect's name to find news articles, reviews, or possible complaints.

Architectural firms range in size from a single architect to more than 100 employees. The average firm employs about ten people. If you are considering a firm with a large staff, be sure to meet and interview the individuals who will be working on your project. No matter how well known and prestigious the architectural firm may be, the success of your project depends on your having a good relationship with your designer and construction manager.

Finding a green contractor

Once you have found an architect, you will need a contractor or construction manager to supervise the building process. Design/build firms combine architects, engineers, and contractors and take responsibility for the entire project from beginning to end. Your architect may be able to recommend a contractor or give you a list of preferred contractors. You can also search for contractors through local professional organizations and through the green building directories mentioned above.

TIP: Search each contractor's name

Type each contractor's name into a search engine and see what kind of results turn up. You will probably find only business information. If your search pulls up notices of legal action against a company, blog entries complaining about a contractor's work or business ethics, or news articles pertaining to complaints, you should seriously consider using a different contractor. You should also look for complaints or comments on the website of your local Better Business Bureau (**www.bbb.org**).

Interview several contractors before making a decision so you have a good understanding of what each one offers. Remember that the cheapest con-

tractor is not necessarily the best. An experienced contractor will be able to save you money on building materials and avoid mistakes and delays.

When interviewing a contractor, ask these questions:

- How long have you had your firm?
- What type of insurance do you have? Are you bonded?
- What types of projects do you prefer to work on?
- How many projects are you working on at any one time?
- What trades do you have on staff and which do you subcontract out? How long have these subcontractors been working with you? Do you have any trade licenses (such as plumber or electrician)?
- Have you ever been the subject of legal action by a client?
- Do you have references? Can I go and see some samples of your work? (If possible, visit a site in progress. Look carefully for the quality of workmanship, neatness, and organization.)
- How do you plan to reduce the amount of building materials, energy, and resources needed for this project?
- How do you plan to organize recycling and waste disposal on the building site?
- What kind of experience do you have with green building?
- Have you attended any green building seminars or workshops? Do you have any certifications?

Ask for proposals, or bids, with itemized breakdowns of the materials and services provided. When comparing bids from several contractors, check carefully to make sure you are comparing the same items; for example, one contractor's price might be lower because he or she uses a lower-quality material or because the cost of waste disposal has been left out. Clarify who is responsible for getting permits and scheduling inspections.

Look for a contractor who has an open mind.

Try to put together a team of tradesmen who are willing to work with others and consider new ideas. An overbearing "expert" who always does things a certain way might miss opportunities to economize by trying new techniques or making slight alterations.

The Charette

Once the project team has been assembled, the green design process begins with a brainstorming session called a **charette**. Everyone involved in the project, including the homeowner(s), architect, contractors, builders, tradesmen such as plumbers and electricians, and any specialists such as landscape architects, solar contractors or HVAC engineers, is assembled in one place. The homeowner(s) and the architect explain the basic plans and the project goals. When everyone understands the homeowner's or builder's priorities and expectations, the plans are reviewed step-by-step, and participants are invited to offer suggestions and ideas for achieving the project's objectives. Goals are set for each objective, and the team determines ways of measuring how well they have been achieved. During the charette, the architect and builder establish a design schedule for the project and identify points at which the designer, builder, and tradesmen will need to collaborate on designing specific areas of the project. For example, the carpenter will have to leave openings in the wall or floor for the plumber's gray water system.

The outcome of a charette should be a set of guidelines and objectives that will guide everyone's decision making throughout the project. A pre-design brainstorming session ensures that everyone understands the builder's objectives and will not undermine them during construction — for example, by substituting a high-VOC paint for a more expensive low-VOC paint. The designer is able to access the expertise of the contractors and make the design as efficient as possible. A solar contractor can calculate how much space is needed on a south-facing roof for solar panels, suggest the placement of architectural features containing PV cells, and request a well-ventilated storage area for a battery backup unit.

A landscaper can suggest ways to collect rainwater, incorporate a vegetated roof or roof garden, or use trees and hedges to cool a house. The HVAC contractor can reduce the size of the air conditioning unit because the home is more energy efficient and recommend locations for vents and ducts.

If you are seeking LEED, NAHBGreen, or Green Globes certification, it is important that everyone on the design and construction team understands the rating system and the certification system so they do not inadvertently lose opportunities to gain points.

Location and Orientation

Crucial decisions made early in the design process, such as the orientation of the building on the site, its size, its shape, and the distribution and purpose of its rooms, have the greatest influence on energy consumption over the lifetime of the building. An energy-efficient home is also a comfortable home; its occupants do not experience extremes of heat and cold, dry air or excess humidity, and they can use natural light during most of the day.

Southern exposure

In the Northern Hemisphere, the south side of a building receives the most sunlight during the day as the sun travels across the sky from east to west (or as the earth rotates around the sun). Large, south-facing windows al-

These large south-facing windows also allow this room to serve as a temporary greenhouse during the winter months.

low sunlight and warmth into a house during the winter, and south-facing walls absorb the most heat. During the summer, south-facing windows must be shaded to keep the house cool. Solar panels must have unobstructed southern exposure in order to work efficiently. Simply orienting your house to take advantage of southern exposure and controlling the amount of solar radiation that enters your house can reduce your energy needs by 30 percent. In climates with harsh winters, patios and outdoor seating areas located on the south side of the home provide sunny outdoor living space even when the weather is cool.

The southern side of the house does not have to face directly south — optimum solar gain can still be achieved if the orientation of the building deviates up to 10 degrees to either side of true south. At 22 degrees from true south, the side of the house still receives about 92 percent of the solar radiation. A deviation of more than 10 degrees can cause overheating in the

summer because the east and west sides of the house are then pointed more directly at the sun during the early and late parts of the day. The sun's rays falling directly on the east and west sides of the building raise the interior temperature several degrees.

True south is not magnetic south

The needle of a magnetic compass does not always point directly to the South Pole. Iron-bearing minerals in the earth's crust cause it to deviate from a true southerly direction, especially in the western United States.

In planning the orientation of your building, use true south and not magnetic south. You can use the shadow cast by a plumb-bob string or the vertical edge of a building to determine true south. A shadow cast by a vertical object at solar noon runs true north-south. Determine the local time that corresponds to solar noon by looking up the times of sunrise and sunset in a current local paper or on a GPS set to your time zone. Solar noon is exactly halfway between sunrise and sunset. The NOAA solar time calculator also gives the local time for solar noon at your location: **www.srrb.noaa. gov/highlights/sunrise/sunrise.html**.

Shape

A building's shape also determines how much solar heat it absorbs and the amount of energy required to heat or cool it. In the Northern Hemisphere, long, rectangular buildings with the long wall facing south absorb the most heat and are more energy-efficient in cold climates. In hot climates, the house should be shaped to minimize exposure to the sun and oriented to take advantage of cooling breezes and natural shade. For example, a house could have a corner or a short wall facing south or a design with a south-facing alcove or indented curve whose sides block sunlight.

Size

A principle of both energy efficiency and resource conservation is consuming only what is needed. No matter how sustainable it is, a 6,000-square-foot house for two people cannot be considered green. A green home design should provide only the space the occupants need, with functional architectural features that allow for efficient cooling and heating and easy maintenance.

U.S. homes becoming smaller

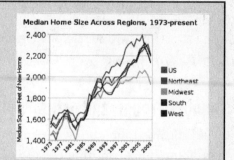

Median Home Size Across Regions, 1973-present

During the 1990s, large (3,000 square feet or more) oversized homes, often referred to as "McMansions," became popular in the United States. Statistical evidence shows that the rise in energy prices and the recent recession have stimulated interest in smaller, more energy-efficient homes. The median square footage for a new home in the United States almost doubled between 1973 and 2005 and has now dropped by about 200 square feet. The chart shows how the median size of new homes in the U.S. is shrinking.

When larger spaces are required, for example for entertaining or to house extra guests at a vacation cottage, there are energy-efficient solutions. For example, indoor furnishings can be easily rearranged, or a section of bedrooms can be closed off from the rest of the house when they are not needed.

The Small House Movement

The small house movement consists of environmentalists and designers who believe that the best way to conserve energy and resources is to live in small structures that provide just enough space for daily activities. Some feel that because there are not enough resources to support our current modern lifestyle for the earth's 6.5 billion people, everyone should minimize consumption. Designers of small houses aim to demonstrate that a small space, if efficient and well organized, can be a comfortable and pleasant living environment. Small houses are also seen as a solution to the shortage of affordable housing in poor countries and urban slums. Some designs use recycled shipping containers or inexpensive prefabricated structures that can be easily transported and assembled.

Small houses range from 100-square foot "tiny houses" to 1,000-square-foot cottages and are designed to be completely energy-efficient and as sustainable as possible. Some can be transported as single units; others are built from prefabricated components. Small houses are often used as vacation homes. Modern "cottage houses" incorporate the architectural features of luxury homes on a small scale. Besides being energy efficient and sustainable, small houses cost less, and the property taxes on them are low.

You can find more information about small houses on the websites of the Small House Society (**www.resourcesforlife.com/small-house-society**) and the Small House Style magazine (**www.smallhousestyle.com**).

Layout of rooms and natural light

A well-planned interior layout contributes significantly to energy savings in a house by maximizing the use of natural light and heat. Exposure to natural light inside a house contributes to the occupants' well-being and peace of mind and makes electric lights unnecessary for much of the day. Think about the times of day that different areas of the home will be in use and where the sunlight will fall at those times. A kitchen should be located on the southeast side of the house, where it will receive warmth and light in the morning. A living room or family room should be on the southwest side where it will receive sunlight later in the day. A good location for the master bedroom is on the northwest side because it will not be used as much during the day and the early morning sunlight will not strike the windows. Other bedrooms can be located on the north side, and bathrooms, laundry rooms, and utility rooms should be on the north side or in the interior of the building because they are not occupied much during daylight hours. A garage on the east or west side helps to buffer the house against the heat of the summer sun or cold winter winds.

To minimize glare and avoid direct sunlight shining in through the windows in the mornings and late afternoons, windows on the east and west side should be avoided if possible. Skylights and solar tubes can bring natural light into deep interior spaces such as hallways.

The placement of electrical lighting fixtures should not be decided until after the natural lighting in the home has been designed. In conventional homes, lighting fixtures are often placed automatically in standard positions such as the centers of ceilings, and the type of fixture is often dictated by what happens to be in style at the moment. Instead, lighting should be placed where it is needed, and the brightness and type of fixture should match its purpose.

Water management

Managing groundwater and surface water on the site should be part of the early design process. **Groundwater** is the water that flows and seeps through the soil and rock underground. Groundwater always flows downward in the direction of the water table, the point at which the ground is totally saturated. Think of digging a hole in the beach near the edge of the water; when you dig down a few inches, the hole fills with water. The level of the water table can rise during the rainy season or when the water level in nearby lakes and rivers rises. As the water table rises, groundwater can seep through a slab or through foundation walls.

Surface water is the water that runs across the ground when it rains or when snow melts. A number of factors influence the flow of surface water, including the placement of landscaping features, concrete slabs or structures on the site, paved areas and driveways, and the type of soil. If surface water does not drain away from your house naturally, it will collect in low spots and may cause flooding. If your site slopes downward toward your building, you must direct surface water around the house. When native vegetation is removed from the site during construction, the natural flow of water may be disturbed. You must also think about access to your home during wet weather — you do not want to have to wade through water to get to your front door or drive through a deep puddle in your driveway.

When considering water management when designing your green home, answer the following questions about your site:

- How high is the water table, and does it rise and fall seasonally?

- When does it rain or snow, and how much precipitation occurs? What is the maximum amount of precipitation that might occur?

- Does the site have sandy soil that drains easily or clay that holds water?

- Is the site on a slope? Does the slope direct water toward the house?

- Does your site slope enough to naturally drain away the water from gutter spouts and below-grade drainage systems?

- How does surface water travel across the site during a heavy rain? Is any water coming from a neighboring site, a stream, or a nearby storm drain?

If possible, visit your site during a rainstorm to observe how the surface water behaves. Ask nearby neighbors if they have encountered any problems with moisture in a basement, flooding, or pooling during heavy rain or obstruction of storm drains.

Whether the groundwater table rises above the level of your slab, or surface water accumulates in the ground around the foundation, the weight of the water exerts hydrostatic pressure on the outside of the foundation walls. Water 12 inches deep exerts ½ pound of pressure per square inch, but at a depth of 8 feet, the pressure would amount to 500 pounds per square foot. This pressure forces water through seams, cracks, and pores in the slab and foundation. Moisture contributes to heat loss and to the growth of mold and mildew. Even if the foundation is protected with a waterproof membrane on the outside, an underground drainage system, known as a below-grade drain system, is needed in many parts of the country. A **below-grade drainage system** typically consists of a membrane or **a drainage board** (a board that is porous on the outside and contains channels to carry water) on the outside of the foundation that directs the water downward to a **footing drain**, typically a perforated 4-inch pipe filled with gravel and covered with geotextile fabric to prevent clogging, that carries the water away from the structure. If the site does not have enough slope for the water to naturally drain away downhill, a sump pump must be used to mechanically draw the water away through pipes into a rainwater drain. The location of below-grade drains and pipes should be part of the original design so they can be accommodated when the site is graded and the foundation is laid.

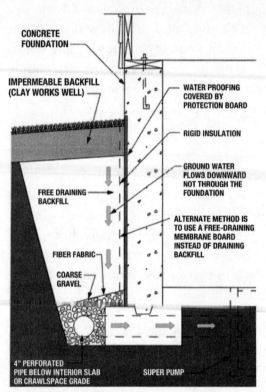

CONCRETE FOUNDATION

IMPERMEABLE BACKFILL (CLAY WORKS WELL)

WATER PROOFING COVERED BY PROTECTION BOARD

RIGID INSULATION

GROUND WATER FLOWS DOWNWARD NOT THROUGH THE FOUNDATION

FREE DRAINING BACKFILL

ALTERNATE METHOD IS TO USE A FREE-DRAINING MEMBRANE BOARD INSTEAD OF DRAINING BACKFILL

FIBER FABRIC

COARSE GRAVEL

4" PERFORATED PIPE BELOW INTERIOR SLAB OR CRAWLSPACE GRADE

SUPER PUMP

Excess water saturating the ground around the foundation runs down a drainage board or moisture barrier to a perforated pipe buried in gravel underground. This pipe carries the excess water off to a collection point where a sump pump moves into the storm drainage system.

You can divert water that runs down a hill or slopes toward the house by digging a swale uphill from the house. A **swale** is a V-shaped trench with a layer of gravel or crushed rock in the bottom. The rock is covered with a **geotextile material** — a fabric that allows water to soak through while blocking soil — and then soil and grass. If the water flow is very heavy, a perforated pipe similar to the footing drain can be placed in the bottom of the trench to carry the water away.

Your roof is typically a large impermeable surface that repels large quantities of water when it rains or snows. Rainwater running off from the roof can be collected and stored in rain barrels for irrigation and other uses instead of going into a storm drain. Rainwater runoff can also be managed with a vegetated, or green roof. *This will be discussed in Chapter 4 in the section on roofs.* Green roofs help to cool and insulate a house, reducing the need for air conditioning. The details of these features can be worked out later in the design process.

Ventilation

In a temperate climate, a house can be cooled during much of the year simply by opening some windows and allowing air to flow through the house. Warm air rises and exits through windows on an upper story or through vents high in the walls or in the attic. Warm air can also be drawn out through a cupola or cooling tower at the top of the house. In hot desert

regions, a house can be cooled at night by drawing in cool outside air. You can supplement natural ventilation by using mechanical fans. If you live in a cold climate, you can conserve heat by keeping the house tightly sealed, and you will need a mechanical ventilation device to supply fresh outside air. Ventilation, including the type and placement of windows, vents, and mechanical devices, should be part of the preliminary design.

Conservation

Architect Frank Lloyd Wright's Fallingwater, a house situated over a small waterfall that integrated the outdoors into its design, has made headlines since it was built in 1935. Conservations argue that the concept for this house is not environmentally sound because it interferes with a natural waterway. A green home should be situated so that it does not interrupt natural systems and has a minimal impact on the surrounding environment. Access roads, storm water runoff, septic tanks, and sewage disposal, and disruption of wetlands and natural communities must be taken into consideration when choosing a location for a house.

Passive Home Design

Passive homes rely almost entirely on solar heat and natural cooling to maintain a comfortable indoor temperature. Passive design cuts energy consumption for heating and cooling to about 10 percent of the energy consumed by a conventional home and delivers excellent indoor air quality. This is achieved by making the house airtight; insulating the foundation, floors, walls, and ceilings; installing high-performance triple-glazed windows; controlling ventilation; and using a mechanical heat transfer system that recovers heat from outgoing air. An energy-efficient heating and cooling system operates only when it is needed.

A homeowner building a new home can determine how to properly position the structure to take maximum advantage of the sun's energy. South-facing windows allow more sunlight to enter the house. Building materials

Modern passive house with a solar water heater in front and PV solar panels on the roof

that absorb heat (known as **thermal mass**) can be placed where the sunlight will hit them during daylight hours. The interior design facilitates convection currents that move warm air to other parts of the house. At night, shutters can be drawn over windows to slow the transfer of warmth out of the house. Passive solar design also incorporates mechanisms for cooling the home during warmer weather, such as overhangs and shutters to shade windows from direct sun and operable windows and screen doors that can be opened to circulate cooler air.

Once a home has been built to use passive solar energy, little maintenance is required. Passive solar design not only reduces dependence on fossil fuels and saves money on utility bills, but it is also cleaner and healthier for the occupants of the house. Warmth radiating from walls or floors is more comfortable than streams of hot, dry air blasting from vents. There is none of the dust and mold that often accumulates in the ducts of heating and cooling systems.

The first passive house was designed and built in 1996 by German Physicist Wolfgang Feist. The Passive House Institute estimates that 20,000 Passive Houses have already been built worldwide, 13,500 of them in Germany alone. Many foreign governments are now adopting passive house standards as part of their building codes. Passive homes have not caught on as quickly in the United States, probably because there is such a wide range of climates. The principles of passive building can be successfully applied in any climate, however, with some adjustments. Existing buildings can be retrofitted with at least some passive design features to slash energy costs.

Many of the design features can be implemented at no extra cost, and the energy savings will pay for any extra expense in a very short time. A passive home that uses solar energy, wind turbines, or some other form of renewable energy to supply all its electricity is known as a **zero-energy building** (ZEB).

Passive solar heating

When you park your car in the sun on a summer day, the temperature inside can quickly rise to 120 or 140 degrees, even with the windows slightly open. The steering wheel becomes so hot you cannot touch it, and metal

seat belt buckles can burn you. You car is acting as a **solar collector** — a box with glass sides that concentrates the sun's light into heat energy. Using passive solar heat involves designing your house as a solar collector, concentrating the energy of sunlight streaming through windows and glass panels and storing that energy in heat-absorbent materials to be released as warmth for many hours afterwards. When you open your curtains on a cool day and let the sun shine into a room to warm it, you are using passive solar energy.

You may not be aware of the many factors that affect the temperature inside your house. A tree that shades your roof for part of the day may lower the temperature in your house several degrees. Cool breezes, rain or snow falling against windows, or cold air seeping into your

Passive solar hot water heater on the roof of a home.

garage can have the same effect. In winter, your house gradually loses heat into the ground through its slab and into the outside air through the walls and roof. Passive design uses building techniques and materials to control unwanted heat loss and prevent overheating.

A passive design makes use of four basic heat movement and heat storage mechanisms:

Conduction: Conduction is the movement of heat through a solid material. Molecules near a heat source begin to vibrate vigorously, and the vibrations spread to neighboring molecules, which transfer heat further and further from the source.

Convection: Convection is the circulation of heat through liquids and gases. As fluid or air is heated, its molecules spread apart and it becomes lighter. Warmer, lighter fluid and air rise, and cooler, denser fluid and air sink. This is why heat rises to the second floor of a home while the bottom floor stays cool.

Radiation: When heat radiates, it moves through the air from warmer objects to cooler ones, like heat from a fireplace that warms the people sitting in front of it. Passive solar design incorporates two types of radiation: solar radiation and infrared radiation. When radiation strikes an object,

it is absorbed, reflected, or transmitted, depending on that object's physical properties. Depending on their color, opaque objects absorb 40 to 95 percent of incoming solar radiation from the sun. Darker colors typically absorb a greater percentage than lighter colors. Bright-white materials or objects reflect 80 to 98 percent of incoming solar energy.

Infrared radiation occurs when heat radiates from warmed surfaces toward cooler surfaces. Clear window glass allows 80 to 90 percent of solar radiation to pass through into a house and absorb or reflect only 10 to 20 percent. After solar radiation passes through the glass and is absorbed by materials in the home, it is radiated again from the interior surfaces as infrared radiation. Although glass allows solar radiation to pass through into the house, it absorbs the infrared radiation from the interior surfaces and then radiates part of that heat back to the home's interior.

Thermal capacitance: Thermal capacitance refers to the ability of materials to store heat. Thermal mass — the materials used to build the home — changes its temperature either by storing heat from a warm room or by converting direct solar radiation into heat. The more thermal mass, the more heat can be stored for each degree rise in temperature.

In addition to orienting a house to take advantage of southern exposure and natural ventilation, passive design incorporates the following features:

Using shading and overhangs to control solar gain

Solar gain is the heat that accumulates inside the house when the sun's radiation passes through the windows. In the summer, solar gain can cause the house to be too hot. Overhangs and architectural features that partially shade windows cut down on the amount of sunlight entering at certain times of day.

Correct placement of thermal mass

Thermal mass is any dense substance that absorbs and stores heat. Some thermal mass, called "free" or "incidental" mass, is automatically present in drywall, framing lumber, doors, and furniture. Intentional mass is deliberately located in strategic places in a building to absorb solar radiation. Brick, concrete, concrete blocks, tile, and earthen materials are all forms of

thermal mass that also serve architectural functions within a house. Thermal mass absorbs and stores heat from solar radiation, from warm air circulating around it, and from other heat sources within a house such as fireplaces. Some of the heat immediately radiates back into the room, and some of it migrates inward where it remains until the temperature in the room falls below the surface temperature of the thermal mass. Then it is slowly released back into the room. Thermal mass also helps to cool a home by absorbing heat during the day.

In most passive homes, thermal mass is located inside the structure where it absorbs solar radiation coming into the house through the windows. This is known as a direct gain system. In some houses, such as adobe and rammed earth houses, the exterior walls absorb solar radiation and slowly transfer heat to the interior of the house. An indirect gain passive solar heating system, also called a trombe wall or a thermal storage wall, is a south-facing glazed wall that absorbs sunlight and heats up slowly during the day. As the wall cools during the night, it slowly releases heat into the building interior. Thermal walls are usually made of heavy masonry, but sometimes contain tanks or pipes filled with water or **phase change materials** (materials capable of storing and releasing large amounts of energy as they freeze and melt). Isolated gain, or sunspace, heating collects heat from solar radiation in an area such as a sun room or foyer that can be shut off from the rest of the building. During the day, doors and windows opening from the sunspace into the rest of the building allow the accumulated heat to circulate out into the building. At night when it cools, the windows and doors are shut, and the area is closed off from the building.

Eco-friendly wall insulation in a home remodeling project

Thermal mass can be concentrated in one or two areas to heat specific parts of the house, or it can be distributed throughout the house as plaster or wall covering to maintain a uniform temperature. A combination of concentrated and distributed thermal mass works best. Thermal mass placed directly in the path of the sun is much more effective than thermal mass that absorbs warmth from the air circulating around it. Tile, brick, flagstone, or stained concrete floors absorb heat from sunlight falling on

the floor. Planters and low barrier walls can also be strategically placed to absorb heat. Light-colored walls can be used to reflect solar radiation to thermal masses deeper within a house.

Thermal mass: Not too much and not too little.

An inadequate amount of solar mass can make a home uncomfortable — it releases heat too quickly during sunny days. It brings temperatures inside the house up to the mid-80s and dissipates heat too quickly at night, which makes extra backup heating a requirement. Architects apply "glass-to-mass" ratios to determine the correct amount of thermal mass for the amount of sunlight entering through south-facing windows. Thermal mass stores heat effectively up to a depth of about 4 inches; making it 2 inches thicker only increases heat absorption by another 8 percent. Because installing thermal mass tends to be expensive, it is better to have a large surface area of 2-inch thick thermal mass than a small area covered with 6-inch-thick thermal mass.

Using insulation to maintain the interior temperature of the house

Heat leaves and enters a house through walls, ceilings, floors, foundations, and windows. Successful passive heating and cooling relies on insulation to maintain the indoor temperature and prevent unwanted heat loss or gain. Walls and ceilings are insulated, and in cold climates the slab, foundation, and basement are also insulated to prevent heat from transferring out of the house into the cold ground. Insulated shades, drapes, or shutters are used to cover the windows at night and when rooms are not in use.

Protecting the insulation from moisture

In most climates, the air inside a house contains more moisture than the air outside. Moisture from cooking, showering, plants, pets, people, aquariums, and washing machines evaporates into the air, especially when the inside air is warmer. Water vapor tends to migrate from an area of high concentration to an area of lower concentration, passing outward through ceilings and walls, as well as through seams and cracks around doors and windows, electrical outlets, and other openings. When the escaping moisture encounters a cold surface such as an outer wall or roof decking, it condenses there and wets the surrounding insulation, wood, and drywall. Moisture causes insulation to become ineffective, breeds mold and mildew,

and rots wood. In passive homes, vapor barriers are installed to protect insulation, and exhaust fans remove water vapor from cooking and showers.

Sealing against air leaks and controlled ventilation

To prevent unwanted hot or cold air infiltration, a passive home is tightly sealed against air leaks around windows, doors, foundations, and holes for electrical wiring and plumbing. Operable windows can be opened for natural ventilation, and a mechanical ventilation system continually brings fresh air into the house when needed.

Using an HRV or ERV to recover heat from outgoing air, or cool incoming air

In climates with extreme winters or summers, a heat and energy recovery ventilation system (ERV or HRV) heats or cools outside air as it enters the ventilation system by transferring energy to or from the outgoing air. Energy recovery systems employ a number of methods, including run-around coil systems that recover energy during the process of cooling water and use it to heat water and air; regenerative heat wheels, which treat outside heat and moisture; and heat pipes, which absorb energy from exhaust streams and transfer it.

An ERV is more expensive to install than other ventilation systems but has a payback period of several months to three years. According to the U.S. Department of Energy, most energy recovery ventilation systems can recover about 70 to 80 percent of the energy in the exiting air and deliver that energy to the incoming air.

Giving each room access to solar heat

Passive homes are designed so every room has access to sunlight, and rooms requiring the most heat and light are on the south side of the building. The ideal design is a linear building that is only one room deep, but this arrangement may not fit an urban lot size and may interfere with the smooth flow of traffic inside the house. For this reason, passive houses are often rectangular or square. Each room is a self-contained solar unit. Open floor plans, in which the main areas of the house are separated by counters, low walls, or furniture instead of dividing walls, are also effective because they

allow the whole area to be warmed naturally by convection but may require additional backup heating or cooling because individual areas cannot be closed off.

Creating sun-free spaces

Though solar radiation is being used for heat and light, too much light can be overwhelming and cause glare. Every home needs spaces that are sheltered from sunlight, for offices, computers, and televisions. It is important to include areas in the design that are sheltered from light by architectural features, planters, and interior walls.

Using properly-sized, energy-efficient backup heating and cooling

Most local building codes require a building to have a backup heating system even if it is designed to rely on solar energy for heat. It is important that the heating system is the correct size to provide the required heat. An oversized system costs more and will waste energy by turning on and off too frequently. An oversized cooling system will generate excessive moisture and make the home uncomfortable. The HVAC contractor must have experience with passive design in order to accurately calculate the capacity of the backup system.

Using landscaping to protect from heat loss or gain

Cold winter winds quickly strip heat away from the exterior of your house, and baking sun on your walls and roof raises the temperature inside during the summer. Passive design uses landscaping and earthworks to shelter the house from sun and wind.

Windbreaks

A windbreak can reduce the wind chill near your home during cold winter months. To plant an effective windbreak, you need to know which plants grow best in your region and what direction the wind comes from around your house. Trees and shrubs with low crowns work best because they block wind close to the ground. Trees, bushes, and shrubs are often planted together to create a wind barrier from the ground up. The most common type of windbreak consists of dense evergreen trees and shrubs planted to the north and northwest of a home. Evergreen trees combined with a wall, fence, or man-made earth berm can deflect or lift the wind over the home.

A windbreak will reduce wind speed for a distance of as much as 30 times the windbreak's height. For maximum protection, your windbreak should be planted at a distance from your home of two to five times the mature height of the trees. Be careful not to plant the trees too close to the house where they will block the winter sunlight or cast shade on your solar panels.

Summer winds can have a cooling effect, especially at night. However, if summer winds are hot and you live in a climate where you use air conditioning all summer, you may want to block those winds from circulating near your home.

Insulating with landscaping

Planting shrubs, bushes, and vines next to your house creates dead air spaces around the walls that insulate your home in both winter and summer. Place plants so that there will be at least at least 1 foot of space between them and the wall when they are fully grown.

These south Florida home owners maximized the shade from the trees in their yard when building their home.

Shading

Shading and **evapotranspiration** (the process by which a plant actively moves and releases water vapor) from trees can reduce surrounding air temperatures as much as 9 degrees F (5 degrees C). Because cool air settles near the ground, air temperatures directly under trees can be as much as 25 degrees F (14 degrees C) cooler than air temperatures above nearby blacktop.

To use shade effectively, you must know the size, shape, and location of the shadows cast by your trees and plants as the sun moves across the sky during the day. Trees can be found with appropriate sizes, densities, and shapes for almost any shading application. You must also know which trees grow well in your region. Deciduous trees block solar heat in summer but let sunlight through in winter when they lose their leaves. Evergreen trees provide shade year-round. Homes in cooler climates may not need shade at all. Shading an air conditioner can increase its efficiency by as much as 10 percent. Trees, shrubs, vines, and groundcover plants can reduce heat radiation and cool the air by shading the ground and pavement around

your home. A patio or driveway can be shaded with a large bush or row of shrubs, a hedge, or vines on a trellis.

Solar energy absorbed through your roof and windows increases the heat inside your home during the summer, but shade in the wrong places may interfere with the operation of solar panels on your roof or with passive solar heating in the winter. Place trees where they will not block sunlight falling where you need it. Even the bare branches of deciduous trees can block enough sunlight to reduce the efficiency of solar panels. Deciduous trees with high, spreading crowns to the south of your home will provide maximum shade for your roof during summer. Trees and shrubs planted to the west will protect your home from sun angling toward the windows during the afternoon.

Earth sheltering

Earth sheltering is burying a house under soil that is then seeded with grass or plants. A house can also be built up against a hillside with dirt covering a specially constructed roof. Because the temperature of the earth below the frost line stays around 50 degrees F, earth-sheltered houses require only a small amount of additional heat to maintain a comfortable temperature. The earth covering prevents heat loss due to wind.

Earth berming is burying the lower parts of a house's walls, typically with 3 or 4 feet of earth. Earth berming protects against heat loss when a house is built on flat terrain.

Passive design for existing homes

Owners of existing homes can make minor changes to take advantage of passive solar energy. Modest levels of passive solar heating, also called sun tempering, can reduce building auxiliary heating requirements from 5 percent to 25 percent at little or no extra cost. More aggressive passive solar heating can reduce a building's heating energy use by 25 to 75 percent over a comparable structure.

Adding or enlarging south-facing windows will increase the amount of solar energy entering the house. Thermal mass can be added by covering a sunlit wall with a heat-absorbent material such as stone or brick. Insulation can be retrofitted to the foundation and basement and increased in the walls and attic. Passive cooling can be achieved by installing screen windows that can

open to allow outside air to cool the house. Homeowners can also use passive design by increasing attic ventilation to draw off heat during the summer. *Chapter 4 describes how you can seal up leaks and make your home airtight.*

If you do not want to undertake a major home improvement project, there are still small changes you can make to implement some principles of passive solar design. During the summer, a room facing south will probably be uncomfortably warm. To diminish the amount of sun and heat entering that room during the summer, tint the windows or hang awnings outside. Outdoor shades on south-facing windows help block the sun's heat.

Landscaping is another passive solar solution. Planting trees or hedges near your windows will help to lower your air conditioning costs. Plants and trees can also help keep your home warmer during the cold months. Take an inventory of where your home seems the hottest during the summer. For instance, if your family room feels like a sauna even when your thermostat is set at 76 degrees, the room may be getting too much heat from the sun to allow your air conditioner to work properly. A well-placed tree outside the room's windows will help cut the amount of solar radiation entering the room and make it much cooler. In the winter, observe where the wind is strongest on your property and plant a few strategically placed trees to create a windbreak.

Conclusion

Green building strives for maximum efficiency in every way, starting with the design process. One of the innovations of green building is a collaborative design process that involves all the stakeholders — the building owners and occupants, architects, engineers, tradesmen and landscapers — from the beginning. This ensures that everyone understands the project goals and allows designers to create interactive systems that increase efficiency.

The choice of a location and the orientation of a building on the site are crucial to achieving maximum energy efficiency and comfort. Green building makes the most of passive heating and cooling, natural ventilation, and daylight. In an existing home, insulation, windows, doors, flooring, and landscaping can be altered to increase the home's energy efficiency and improve indoor air quality.

Chapter 4

The Building Envelope

The **building envelope** is the space between the interior and exterior environments of a building — the slab, foundation, floors, walls, and roof. The design, construction, and quality of the building envelope determine the building's energy efficiency, interior air quality, interior temperature, and durability. The building envelope is a crucial component of green building. The previous chapter discussed the role of the building envelope in conserving energy: an airtight, well-insulated building envelope drastically reduces energy consumption by preventing heat or cold air from escaping.

Green building is also concerned with the sustainability of the materials used to construct the building envelope: where they come from, how they are produced, whether they are renewable, how far they are transported, how much of them is used, how long they last, and what is done with them when the building is taken down. The materials used in the building envelope also affect the indoor air quality of the building — they might contain toxins or harmful chemicals that leach into the soil or circulate in the air.

The best green construction practices and materials for your particular building envelope will be largely determined by your geographical location. Regional building codes typically require specific insulation R-values, drainage arrangements, and wind resistance and load-bearing capacities to accommodate local soil and weather conditions. Green building strives to go beyond building codes, exceed requirements, and fine-tune a home ac-

cording to the specific characteristics of the building site. Some building codes have not been updated to include the newest materials and technologies, and it may be necessary to negotiate with your zoning department to have them approved. An experienced green contractor will know what can and cannot be done.

The Foundation

The primary role of a foundation is to support the weight of the building. Depending on the climate and soil conditions where you live, a conventional foundation can be a concrete slab poured directly on the ground (grade); concrete blocks laid on a poured concrete footing; or a basement with 8-inch-thick concrete walls standing on a poured concrete footing.

Concrete

Although concrete is made from natural materials such as sand and rock minerals, it cannot automatically be categorized as a sustainable building material. Concrete is made by mixing a variety of materials, including water, sand, stone, and Portland cement. Producing Portland cement requires a significant amount of energy and generates large volumes of air pollutants such as concrete dust and greenhouse gases.

To produce every ton of cement, 6,000 BTUs (British thermal units) of energy are required. The environmental impact of using concrete becomes apparent when you consider that about 2.5 billion tons of concrete are produced each year. The burning of fossil fuels to produce this energy also produces greenhouse gases and other air pollutants, many of which are hazardous to the environment and to people, animals, plants, and ecosystems.

Concrete also contributes to nearly half of the waste produced by construction each year. Although concrete is recyclable because it is made from natural materials, it is rarely recycled. Green building practices aim to make the most of the concrete being used for the foundation, walls, and architectural features.

Chapter 3: Planning and Designing Your Green Home Project   51

Chapter 4: The Building Envelope   81

Chapter 5: Heating, Ventilation and Air Conditioning (HVAC)   143

Table of Contents

Make the foundation fit the building

Conventional builders tend to build foundations according to standard specifications without considering the actual weight and structure of the buildings sitting on top of them. As a result, foundations are often much heavier and thicker than they need to be, which wastes concrete and money. Green builders conserve resources by tailoring the foundation to match the requirements of a building.

Use fly ash

Every year, millions of tons of fly ash, a fine, glass-like powder recovered from gases emitted during coal-fired electric power generation, is produced by U.S. power plants. Much of this fly ash is dumped into landfills, but it can be used as an inexpensive partial replacement for the Portland cement in concrete. Fly ash actually increases the concrete's strength, improves segregation, and makes pumping easier. Fly ash is also an ingredient in brick, block, paving, and structural fills. Fly ash is environmentally friendly because it is recycled and has low embodied energy.

Pre-cast foundations

Pre-cast foundations, already used for decades in commercial building, are quickly becoming accepted for residential construction. The foundations are cast in sections at a manufacturing facility then transported to the building site where they are assembled on top of a bed of crushed stone. Pre-cast foundations come with a built-in footing and offer many advantages:

- The walls are made with 5,000 psi concrete reinforced with vertical steel bars; most poured foundations use only 3,500 psi concrete.

- The sections are cast in one continuous pour under ideal conditions at a factory. This avoids many of the problems with poured concrete or block foundations, such as mistakes made by inexperienced workers mixing mortar or cement, the hardening of one section before the next is poured, a foundation that is not level or not square, and delays and damage caused by rain or cold weather.

- An average pre-cast foundation system can be installed by a trained crew in about five hours, regardless of most weather conditions. **Backfilling** (filling in earth around the outside of the foundation) can begin as soon as the floor is poured and the subfloor is properly attached to the top of the wall system. The panels are cured before they are brought to the site, so construction work can begin immediately.

- Pre-cast foundations have 1-inch foam insulation with an R-5 rating built in; additional insulation can be added between the studs to increase the R-value up to R-26. **R-value** is a measure of a material's resistance to heat transmission. *See the following section on insulation for an explanation of R-values.* The panels are bolted together and the seams are waterproofed with special high performance urethane caulks. Once the pre-cast foundation is installed, it is fully insulated and watertight.

- The sections are custom-made in heights from 4 feet to 10 feet and can be made in any shape. Window and door openings can be included, and wiring and plumbing are accommodated with holes in the studs. The exterior is faced with concrete, and the interior of each stud has a wooden strip to which wall finishings can be directly attached.

- The wall panels come in heights from 4 feet to 10 feet. Foundations can be built in any shape or size, and window or door openings can be included. The panels are bolted together, then waterproofed with special high performance urethane caulks.

- A simple and economical ventilation system using an inline fan and piping can be easily installed to remove contaminated air and radon gas from the basement. The crushed rock base allows the free flow of earth gases into the exhaust system, and the walls of the foundation are highly impermeable.

- The foundation is manufactured off-site, minimizing waste, water run off, and damage to the building site.

Pre-cast foundation manufacturers

Superior Walls (www.superiorwalls.com/consumers.html#) has been manufacturing pre-cast foundations since 1986. Its products are available through representatives throughout the United States. Superior Walls was one of the first 25 manufacturers to have products approved to earn points toward the NAHB Research Center National Green Building Certification.

Kistner Concrete Products Inc. (**www.kistner.com**) produces Thermal-Krete Precast Concrete Foundations.

The foundation as part of the whole-house system

A **whole-house system** views the building envelope as a single insulated unit and aims to prevent heat transfer through any part of the structure. The foundation is a weak point in the building envelope because it is thermally connected to the walls and floor of the house, and heat dissipates through it into the surrounding cold earth, just as heat dissipates through uninsulated walls and ceilings. A tight building envelope includes a foundation that is insulated against outside temperatures.

In **heating climates** (cold climates where heating is required during part of the year), the foundation should be insulated with at least 2 inches of closed-cell rigid foam insulation applied over the moisture-proofing on the outside of the foundation from the footer up to the top of the foundation wall. Putting insulation on the outside of the foundation makes the concrete or block foundation part of the conditioned space in the house and reduces the risk of moisture condensing on the insulation.

Check to see if local building codes require termite barriers.

The layer of foam insulation can act as a channel for termites in some areas. It may be necessary to install a **termite barrier**, a thin sheet of metal along the top of the foundation wall that covers the space where the foam meets the wall. Check your local building code to see what kind of termite barrier is required.

Slabs are typically not insulated, even though they conduct heat in and out of a house. In hot climates, it is estimated that heat gain from warmth absorbed by the edges of the slab account for 15 percent of cooling costs. In cold climates, the rooms around the outside of the house have cold floors.

A simple solution is to install at least 1 inch of closed-cell rigid foam insulation around the edges of the slab. The insulation should be placed inside the concrete form before the concrete is poured, and any exposed insulation covered with flashing, stucco or cement board when the slab is completed.

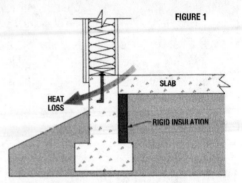

FIGURE 1

Insulating the entire underside of a slab is even more effective but costs more initially. It is essential to insulate the whole slab if you plan to use radiant heating (tubing or cross-linked polyethylene imbedded in the floor to provide heat.)

Failure to insulate the edge of the slab results in cold floors near exterior walls in the winter and higher heating costs as heat penetrates from the ground outside in the summer.

Frost-protected Shallow Foundations (FPSPs)

In northern climates, frost heaving can damage foundations and other concrete structural components. **Frost heaving** occurs when accumulations of water in the ground expand as they freeze, forming ice lenses

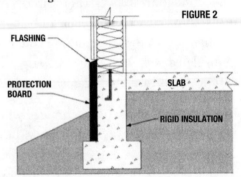

FIGURE 2

Rigid foam insulation on the outside of the slab, extending up to the wall, prevents heat transfer around the edges.

that push up the soil and displace the structures on top. To avoid damage, the footers of building foundations must be placed below frost line, which requires deep excavations and extra concrete.

Frost-Protected Shallow Foundations (FPSFs) provide protection against frost damage without excavating below the frost line. Frost-protected shallow foundations are wrapped with insulation that channels heat escaping from the building to warm the earth beneath the foundation and prevent frost from forming there. In colder climates, the footing or foundation depth is reduced from 48 inches to 16 inches, which reduces the amount of concrete needed. The foundation can be installed with simpler equipment, such as a trenching machine, and the foam insulation serves as a stay-in-place form for pouring the concrete.

According to the NAHB, more than 1 million homes have insulated shallow footings in Norway, Sweden, and Finland where they are included in building codes as standard practice. The NAHB estimates that more than 5,000 buildings in the United States have successfully used frost protected shallow foundations. The NAHB Research Center has published a *Design Guide for Frost Protected Shallow Foundations* (**www.toolbase.org/PDF/ DesignGuides/revisedFPSFguide.pdf**) containing detailed drawings of the prescribed methods of construction.

Poured concrete slabs waste wood

Although reusable forms are available for pouring concrete basement walls, many slabs are poured using 2 x 12 wooden boards supported by stakes. These boards are old-growth timber. They can be reused two or three times but eventually become caked with cement and saturated with release agents (chemical coatings that prevent the concrete from sticking to the wood) and must be discarded, which wastes timber.

Insulated Concrete Forms (ICFs)

Insulated concrete forms (ICFs) are lightweight blocks or panels made of expanded polystyrene (EPS) or extruded polystyrene (EXPS) that can be assembled to make forms for poured concrete walls. They are easy to transport and put together. The forms are left in place after the concrete is cast and serve as built-in insulation on both the interior and the exterior of the wall. ICFs are used for both foundations and walls. The R-value of an ICF system is between R-18 and R-35. *Read more about R-values in the following section on insulation.*

When ICFs are used below-grade for foundations, special care must be taken to protect them from termites. More than 23 companies in North America manufacture and distribute ICFs.

Durisol Wood Concrete Insulated Forms

Durisol cement-bonded wood fiber ICFs (www.durisolbuild.com) are made of 80 percent recycled material. Softwood aggregates, by-products of the lumber industry, are chipped, mineralized, and bonded together with Portland cement into a variety of shapes. No post-consumer waste or recycled demolition material is used, which ensures Durisol does not contain any toxic or other unhealthy ingredients. They contain no plastic, foams, or polystyrenes.

Durisol ICFs have been used for more than 50 years. Lightweight and durable, they are vermin, termite, and insect proof, will not support fungus growth, and do not rot or decay. Durisol is easily cut, nailed, and screwed with simple carpenter tools. Interior and exterior finishes are applied directly to the Durisol material, and drywall can be attached anywhere on the Wall Form surface. Durisol insulated concrete forms are 100 percent recyclable.

Crawl space foundations

The foundations for many houses in the United States are low walls that allow just enough space between the ground and the floor for someone to crawl around underneath and for ductwork, wiring, and plumbing. Most building codes specify that a crawl space should be a minimum of 18 inches high, but increasing the height to 24 inches gives more room for insulation under the floor and allows workers more space to move around. Installing insulation under the floor keeps the floor warm, but any ductwork or plumbing running through the crawl space is subject to heat loss and air leaks. Ideally, the exterior of the walls around a crawl space should be insulated to retain heat and make the entire crawlspace a conditioned area.

Framing

Natural building refers to using natural materials for a building structure. Many methods of natural building have been used for centuries and are popular now because they use inexpensive materials that are locally available and that decay or disintegrate naturally when the building is no longer in use. The following are some items you can use to construct the frame for an environmentally friendly home.

Adobe

Adobe is essentially dirt moistened with water, sometimes with chopped straw or other fibers added for strength, and then shaped and allowed to dry. Common dirt in most parts of the country has adequate proportions of aggregate, sand, silt, and clay, to make adobe, but it is impractical in climates where there are no long dry periods to allow the bricks to dry. The best adobe soil has between 15 percent and 30 percent clay in it to bind the material together. Sometimes additives such as cement or asphalt emulsion are included in the mixture to make it more waterproof.

Adobe is molded or pressed into blocks that are sun dried and stacked like bricks to make walls and can also be piled up and dried in layers. The mor-

tar used to lay the blocks is made from the same soil with the stones screened out. This creates a homogeneous wall that is stronger than its individual parts. Only a few rows of blocks can be applied at a time; the wall must be allowed to dry out before the next layer is applied. Adobe has an aspect ratio of 1/10, which means the height of the wall can be ten

Close-up of adobe wall texture.

times the width of its base. The top of each wall must be secured with a bond beam of concrete, steel, or wood to help hold the wall together and support any roof loads. Unlike bricks, adobe blocks are easily cut to fit doors and other openings. Adobe can also be used for floors, colored with a thin slip of clay and polished with natural oil.

To preserve the adobe, it is often placed on foundations that keep it off the ground, above any surface water, and protected from precipitation by substantial overhanging eaves. Sometimes the outside is plastered with cement or a stabilized adobe; otherwise the external finish must be regularly reapplied.

Adobe is a good thermal mass because it absorbs and holds heat well, but it does not insulate well. Adobe walls are often insulated either by attaching an interior surface such as sheets of drywall and filling in the space between the interior surface and the outside wall with insulation or by putting insulation on the outside.

Although adobe itself is very cheap, building with adobe is labor-intensive. It is typically regarded either as a luxury or as a do-it-yourself project. Building the walls is relatively simple, but it can take a long time to work out the electrical wiring, plumbing, and interior fittings.

Rammed earth

Rammed earth walls are created by compressing or tamping soil that is mostly clay and sand into forms that create very flat vertical surfaces. Historically, rammed earth techniques have been used successfully in a wide range of environments on six continents. As with adobe, rammed earth walls must be protected from surface water and driving rain by raising them on concrete foundations and covering them with overhanging eaves. Rammed earth walls are normally at least 1 foot thick to give stability and provide thermal mass.

Modern rammed earth walls are typically made using heavy mechanized equipment to move and compress the material. Insulation applied to the exterior of the walls helps to keep the interior temperature constant. The heavy thermal mass can lead to overheating in hot climates if too much sunlight is allowed into the house. The interior walls can be finished naturally by oiling them or covered with standard wall finishings. Rammed earth houses shut out external noise and are quiet inside.

Poured earth

Poured earth, a technique developed by architect Michael Frerking, uses ordinary soil mixed with Portland cement poured into forms to create walls. Poured earth walls have a high degree of resistance to water and sun and require little maintenance. Rigid insulation can be inserted within the poured wall, which creates a thermal break and allows the interior portion to serve as thermal mass for passive heating.

Straw bale

The technique of building with bales of straw was pioneered by Nebraska settlers about a century ago using the bales of grass produced by newly invented steam- and horse-powered baling machines. The bales of straw were stacked to form walls and plastered on the inside and outside with mud or cement. This technique was revived in the Southwestern United States during the 1980s and is now used worldwide. Many localities in the Southwest now have building codes for straw-bale construction.

Straw is a renewable resource and a good insulator. Straw bales are rectangular blocks of straw, tightly compressed and bound with twine or baling wire. The bales are not uniform and bale length may vary by a few inches. There are two types of straw bale construction: load-bearing and non-load bearing. In load-bearing, also known as Nebraska-style, straw bale construction, some or all of the weight of the floors, roof, and ceilings is carried by the straw bales. Load-bearing construction must account for the possible settling of the straw bales as the weight of the roof compresses them. In non-load-bearing straw bale construction, a timber frame supports floors and ceilings, and the straw bales are used as infill. Many building authorities will only allow non-load-bearing construction of straw bale homes. A non-load-bearing straw bale house saves only about 15 percent of the timber used in a conventional framed house and typically costs more to finish because of the specialized labor required to finish the interior and exterior. However, the construction work goes quickly, and the superior insulating qualities of straw bale save on heating costs. During construction, the straw bales are "notched" to create conduits for plumbing and wiring.

The moisture content and quality of straw bales varies and should be checked and measured during construction. If the straw inside the walls is not kept dry, it will eventually rot, so it is essential not to install any moisture barrier that might cause condensation. The straw must be in direct contact with the surface plaster so that it can breathe. Water vapor is allowed to pass in and out through the walls, but the straw inside must be protected from any kind of direct water leak. A water barrier between the foundation and the bottom of the straw wall prevents moisture from being wicked up into the straw.

In all straw bale construction, the straw is covered with a "skin" of gypsum or stucco cement. These interior and exterior wall coverings must resist rodents or insects that might try to nest inside the straw. Once the plaster skin hardens, it forms a sort of sandwich with a hard skin on the outside and the soft straw inside. Any additional stress or weight is borne by the hard plaster skin.

Cordwood, or stackwall

Cordwood, or stackwall, is an ancient form of construction that

Cordwood Lodge,
Photo provided by Richard Flatau.

uses short, round pieces of wood, similar to firewood. The short logs are stacked and aligned with their ends sticking out of the wall on each side and are cemented together with mortar or concrete around the end of each log. Other objects such as glass bottles can be inserted among the logs. The cordwood is typically wood that would otherwise have been wasted, such as offcuts from timber yards or furniture factories.

Cordwood wall provides both insulation from the wood and the cavity between the interior and exterior wall faces and thermal mass from the masonry mortar that is used to cement the logs together. The cordwood method creates a strong wall that could support a considerable load, but many building authorities require a timber frame or similar supporting structure with the cordwood used only as an infill. The logs are not coated with a moisture barrier, but are allowed to breathe. Bark must be removed from the logs to prevent insects from entering the wood. In dry climates, the wall may need to be "chinked" with mortar around the edges of the logs after a year or so, when the logs have dried out.

Earthships: Extreme Green

For more than 25 years, the architect and builder Michael Reynolds has been promoting earthships, substantially bermed, passive solar houses built with locally available materials including used tires and aluminum cans. Entire communities of earthships exist in the Southwest United States, and the designs have been adapted for use in many parts of the world. Earthships can be designed to function in any climate and embody these principles:

- **Thermal/solar heating and cooling** — They are embedded in the earth to take advantage of natural heating and cooling tendencies and use regulated solar heating and thermal mass to maintain comfort in the home.

- **Solar and wind electricity** — Where appropriate, earthships are powered by solar or wind energy. Very little energy is required because most of the heating and cooling is passive.

- **Contained sewage treatment** — Earthships often incorporate composting toilets or enhanced septic systems.

- **Building with natural and recycled materials** — Houses should be built with locally available materials made with as little energy as possible and by using techniques that are simple enough for an ordinary person to learn. In the past, houses were built using natural materials such as wood and earth. Today we are also surrounded by manufactured trash — bottles, tires, aluminum cans — that can be recycled as building materials. Many earthships are built using adobe. A signature feature of earthships is rubber tires filled with rammed earth to make building blocks that provide outer walls thermal mass. Adding exterior insulation to these rubber-tire walls has made them efficient.

- **Water harvesting** — Water shortage is one of the world's most serious problems. Earthships employ systems to capture water from precipitation or condensation and recycle gray water as many as four times using filters and botanical cells.

- **Food production** — Many earthships incorporate indoor gardens or edible plants for landscaping.

Wood framing

Wood is ideally suited for building. It is durable, easy to work with, and nontoxic (except when it is treated with toxic chemicals). If properly protected from weather and insects, it can last for hundreds of years. A majority of the homes in the United States are built using wood.

In many areas, wood for construction is locally available and has low embodied energy. Trees produce wood using solar energy, and relatively small amounts of energy are consumed maintaining the forest, felling trees, and transporting them. Producing a cubic meter of steel requires about 320 times more energy than producing a cubic meter of wood. Processing and manufacturing wood products also requires far less energy than manufacturing other building materials. Wood is also one of the most renewable construction materials, if it is grown and harvested responsibly.

Sustainable wood products

Irresponsible and unregulated harvesting of wood is an environmental tragedy. The wood you purchase might have been harvested by clear-cutting forests, which involves destroying an entire forest and prevents its future growth. It takes 1 acre of clear-cut forest to build a 1,760 square foot house.

Clear-cutting diminishes future wood supplies, depletes oxygen in the Earth's atmosphere, disrupts and kills ecosystems, and displaces thousands of animal, plant, and bird species. This is particularly true for tropical and exotic woods, which come from rain forests. In countries where there government oversight is lax or poorly organized, forests are rapidly disappearing. Between 1960 and 1990, developing countries lost one-fifth of their natural tropical forest cover.

In some parts of the world, timber harvesting is associated with social injustices. Timber cutters are underpaid and forced to work in dangerous conditions with no compensation for illness or injuries. Local inhabitants are displaced and lose their livelihoods when their forests are cut down. Farmers move into the clear-cut areas and deplete the nutrients in the soil. Within a few years, the land is barren and abandoned, and loose silt begins to erode and clog streams and rivers.

A building cannot be considered green if it is built with wood that was harvested under these circumstances. How do you ensure that the wood you are buying has been harvested in a socially and environmentally responsible manner? Two independent organizations, the Forestry Stewardship Council (FSC) and the Sustainable Forestry Initiative (FSI), provide verification that a particular wood product comes from a responsible source. A handbook produced by the World Business Council for Sustainable Development (WBCSD) and the World Resources Institute (WRI) in 2007, *Sustainable Procurement of Wood and Paper-Based Products* (2007), (**www.sustainableforestprods.org/**) tells homeowners and builders how to verify that wood products come from sustainable sources.

FSC-certified wood products cost more than uncertified wood. If you are seeking LEED certification for a home, the MR7 LEED point requires that more that 50 percent of the value (not the quantity) of permanently installed wood and wood fiber be FSC certified. Some builders cut costs by framing a house with uncertified wood and buying expensive FSC-certified finished wood products for the interior of the home to meet the LEED requirement.

Third-party certification of wood products

More than 50 different systems exist worldwide for certifying that wood is responsibly harvested. In North America, the most widely recognized is the Forestry Stewardship Council (FSC) (195 million acres certified); the Sustainable Forestry Initiative (SFI) (135 million acres certified); the American Tree Farm System (ATFS) (3.15 million acres certified); and the Canadian Standards Association (170 million acres certified). The Programme for the Endorsement of Forest Certification (PEFC) (**www.pefc.org**), an international umbrella organization based in Switzerland, evaluates and endorses national forest certification systems using Sustainability Benchmarks that allow the systems to be compared.

Forestry Stewardship Council (FSC)

The Forestry Stewardship Council (FSC) (**www.fsc.org**) is an independent, non-governmental, not-for-profit organization established in 1993 to promote the responsible management of the world's forests. A response to concerns over global deforestation, it is a pioneer global forum seeking to define and implement environmentally appropriate, socially beneficial, and economically viable forest management. FSC is nationally represented in more than 50 countries around the world.

FSC certification is a voluntary, market-based program that supports responsible forest management worldwide and enables consumers and businesses to make purchasing decisions that benefit people and the environment, as well as provide ongoing business value. FSC certified forest products are verified from the forest of origin through the supply chain. The FSC label ensures forest products used are from responsibly harvested and verified sources.

FSC certification guarantees that civil and indigenous rights of local residents and workers are respected, areas of high social and environmental conservation value are maintained or enhanced, natural forests are not converted to plantations, highly hazardous pesticides and genetically modified trees are prohibited, and harvesting is done according to the requirements of national laws and international treaties.

The certification process is carried out by independent organizations accredited by the FSC, who have to comply with an extensive set of rules. FSC owns three trademarks: the initials "FSC," the words "Forest Stewardship Council," and the FSC Logo. The FSC trademarks offer a guarantee that wood products come from responsible sources.

Sustainable Forestry Initiative Inc. (SFI)

The Sustainable Forestry Initiative Inc. (SFI) (**www.sfiprogram.org**) is an independent, non-governmental, not-for-profit organization that promotes sustainable forest management by working with conservation groups, local communities, resource professionals, landowners, and other organizations and individuals concerned with responsible forest management. The SFI program only certifies lands in the United States and Canada, where social concerns are addressed through extensive forest regulations, effective enforcement, and an open, democratic governance system. The SFI forest certification standard is based on principles of sustainable forest management, including protection of water quality, biodiversity, wildlife habitat, species at risk, and forests with exceptional conservation value. Program participants must comply with laws covering civil rights, equal employment opportunities, anti-discrimination and anti-harassment measures, workers' compensation, indigenous peoples' rights, workers' and communities' right to know, prevailing wages, workers' right to organize, and occupational health and safety. SFI program participants must also take steps to show that fiber they buy offshore is from responsible and legal sources.

The Sustainable Forestry Initiative® (SFI®) label indicates you are buying wood and paper products from a responsible source, backed by a rigorous, third-party certification audit.

The American Tree Farm System

The American Tree Farm System® (ATFS) (www.treefarmsystem.org), a program of the American Forest Foundation's Center for Family Forests, is committed to sustaining forests, watershed, and healthy habitats through private stewardship. Since 1941, ATFS has certified 24 million acres of privately owned forestland and more than 90,000 family forest owners in 46 states. Tree Farmers share a unique commitment to protect wildlife habitat and watersheds, to conserve soil, and to provide recreation for their communities while producing wood. Private forest owners must develop a management plan based on strict environmental standards and pass an inspection by an ATFS volunteer forester every five years. Tree Farms are varied in nature and contain many different habitats and stages of forest regeneration, from seedlings to mature timber. Biodiversity is a critical component of a certified Tree Farm. Tree Farmers must maintain natural forest buffers and practice other conservation techniques.

Timber framing and post-and-beam construction

Timber framing construction is an ancient craft that has regained popularity over the last 25 years. The frame of a house is built of precisely shaped wooden posts and beams carefully fashioned to fit together and joined with traditional mortise and tenon and dovetail joints and pegs. Timber framing uses fewer, larger wooden

members (6-inch to 12-inch) than stick framing, and a variety of engineering techniques to carry the weight of the structure. The beautiful timber framework is often left exposed in the interior of the building.

Today, timber framing is done with assistance of computer aided design (CAD) and computer numerical control (CNC) manufacturing. Most manufacturers cut and assemble the frame in the factory, then take it apart and ship it to the building site. The frame is often covered with manufactured panels, such as SIPs (structural insulated panels), that are energy efficient and easy to install. Straw bales or conventional insulation can also be used to fill in between the posts.

Because timber framing uses more wood than is used in a conventionally framed house, it could be considered to be less green unless the wood is carefully sourced. Wood can be regarded as a renewable resource if the timber is salvaged, FSC-certified, or cut from standing dead wood.

Post-and-beam framing resembles timber framing except that metal fasteners, bolts, and steel plate connectors are used to join adjacent pieces together. The frame is constructed using heavy posts (vertical members) and beams (horizontal members), and the metal connectors may be hidden or exposed as decorative elements. The strength and size of the posts and beams allow for wide spans between the posts, conserving lumber. The structure leaves large open spaces in the interior of the building, allowing for easy and inexpensive renovations as housing styles change over time. Wood post and beam frames usually require additional structural elements such as diagonal braces, shear panels, and infill framing to create a stable structure.

Advanced framing

Ninety-five percent of new homes in the United States today are stick framed. The "sticks" are lumber cut in standard dimensions that are nailed or fastened together vertically and horizontally to form a frame that supports the walls and roof of the house. Interior and exterior walls are attached to the sticks (also called studs), which are placed at regular intervals and reinforced with diagonal braces or plywood siding. Wherever there is a joint, corner, window, or door, the studs are doubled or tripled to provide nailing support for window frames and other structures.

There are several disadvantages to stick framing:

- Not enough tradesmen are trained to frame correctly, with the result that they overcompensate by adding extra studs or create complex arrangements that are difficult to insulate.

- Too much wood is used because standard practices are followed and studs are often placed too close together or unnecessarily doubled up.

- Stick frames are difficult to insulate properly. Insulation loses its effectiveness when it is compressed in tight corners or cannot be made to fit into some spaces.

- Each stud acts as a thermal bridge between the interior wall and the exterior wall of the building; the more studs used, the more thermal bridges conducting heat through the building envelope.

- There are too many places where moisture can infiltrate wall cavities.

- The quality of the structural material on the market has decreased over the last decade.

- The system is only built to last 30 years.

- Plumbers, electricians, and HVAC contractors often weaken the structure inadvertently by cutting into studs to place conduits.

In the 1970s, the NAHB Research Foundation conducted studies to see how more insulation could be inserted in wall cavities to improve energy efficiency. The study found that, on average, about 20 percent of the wood used in traditional framing could be removed without compromising the structural integrity of a building. The result was advanced framing, or optimal value engineering (OVE). Advanced framing matches the size and placement of framing components to their functions and the weight they must carry and eliminates excess or unnecessary studs. In a 28-foot by 40-foot two-story house, the savings are equivalent to eliminating about 35 studs.

Structural building components

Structural building components are prefabricated framing elements such as roof trusses, floor trusses, and wall panels. Using structural building components cuts down on waste and on the labor required to frame a building. The efficiency of structural building components was tested during *Framing the American Dream*®, a project sponsored by the Wood Truss Council of America (WTCA), individual component manufacturers, supplier companies, and the Building Systems Council of NAHB. Two 2,600-square-foot homes were built simultaneously, one using wood component systems framing, and the other using fully engineered conventional stick framing. The results:

- Builders spent 148 hours framing the home with components; the conventional home took 401 hours, 67 percent longer than framing with components.

- 15,100 board feet were used to frame the component home, while 20,400 board feet of lumber were used to frame the conventional home — 26 percent more lumber than in the component house.

- Scrap generated was 4 yards for the component home and 17 yards for the conventional home.

Building components can be designed specifically for a house, constructed, dried, and tested at the manufacturing facility and delivered to the building site ready to be assembled. Leftover wood scraps at the factory can be used in the manufacture of other components.

Engineered wood

Engineered wood, also called manufactured or composite wood, is made using scrap wood from sawmills and salvaged wood (such as wood from pallets or demol-

A close up of the texture of fiberboard.

ished buildings). It is environmentally friendly because it reuses material that would otherwise end up as waste and reduces the need to harvest more timber. In some applications, it is superior to natural timber.

Engineered wood can be manufactured to exact specifications and is free of many natural anomalies, such as knots, soft spots, burls, and splits. It is used for ceiling and floor joists, which benefit from the strict adherence to specified dimensions, strength, and trueness of the planks; glue laminated (Glulam) timber beams that have exceptional strength ideal for spanning long distances; oriented strand board (OSB); and a variety of siding products. Finger-jointed studs, made by joining short pieces of wood together into a longer stud, are made from cured wood and do not warp, twist, or split like studs made from sawn green lumber.

All engineered wood products contain binders or adhesives. Some of the adhesives used in the bonding process may be toxic, and construction workers may have to wear PPE (personal protective equipment) such as respirators when cutting to avoid inhaling any potential toxins. Any product with an APA stamp from APA-The Engineered Wood Association (**www.apawood. org**) uses phenolic resin, which is not the same as the urea-formaldehyde used for particleboard and medium density fiberboard (MDF). Phenolic resin offgasses only a minute percentage (4 percent) of the formaldehyde emitted by those products.

Autoclaved Aerated Concrete (AAC)

Autoclaved aerated concrete (AAC), also called autoclaved cellular concrete, is a precast structural product made with all-natural raw materials. It is manufactured as a solid block that provides thermal and acoustic insulation, as well as fire and termite resistance. It is both economical and sustainable. AAC is available in many shapes and forms, ranging from wall and roof panels to blocks and lintels.

A popular building material in Europe for more than 50 years, AAC has only been introduced in the United States during the past 20 years. AAC is made by mixing Portland cement with lime, silica sand, or recycled fly ash, water, and aluminum powder or paste. The resulting mixture is poured into a mold. A chemical reaction between aluminum and concrete forms microscopic hydrogen bubbles that expand the concrete to about five times its original volume. After the hydrogen evaporates, the aerated concrete is cut to size and formed by steam curing in a pressurized chamber to produce a non-organic, nontoxic, airtight material that can be used for many purposes. Blocks can be cut on site and laid like concrete blocks. AAC replaces wood, house wrap, insulation, and drywall with a single block.

AAC has an R-value of approximately 1.25 per inch, dependent on density, significantly outperforming conventional concrete block or poured concrete. It serves as a suitable thermal mass for passive solar heating.

Steel frames

Studs made of recycled steel are lighter than wood and guaranteed to be straight. Steel framing components are manufactured to strict tolerance levels, which results in consistent strength, straightness, and dimensional stability. The inherent strength of steel allows it to span longer than wood, and resist wind and earthquake loads. It is resistant to corrosion, warping, and termites.

All cold-formed steel framing contains a minimum of 25 percent recycled steel and is 100 percent recyclable. Because the components are pre-cut to specified sizes and shapes, only about 2 percent of the material is wasted at the job site during construction compared to about 20 percent for wood stick framing. A steel-framed structure can be made airtight, which conserves energy, and is durable, which reduces the need for future building resources.

Metal conducts heat, so steel studs and the screws that fasten them to walls can act as thermal bridges in exterior walls. The Oak Ridge National Laboratory found that exterior steel framing reduces the effectiveness of cavity insulation by as much as 50 percent. A steel-framed structure should be insulated with a layer of rigid foam insulation attached to the outside of the building. Steel framing is efficient for inside walls and can be put in place more quickly than wood framing.

Structural insulated panels (SIPs)

Structural insulated panels (SIPs) are high performance building panels used in floors, walls, and roofs. SIPs provide structural framing, insulation, and exterior sheathing all in one solid, one-piece component and can be custom designed for each home. Typically, a core of rigid foam plastic insulation is sandwiched between two structural skins of oriented strand board (OSB), but other materials can be used for the skin and the cores are sometimes made of agricultural fiber with similar thermal properties. The result is a building system that is extremely strong, energy efficient, and cost effective. Building with SIPs will save you time, money, and labor.

Some panel manufacturers use machines that automate forming and cutting according to dimensions downloaded from digital floor plans. Manufacturers can also produce curved walls or other customized architectural features. Workers can assemble the precut panels at the job site without extensive training. The exterior building envelope is quickly completed, making construction much easier in cold weather.

Bonding the foam core to the stiff outer skins creates structural strength that can withstand high wind and seismic forces. Properly designed and assembled SIPs replace conventional framing. Openings for doors and windows are framed with dimensional lumber or with insulated headers using sandwiched foam that has been specially designed to use in conjunction with SIPs. SIPs are more airtight overall and provide better thermal performance than conventionally framed walls because they form a dense, uniform, and continuous air barrier with few thermal bridges, and no opportunity for internal convection.

SIPs are typically manufactured with channels through the foam to accommodate electrical wiring. Electrical contractors should be made aware of these channels, and the manufacturer should be informed if additional channels are needed. The SIPs must be protected from water with a waterproof membrane and flashing, or they will lose their strength.

Insulation

Insulation is a crucial component of your green home project because proper insulation is essential for maximum energy efficiency. Quality insulation combines products and construction techniques that protect a home from outside hot or cold temperatures, control moisture, and protect it against air leaks. A variety of insulating products and technologies exist. In selecting the best insulation for your project, you will need to consider a number of factors: the climate in your area (which determines how much insulation you need); your construction budget; local building codes; the skills and experience of your building contractor; whether certain materials and technologies are available in your area; and the way insulating materials may affect indoor air quality.

Insulation's resistance to heat transfer is measured in R-values. An R-value is expressed as the thickness of the material divided by the thermal conductivity. The higher the R-value of your insulation, the better your walls and roof will resist the transfer of heat. Increasing the thickness of an insulating layer increases the thermal resistance.

The type of insulation you choose determines how your building will be framed and how it will be detailed on the outside. Different types of insulation have different R-values. Studs must be sized and placed to achieve the required R-value for walls and ceilings. The thickness of an exterior insulating wrap affects siding, windows, and doors. Your choice of insulation will also ultimately determine the size of your HVAC system because an airtight, heavily insulated building requires a smaller system.

The amount and type of insulation to use depends on the climate, the type of building, and the part of the house being insulated. Building codes normally specify the R-values that will achieve an acceptable level of energy efficiency under local conditions. Green buildings should exceed these standards by 50 percent; however, excessive and unnecessary insulation wastes money and resources. The DOE ZIP Code Insulation Calculator (**www. ornl.gov/~roofs/Zip/ZipHome.html**) shows the amount of insulation appropriate for your geographical location.

Insulation does not always perform up to its stated R-value. If it is compressed into corners and small spaces, it loses resistance to heat. Over time, insulation may subside and become thinner. Moisture also makes insulation ineffective. Heat can flow around insulation through joists and beams, around windows and doors, and in places where the insulation does not reach. Insulation that is not properly installed does not achieve its specified R-value. In a stick-framed building, heat transfer through the wood studs lowers the R-value by an average of 15 percent. Steel framing can lower it by as much as 50 percent.

There is no single rule for choosing the "greenest" insulation because several factors must be considered. The first is energy efficiency: how well the insulation performs, its durability, its resistance to movement of air and moisture. Another consideration is the amount of recycled material the insulation product contains. In the United States, most fiberglass insulation has a minimum of 20 to 30 percent recycled content. Slag wool (insulation made from mineral fibers), cotton, and cellulose use 75 percent recycled content. The durability of the insulation is important: how long before it has to be discarded and replaced? Also, can it be recycled when it no longer serves its purpose? Finally, there are concerns about off-gassing and the chemical content of the insulation material and whether it is made from renewable materials.

Insulation recycling statistics

According to the National Association of Insulation Manufacturers (NAIMA) (www.naima.org/pages/benefits/environ/recycled.html):

- In the last decade, manufacturers of fiberglass and slag wool insulation have diverted more than 20 billion pounds of glass and blast furnace slag from America's solid waste stream.

- The slag wool industry consumes a significant portion — approximately 6 percent — of the blast furnace slag produced in the United States that might otherwise end up in a landfill.

- Fiberglass insulation manufacturers recycle more material by weight than any other type of insulation used in the building and construction sector. In the last ten years for which data is available, nearly 9.5 billion pounds of recycled glass and nearly 11 billion pounds of recycled blast furnace slag have been used in the manufacture of fiberglass and slag wool insulation.

- More than 90 percent of slag used in slag wool insulation is purchased from manufacturers and the remaining 10 percent mined directly from waste disposal sites.

- On average, slag wool insulation contains 75 percent recycled content.

- Many fiberglass insulation products now contain up to 40 percent recycled materials, depending on where they are produced.

- Fiberglass insulation is highly compact and requires fewer packages to be transported and used for each building insulated.

- An added environmental benefit of mixing recycled materials with raw materials is that insulation manufacturers are able to use less energy during production than by using raw materials alone.

There are four basic types of insulation:

Rolls and batts

Rolls and batts are flexible blankets made from mineral fibers and are sold in widths adapted to standard spacings of wall studs and attic or floor joists. Fiberglass batts are the most widely used type of insulation in the United States but must be installed carefully to prevent air leaks around windows, vents, electrical outlets, and other openings. Some brands of fiberglass batt contain formaldehyde, and there are concerns about possible harmful effects of glass fibers in the air.

Batt insulation is also made from mineral wool (rockwool or slag wool), as well as from natural cotton and sheep's wool. In the United States, mineral wool insulation is more commonly used for industrial and marine purposes. Cotton and sheep's wool are environmentally appealing but cost more and are more difficult to obtain.

Batt insulation performs most effectively when it is properly installed. It should fit exactly between studs and cover the entire area being insulated right up to door and window frames. It should be neatly cut to fit around obstructions such as pipes and electrical wiring in the walls. Studies have shown that even a small gap in batt insulation can reduce energy efficiency by as much as 50 percent. Batt insulation must also maintain its loft, or depth. It loses R-value when it is crammed or compressed into a small space such as the corner of an eave. Properly installing batt insulation requires time and attention to detail. Sometimes contractors are in a hurry and fail to close up all the gaps.

Insulation made from recycled blue jeans

UltraTouch™ Denim Insulation (http://bondedlogic.com) is made from 90 percent recycled post-consumer denim. It contains no chemical irritants, does not cause itching, is easy to handle, and is 100 percent recyclable. It comes in batts made to fit inside 2x4 and 2x6 walls, with R-values ranging from R-13 to R-21.

Loose-fill insulation

Usually loose fibers or fiber pellets made of fiberglass, rock wool, or cellulose, loose-fill insulation is blown into spaces using special pneumatic equipment. It conforms easily to building cavities and attics.

Rigid foam insulation

Rigid foam insulation is more expensive than fiber insulation but is effective in buildings with space limitations. Foam insulation R-values range from R-4 to R-6.5 per inch of thickness, up to 2 times greater than most other insulating materials of the same thickness. Rigid foam insulation is used to insulate around foundations and under slabs.

Foam-in-place, or spray foam insulation

Foam-in-place insulation is a foam that can be blown into wall cavities. It has an R-value of up to 6.5 per inch and is effective as both a thermal barrier and an air barrier. It prevents air from moving through walls and reduces air leakage around window and doorframes by filling in cracks and small gaps around corners and around electrical boxes.

Spray-in foam must be applied by a skilled professional using special equipment. As the liquid spray hardens, it expands to fill the wall cavity. The excess foam is trimmed off, a thermal barrier is applied, and then the wall, floor, or ceiling area is enclosed. There are two types of spray-in insulation: low-density open cell and high-density closed cell, which has a higher R-value. Both types expand on contact to fill in empty spaces and small cavities, but different types of blowing agents are used for the process. Open cell spray foam insulation uses water as a blowing agent, which reacts with air to produce bubbles of CO_2. These bubbles expand rapidly and burst before the plastic sets, creating a spongy, lightweight foam that allows some vapor to pass through it while still providing an air barrier. Open cell insulation has lower R-values than closed-cell insulation, but it is ideal for hot, humid climates where less insulation is required. It has almost twice the noise-reduction coefficient as closed cell foam. Closed cell spray foam uses hydroflourocarbons (HFCs) as blowing agents. Instead of bursting, the gas bubbles become trapped in the plastic as it sets, forming an impermeable barrier to both moisture and air. Closed cell insulation costs 20 to 30 percent more than open cell but requires little trimming, so only a small amount is wasted. It adds to the structural strength of the building and is recommended for areas prone to flooding because it is resistant to moisture.

Open cell foam can expand as much as 100 percent, and the denser closed cell foam expands about 30 percent. To create a thicker layer of insulation and prevent thermal bridging in a stud-framed wall, light metal channels can be nailed horizontally across the inside of the studs to hold the foam. The foam quickly hardens into a smooth layer of insulation that covers the studs as well as the cavities. To comply with building codes, all insulation must be covered with a thermal barrier such as drywall.

The Difference Between Open-Cell and Closed-Cell Spray Foam Insulation

Steve Easley is a construction quality consultant who specializes in solving building science-related problems. He provides consulting and seminars on topics such as better building practices, energy efficient construction techniques, and cost-effective green building. Contact him at steve@steveeasley.com or visit **www.steveeasley.com**.

The following is an excerpt from his article, "Pros and Cons of Closed and Open Cell Spray Foam Insulation," in the August 2007 issue of LBM Journal (**www.LBMJournal.com**)

Spray foam costs more than traditional insulation, but it can be a cost effective way to build high-performance homes and meet stricter energy codes. The two basic families of spray foam are typically classified as either open cell spray foam or closed cell spray foam. I prefer closed cell spray foam products because of its superior properties.

To understand the differences between these two spray foam product families, it's important to understand what makes traditional insulation such as fibrous, cellulose, and open cell spray foam resist heat flow. Those items work because of their ability to trap air. The greater the number of air pockets, the higher the R-value. What makes closed cell spray foam superior is that in addition to trapping air, it also prevents air from flowing through it and therefore reduces the heat scavenging effects of wind-washing. It's like putting a windbreaker over a sweater. When it comes to spray foams, their performance is governed by:

- The number and size of bubbles or pockets
- What the bubbles are filled with

In open cell spray foam insulation, the bubbles are cross-linked or connected by air pockets and typically have R-values around 3.5 per inch, about the same as fiberglass. Closed cell spray foam uses blowing agents that create millions of tiny bubbles that are filled with gases less conductive than air. The result is an aged R-value of around 6 to 6.8 per inch. The gas inside the closed cell foam works on the same principle as the inert gases used between the panes of glass on a high-performance window.

Closed cell spray foam is very strong and has a much higher compressive and tensile strength than do open cell foams. Some studies have shown that closed cell spray foam insulation increases the **racking strength** (a measure of walls' ability to resist wind loads) of walls as much as 300 percent. Essentially, by using closed cell foam, you are gluing a house together with high R-value insulation that is highly water-resistant. In fact, closed cell spray foam has been used on the top of roof decks of flat roof commercial buildings for more than 50 years because it absorbs almost no water and does not allow moisture vapor to pass through it. Closed cell spray foam, to my knowledge, is the only FEMA-approved insulation typically used for cavity insulation in hurricane areas. This is because it does not store water.

Open and closed cell spray foams often look alike, and it can be difficult to visually differentiate between the two. Both types come in a variety of colors. If in doubt, simply squeeze a sample and examine it. Open cell spray foam will compress very easily, something like angel food cake. By comparison, closed cell spray foam is difficult to crush. In fact, there are some closed cell spray foams that you can actually stand on.

Both open and closed cell foam are good products if, like any insulation, they are installed correctly. If I were building a home, I would use closed cell spray foam because it has the highest R-value per inch; it seals to reduce air infiltration; it is highly water-resistant; and it does not store water. The product also makes a home more storm-resistant.

Spray foam insulation costs more than other types of insulation, but it ultimately pays for itself in several ways. It reduces energy bills because it is highly efficient. The foam can be installed quickly compared to the painstaking and time-consuming labor of fitting batting around corners and tight spaces. Some builders cut costs by using the foam-in-place insulation in corners and around windows and doors in exterior walls, and insulating the rest of the area with fiberglass batting. Spray-in foam saves on the labor and expense of making a house airtight by eliminating the need to caulk around openings, tape joints, and apply house wrap or vapor barriers.

How green is spray foam insulation?

There is an active debate among environmentalists about whether closed cell spray foam insulation can really be considered "green." It fulfills the criteria of energy efficiency more effectively than any other type of insulation, providing twice the R-value, sealing all corners and tiny openings, and making a building airtight. Because it absorbs no moisture, it does not harbor mold and mildew that contribute to low IAQ. It is durable and adds to the structural strength of the building.

Critics says that the blowing agent used for closed cell spray foam contains large quantities of greenhouse gases that might escape into the atmosphere. According to Environmental Building News, the greenhouse gas in the blowing has a global warming potential (GWP) of more than 1,000. **GWP** is a measure of how much a given mass of greenhouse gas is estimated to contribute to global warming. The gas is compared to the same mass of carbon dioxide, which has a GWP of 1. The environmental payback time — the time it would take for the amount of fossil fuel emissions prevented by using closed cell insulation to equal the greenhouse gasses released if 50 percent of the blowing agent leaks out of the foam over time — for 4 inches of closed cell spray foam insulation is 65 years. In contrast, open cell spray foam, which uses water as a blowing agent, has a GWP of only 1 and a very short payback time. From this point of view, unless a different blowing agent is available for closed cell spray foam, it would be greener to use a less efficient insulation. Spray foam manufacturers point out that the analysis used in Environmental Building News does not consider the air tightness provided by closed cell spray foam insulation. When increased energy efficiency due to air tightness is taken into account, along with the greenhouse gases emitted while manufacturing, replacing, and recycling different types of insulation, manufacturers claim that the payback time for closed cell spray foam becomes half that of cellulose insulation and one quarter that of fiberglass insulation.

Polyurethane foam (SPF) is created by mixing two components known in the spray foam industry as the "A side" and "B side." When the components are mixed, a chemical reaction occurs that releases air bubbles trapped in the hardening plastic. The A half is a petroleum-based isocyanate, and the B half is made up of a variety of ingredients including a blowing agent, catalysts, surfactants, flame retardants, and polyols. The polyols often contain sucrose-based or soy-based agricultural products or recycled products. Many manufacturers market "bio-based" foam products that they claim contain large percentages of agricultural material. In fact, it is only the polyol portion that contains agricultural materials; they make up only 10 to 20 percent of the total foam product. The USDA allows a material to be called "bio-based" if it contains only 7 percent agricultural products. Even though spray foam insulation is more than 50 percent petroleum, it can be considered a more efficient use of petroleum than driving a car. Spray foam insulation has a long life and does not need to be replaced as often as other types of insulation.

GREEN PRODUCT SPOTLIGHT

For those homeowners interested in using energy-efficient spray foam insulation, Icynene (**www.icynene.com**) offers high-performance insulation used in various projects, including The American Lung Association's Health House, Yale University's Yale Building Project, and The New American Home, and has been featured on sustainable building programs on HGTV, the Discovery Channel, and PBS. Icynene's products are sold in more than 30 countries and agencies such as the International Code Council Evaluation Service, European Economic Area, and The Canadian Construction Materials Centre have offered their product approval.

Icynene spray foam being applied to a home's interior

Icynene's light density spray foam insulation has been used in thousands of projects for more than 20 years and is considered the industry standard for quality and innovation that other insulation products are compared against. Using their insulation can provide a 50 percent savings on heating and cooling costs. Aside from the cost and energy savings this spray foam insulation can offer, using this type of insulation is often listed as a selling feature when a home is placed on the market.

Cementitious foam

Cementitious foam consists entirely of air and magnesium oxide (MgO) extracted from seawater. It is blown through a membrane with air as the blowing agent so air bubbles are trapped in the magnesium oxide. A membrane, typically netting or polyethylene, is stretched tightly across the studs, and the cementitious foam is blown in. It is nontoxic even during application, does not emit VOCs, is moldproof, resists insects, and is insoluble in water. It can also be blown into cavities in existing walls and is safer to use than other spray foam insulations because it does not expand rapidly on contact.

Cementitious foam makes an effective sound barrier. It is fireproof and does not give off smoke when it burns. Newly installed cementitious foam contains water and requires a drying period before the wall can be closed up. It does not shrink or settle. To achieve a high R-value, the material must be used at low densities, which makes it **friable** (easily crumbled) when it is dry.

Air-Krete, a manufacturer of cementitious foam, likes to point out that recent studies have proven that (MgO) absorbs CO_2 (carbon dioxide), actually removing greenhouse gases from the atmosphere.

Selecting insulation

When selecting your insulation, you will need to consider a number of factors including your budget, your geographical location, available labor, and the future savings you can realize through energy efficiency. The manufacturer typically provides detailed information on the packaging of insulation products, and you can look for additional details on the manufacturers' websites and industry websites and blogs. These questions will help you select the best insulation for your project:

What is the insulation R-value per inch?

The climate in your geographical location determines how much insulation you need. The DOE ZIP Code Insulation Calculator shows the appropriate R-value for your climate.

What are the air barrier properties/effective R-value under a wind load?

Hot or cold winds blowing around the house can draw off heat or cold through the walls if there is not an effective air barrier. Some types of insulation act as air barriers; others require adding a house wrap or other air barrier.

Does it trap or store water?

Moisture trapped in insulation leads to the growth of mold and mildew, and some insulations lose R-value when they are wet. It is crucial to install the insulation correctly so that it is kept dry, and to use vapor barriers when needed to protect it from condensation.

What is the cost per square foot?

The price of the insulation material is only part of the cost — consider how many hours of labor will be needed to install it and how much you will save on energy bills over time. If the insulation material also acts as an air barrier, you will not have to spend additional money to install a house wrap.

Does it have low permeability?

Permeability is the degree to which air is able to pass through insulating material. Some materials, such as fiberglass batts, are highly permeable. When insulation has high permeability, an additional air barrier is necessary next to the insulation layer.

Does it add structural value to the building?

SIPs combine structural framework with insulation. Rigid foam insulation and spray-in insulation help to stabilize the building frame by providing solid support between studs inside the wall cavities.

Does it maintain its R-value over a wide range of temperatures?

Select an insulation that performs well for the temperature range in your location.

Does it settle or lose its insulation properties?

Loose fill and batting insulations may lose E-value over time as they compress or settle. It may be necessary to increase the R-value to ensure the home is still well insulated after ten or 20 years.

Does it control sound?

Insulation plays an important role in shutting out external noise such as traffic sounds and absorbing sound within a building. If you live in a noisy urban environment, noise control is particularly important.

Does installing the insulation require special equipment or skills? How much clean up is involved?

Your labor costs will be higher if you have to bring in special equipment or a trained contractor to install it. Spray foam insulation involves more cleanup work than batting or loose fill insulation. Make sure that laborers use protective eyewear and masks if recommended and that building occupants or other laborers are not exposed to harmful dust or gases during installation.

DOE Map Showing Recommended Insulation for New Houses

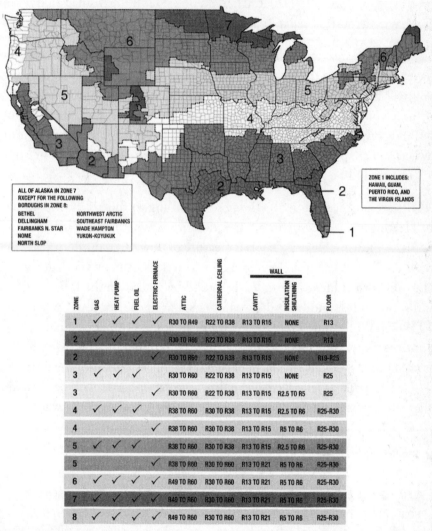

U.S. Department of Energy Recommended* Total R-Values
for New Wood-Framed Houses

ALL OF ALASKA IN ZONE 7
RXCEPT FOR THE FOLLOWING
BOROUGHS IN ZONE 8:

BETHEL   NORTHWEST ARCTIC
DELLINGHAM   SOUTHEAST FAIRBANKS
FAIRBANKS N. STAR   WADE HAMPTON
NOME   YUKON-KOYUKUK
NORTH SLOP

ZONE 1 INCLUDES:
HAWAII, GUAM,
PUERTO RICO, AND
THE VIRGIN ISLANDS

ZONE	GAS	HEAT PUMP	FUEL OIL	ELECTRIC FURNACE	ATTIC	CATHEDRAL CEILING	WALL CAVITY	INSULATION SHEATHING	FLOOR
1	✓	✓	✓	✓	R30 TO R49	R22 TO R38	R13 TO R15	NONE	R13
2	✓	✓	✓		R30 TO R60	R22 TO R38	R13 TO R15	NONE	R13
2				✓	R30 TO R60	R22 TO R38	R13 TO R15	NONE	R19-R25
3	✓	✓	✓		R30 TO R60	R22 TO R38	R13 TO R15	NONE	R25
3				✓	R30 TO R60	R22 TO R38	R13 TO R15	R2.5 TO R5	R25
4	✓	✓	✓		R38 TO R60	R30 TO R38	R13 TO R15	R2.5 TO R6	R25-R30
4				✓	R38 TO R60	R30 TO R38	R13 TO R15	R5 TO R6	R25-R30
5	✓	✓	✓		R38 TO R60	R30 TO R38	R13 TO R15	R2.5 TO R6	R25-R30
5				✓	R38 TO R60	R30 TO R60	R13 TO R21	R5 TO R6	R25-R30
6	✓	✓	✓	✓	R49 TO R60	R30 TO R60	R13 TO R21	R5 TO R6	R25-R30
7	✓	✓	✓	✓	R49 TO R60	R30 TO R60	R13 TO R21	R5 TO R6	R25-R30
8	✓	✓	✓	✓	R49 TO R60	R30 TO R60	R13 TO R21	R5 TO R6	R25-R30

Vapor barriers

A vapor diffusion retarder (VDR), also called a vapor barrier, is a membrane, coating, or sheet of solid material that impedes vapor diffusion in basements, ceilings, crawl spaces, floors, foundations, and walls. A VDR helps to retain heat in a home and prevents walls, wood, and insulation from coming in contact with moisture. VDRs help control moisture in walls, floors, crawl spaces, basements, and ceilings. A typical VDR is a thin sheet of polyethylene film, aluminum foil, or an asphalt-impregnated kraft paper through which water vapor cannot pass easily. Many insulation products come with a VDR attached on one side. If the insulation does not come with a VDR, a separate one can be installed.

Many new homes are built with VDRs, but some older homes may not have these installed. If your home already has a VDR underneath its siding, you will be able to see it by removing a section of your aluminum siding or other outer layer of your home. If your home has a VDR, then your building envelope is tight. It is difficult to add a VDR to an existing home. When you are planning a remodeling project or an addition to your home, a VDR should be included.

VDRs are not needed in all climates. According to the DOE, the number of Heating Degree Days in an area determine whether and how to use a VDR. A Heating Degree Day is a measure of how often outdoor daily dry-bulb temperatures fall below an assumed base, normally 65 degrees F. In climates with cold winters, a VDR should be placed on the interior side of walls, but in hot and humid climates (such as in Florida and Louisiana), a VDR should be added to exterior walls. In some southern climates, homeowners should not use a VDR because the number of days when heating is used roughly equals the number of days when air conditioning is needed. This means that at least half of the time, the vapor barrier will be located in the wrong place and may lead to condensation forming in the walls.

Vapor barriers should be intact

A VDR should be continuous and as close to perfect as possible, especially in very cold climates and in hot and humid climates. Any tears, openings, or punctures that occur during construction should be completely repaired and sealed. All appropriate surfaces must be covered to prevent moist air condensing within the wall cavity and wetting the insulation.

This chart from the DOE (**www.energysavers.gov/your_home/insulation_airsealing/index.cfm/mytopic=11810**) shows where and how a VDR should be installed on your home. A perm at 73.4 degrees F is a measure of the number of grains of water vapor passing through a square foot of material per hour at a differential vapor pressure equal to 1 inch of mercury (1" W.C.) Any material with a perm rating of less than 1.0 is considered a vapor retarder.

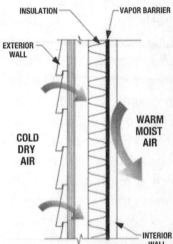

A vapor barrier on the side of the insulation facing the inside of the house prevents condensation from forming inside the exterior wall when moisture-laden air from inside hits a cold surface.

Vapor Barrier Placement By Geographical Location

In most cold climates, vapor barriers should be placed on the interior (warm-in-winter) side of walls. However, the map shows that in some southern climates, the vapor barrier should be omitted, while in hot and humid climates, such as along the Gulf coast and in Florida, the vapor barrier should be placed on the exterior of the wall.

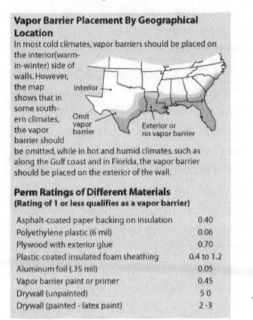

Perm Ratings of Different Materials
(Rating of 1 or less qualifies as a vapor barrier)

Asphalt-coated paper backing on insulation	0.40
Polyethylene plastic (6 mil)	0.06
Plywood with exterior glue	0.70
Plastic-coated insulated foam sheathing	0.4 to 1.2
Aluminum foil (.35 mil)	0.05
Vapor barrier paint or primer	0.45
Drywall (unpainted)	5 0
Drywall (painted - latex paint)	2 - 3

Walls

After a house has been framed, the exterior of the frame is sheathed with solid board, plywood, or oriented strand board (OSB). Sheathing strengthens and stabilizes the building frame. OSB is the greenest choice because it is made from wood fibers instead of whole trees. If plywood or planks are used, they should be FSC-certified. Asphalt fiberboard is also used, but it does not provide as much strength as the wood products, and can outgas asphalt odors. Foil-faced cardboard can also be used for sheathing. A house built with SIPs or ICFs does not need sheathing.

Look for sheathing that does not contain formaldehyde

The glues used to make some plywood and OSB products contain formaldehyde. Though it is used on the outside of the house, offgassing can still affect the indoor air quality of the house.

In a green building, the sheathing is usually covered with a housewrap to promote energy efficiency and protect against water damage. A **housewrap** keeps water from coming into contact with the structural sheathing and framing. It also acts as an air barrier to stop hot and cold air from moving through the wall while allowing moisture vapor to pass through it. Inside an average home, normal daily activities such as showering, cooking, washing clothes and dishes, and even breathing generate 3 to 6 gallons of water vapor each day. Housewrap should permit this water vapor to pass throughout the wall cavity freely so that framing lumber can dry to the outside of the building. Many housewrap products are available on the market. There are two basic types: nonperforated and perforated. Perforated housewraps are either woven or laminated polypropylene films with microscopic punched holes to allow breathability. Nonperforated housewraps are either spun-bounded polyethylene or fiber-mesh-reinforced polyolefin, whose structure enables water vapor to pass through, but inhibits air infiltration. Using housewrap is one of the requirements for the ENERGY STAR® Qualified New Home program as an important element of air sealing and insulating. Various housewrap products also earn LEED-H points. For maximum efficiency, the housewrap must be properly installed with well-sealed seams and no tears or openings.

Siding or cladding

Siding or cladding is the finished surface that covers the exterior of a house. It protects the structure of the house from weather and gives the house aesthetic beauty and architectural character. Traditional wood siding is durable and beautiful but is made from old-growth trees. Modern fiber-cement siding and composites of plastic and wood used recycled materials are durable and do not require painting. Durability is the main quality that makes a siding product "green."

The siding itself does not provide adequate protection from the weather because water from rain and snow can leak behind it. It is necessary to provide a way for moisture that gets behind the siding to evaporate or drain down and away from the building. This can be accomplished with housewrap – Tyvak® and Typar® are two brands of housewrap that shed water while still allowing moisture from inside the house to wick through. An open space can be created behind the siding by nailing thin boards over the housewrap and attaching the siding to them. Special housewraps are available for use behind stucco. Another method is to apply felt paper (usually #15 felt) and cover it with a product that allows water to drain down the wall.

GREEN PRODUCT SPOTLIGHT

Delta®-Dry Rainscreen Systems, made by Cosella-Dörken Products Inc., offer built-in ventilation and drainage layers to prevent moisture from building up behind a home's exterior siding. Cosella-Dörken manufactures nontoxic products that emit zero volatile organic compounds, use high-quality recycled components, are safe to handle and install, and are fully recyclable and sustainable with approximately more than 25 years of expected service. The Delta-Dry system provides drainage and ventilation for water that may be captured in building envelopes and allows water vapor to escape, which minimizes the condensation that can damage the building enclosure.

Illustration of a Delta-Dry rainscreen behind a home's exterior surface.

Including a Delta-Dry system in a home will ensure the wall continues to function as intended and will keep the wall's structural components dry, which will add to its overall life expectancy. Including one of these rainscreens will also yield a healthier home as it will prevent mildew and mold from growing between walls. For more information on Delta-Dry, visit **www.delta-dry.com**.

Delta-Dry ventilated rainscreen on a multifamily home

Wood

Wood siding has been used for hundreds of years, but since modern insulation has made it more difficult for wood to dry out when water gets into wall cavities, wood siding is prone to mold and rot. The only type of wood siding that is durable is cedar or redwood, which seem to resist rot. Several types of FSC-certified cedar shingles are available, but they are expensive and require skilled labor to install. Redwood and cedar planks are still used for siding, but only the wood taken from the heart of a redwood tree resists rot; younger wood is lighter in color and behaves like pine. With any redwood or cedar, the source is questionable unless the wood is FSC-certified. Architectural plywood tends to warp and lose its finish when it is exposed to the elements. In general, unless you can find FSC-certified redwood or cedar, it is preferable to use composite wood or concrete siding.

Stucco

Stucco is a mixture of lime, silica sand, and white cement applied directly to the walls in several layers. It can be applied to block or stone walls, wood sheathing, or rigid foam. A stucco finish should include some kind of drainage plain behind the insulation or between the stucco and

Close up of the texture of stucco.

concrete block. Wooden sheathing is typically covered with tar paper and galvanized mesh or chicken wire before stucco is applied. Sometimes stucco is applied directly to specially prepared masonry surfaces. Stucco should be professionally applied to get a smooth finish. Its application is labor-intensive, which makes it more expensive than other types of cladding. Stucco is guaranteed to last 15 years but can easily last for 50.

Synthetic stucco

For the last half century, a variety of synthetic materials that resemble stucco have been used to finish home exteriors. Exterior Insulation and Finish Systems (EIFS) are composed of three layers: foam insulation board or cement panels secured to the walls; a polymer and cement base coat applied to the top of the insulation and reinforced with glass fiber mesh; and a textured finish coat. The three layers bond to form an airtight surface. There are two types of EIFS — barrier systems and drainable systems. Barrier systems are not suitable for wood walls because they do not allow water drainage that gets behind the surface through fine cracks or window detailing. Drainable EIFS incorporate fiber mesh or grooved foam boards to allow drainage and do not cause wood rot if they are properly installed.

Synthetic stucco is much lighter and softer than real stucco and makes a hollow sound when tapped; real stucco makes a solid sound. The benefit of synthetic stucco is the extra layer of foam insulation on the exterior wall. It must be carefully installed and detailed to prevent damage.

Brick

Brick is often used as a siding over a wood façade. It is durable and requires almost no maintenance. It can be considered a green material because it is baked clay, but the firing process requires more energy than manufacturing other siding materials. It is also heavy and should be purchased locally to avoid transporting it over long distances.

Cement siding

Fiber-cement siding, made with cement, sand, and cellulose fiber, is manufactured to look like various types of wood. It can be colored at the factory or painted. It is guaranteed to last for 50 years, is termite-resistant, water-resistant, and non-combustible. In areas where wildfires are a threat, it prevents fire from climbing up the walls of a house and entering the attic through the soffits. Installation requires some expertise because the siding is brittle.

Vinyl siding

Vinyl siding is widely used because it is relatively inexpensive, durable, and easy to install. It does not have to be painted and is effective in wet climates. Many environmentalists vehemently oppose using vinyl siding because it is made from polyvinyl chloride (PVC). Dioxin, a by-product creating while manufacturing PVC, is an environmental toxin that does not biodegrade. It enters the food chain through waterways and is now globally pervasive. High concentrations have been found in human breast milk. If PVC burns in a house fire or a waste incinerator, hydrogen chloride and dioxin are released into the air. Studies have linked exposure to vinyl chloride and PVC additives to various forms of cancer and other health problems including endocrine disruption, neurological damage, birth defects, impaired development in children, and damage to the reproductive and immune systems. More than 14 billion pounds of PVC are currently produced per year in North America, and about 75 percent of this is used in construction materials. PVC is also difficult to recycle because it has so many additives. Less than 0.5 percent of discarded PVC is recycled each year. In 1998, the Association of Post Consumer Plastics Recyclers declared efforts to recycle PVC a failure and labeled it a contaminant. The environmental hazards posed by PVC far outweigh any benefits from using vinyl siding.

Strawboard panels

Strawboard panels been in used in more than 20 countries for more than 50 years but were only introduced in the United States a few years ago. Strawboard panels are made of solid core, compressed wheat or rice straw. When subjected to high pressure and temperatures (464°F, 240°C), the straw releases a natural resin that binds the fibers together. Then, 100 percent recycled 69# or 85# paper liners are adhered to both sides of the compressed panel with water based nontoxic glue. Strawboard panels replace labor intensive two-by-four stud and drywall construction for interior partition walls and are also used for load and nonbearing ceilings, roofing, doors, flooring, and prefabricated buildings.

Strawboard can be sawn, drilled, routed, nailed, screwed, and glued. Lightweight wall attachments such as shelf brackets, picture frames, mirrors, and towel bars can be attached directly to the panel. A standard straw panel measures 4 feet by 8 feet by 2¼ inches and weighs 140 pounds. Custom panel sizes are available ranging from 1 inch to 3 inches thick and 3 feet to 12 feet long. The panel's high density and low oxygen content does not support combustion. Because the panels do not contain added resins, alcohol, or other chemicals, no flammable vapors are produced. The standard 2-1/4 inch panel has a one-hour fire rating, R-value of 3, and noise level reductions from one side to the other of 32 dB (NTC 0.10).

Sixty million acres of wheat are grown each year in the United States. According to the National Resource Defense Council (NRDC), the byproduct straw is an environmental disposal problem (140 million tons per year) because it is currently being disposed by open air burning. According to a manufacturer, about 10 acres of wheat straw make enough strawboard to build a 1,760 sq. ft. house.

Roofs and Attics

The roof is an integral part of a whole-house system because it acts as a barrier to heat and cold, protects the interior of the building from moisture, helps to regulate the flow of air through the building, and directs storm water runoff when it rains or snows. A roof is also an ideal location for solar panels or a solar water heating system.

Roofing styles and materials are largely determined by geographical location. In cold climates, dark materials are used to absorb heat, and high peaks and steep angles avoid the build-up of heavy snow on the roof. In hot climates, light materials reflect light and heat away from the house. In areas prone to hailstorms, tornados, or hurricanes, roofing material must be resilient and building codes require extra protection from wind damage.

What makes a roof green?

The "greenness" of a roof is determined primarily by the materials that go into it and how efficiently it regulates the house's interior temperature. The roof structure is also important because a properly constructed roof keeps moisture out of walls, prevents mold and mildew, and preserves the building in good condition. The roof structure also affects the insulation's performance. In a green home, the space between the roof and the ceiling acts as a buffer between the interior of the house and the outside climate.

Durability

The longer a roof lasts, the greener it is. An asphalt shingle roof that has to be replaced every 12 to 20 years is not environmentally friendly because the shingles are rarely recycled and end up in landfills. The cost of periodically replacing shingle roofs adds significantly to the cost of home ownership. If the roof is not replaced when it deteriorates, the interior of the house will be damaged by water leaks.

Chemical runoff

Petrochemicals in asphalt shingles, preservatives in wood shingles, and copper and zinc from metal roofs can gradually leach out in rainwater and end up in our waterways, where they are toxic to aquatic life.

Source of materials and embodied energy

Wood from old-growth trees, petroleum products, and products manufactured using large quantities of energy from fossil fuels cannot be classified as sustainable. Manufacturing processes for some products release toxic emissions or greenhouse gases. The energy required to transport materials from the factory to the job site should also be taken into consideration. Materials made from petroleum or with manufacturing processes that use fossil fuels can be justified as "green" if they make a house energy efficient and last a long time.

Energy efficiency

Insulating the roof and attic is an important component of an energy efficient house. A number of techniques and materials are used to insulate roofs and attics. Air leaks often occur in corners and places where drywall is attached to studs and trusses.

Indoor air quality

A well-constructed roof plays a role in protecting indoor air quality by preventing moisture from entering the walls and insulation. Moisture in the walls and ceiling promotes the growth of mold and mildew that release toxic spores into the air. Green roofing materials do not off-gas toxic substances such as formaldehyde.

Maintenance

A green roof requires little maintenance and is easy to clean and repair.

Roofing materials

Apart from its practical functions, roofing material is part of the aesthetic appeal of a house. When selecting a roof for your green home, be sure to review local building codes and also the requirements of your homeowner association (if you have one).

Sheathing and membranes

This site has several helpful illustrations . ***http://homeconstructionshop.com/
instruction/home-construction-shop-and-steps-to-shingle-a-roof***

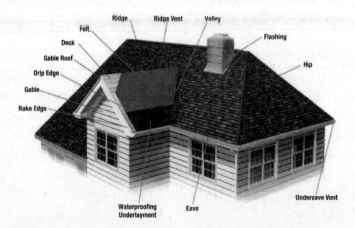

A roof consists of several layers, each of which contributes to the greenness of the whole-house system. The first layer is a sheathing or roof deck attached to the frame. The decking is typically sheets of plywood or OSB (oriented strand board) or tongue-and-groove planks. OSB is the greenest choice because it is made from wood fibers instead of whole trees. If plywood or planks are used, they should be FSC-certified. Other products such as SIPs that integrate insulation with panels can also be used as decking.

OSB (oriented strand board)

The second layer is a waterproof membrane that covers and protects the roof deck. This is usually overlapping sheets of 15- to 30-pound tar paper laid over the decking. Self-adhesive membranes that automatically seal around nails and other penetrations in the roof decking are often used along the edges of roofs and in roof "valleys" — areas where water might back up under the shingles during storms. The extra seal prevents the decking from leaking. In climates with high winds, self-adhesive membranes are sometimes used over the entire roof decking. Some membranes have an extra layer of asphalt-impregnated felt.

Finally, the roof is covered with a surface of shingles, tile, metal, stone, or other material.

Asphalt shingles

Asphalt shingles make up about two-thirds of the U.S. roofing market. Asphalt roofing shingles are made of a felt mat saturated with asphalt with small rock granules added. Asphalt shingles are popular because they are relatively inexpensive and easy to install. They are also resilient to hail.

The National Association of Home Builders (NAHB) estimates that 7 to 10 million tons of shingle tear-off waste and installation scrap are generated from roof installations every year. As with any petroleum-based product, it is necessary to weigh the use of a non-renewable resource against the benefits it conveys. Manufacturing a roof that lasts two or three decades is a more efficient use of petroleum than burning gasoline to run errands in your car. The least expensive asphalt shingles last 12 to 20 years, but shingles are now being manufactured with a 50-year warranty. Though they cost more initially, these shingles avoid having to replace a cheaper roof twice. Initiatives are underway to recycle asphalt roof shingles into fuel or paving materials for roads, The U.S. Environmental Protection Agency's (EPA's) Region 5 (Illinois, Indiana, Michigan, Minnesota, Ohio, and Wisconsin) has begun developing a network of waste recyclers, roofing contractors, roofing manufacturers, paving companies, and regulators to consider recycling options. The Asphalt Roofing Manufacturers Association (ARMA), Construction Materials Recycling Association (CMRA), National Asphalt Pavement Association (NAPA), Asphalt Emulsions Manufacturers Association, and Asphalt Recycling and Reclaiming Association (ARRA) are promoting waste-reduction and recycling programs.

Wood shingles

Good quality wooden shingles are attractive and durable when they are cor rectly installed. Wood shingles need to "breathe" and should be installed so some air can circulate underneath them using either strips of sheathing boards or modern products such as Cedar Breather®, a nylon mesh that goes under the shingles.

The problem with wood shingles is the source of the materials. The best cedar shingles are manufactured from the heartwood of old-growth trees, which is insect- and rot-resistant. Good-quality shingles are also made from southern yellow pine, which is renewable but is often treated with preservatives and fire-retardants that leach chemicals into rainwater runoff. Use shingles that have been certified by the FSC.

Another consideration with wood shingles is the labor involved in installing them. The installation process is time-consuming and requires skill and experience.

Clay tile

Clay tiles are one of the oldest known roofing materials. A clay tile roof can last more than 100 years if it is well maintained. Clay tiles are popular in the hot climates of Florida and the Southwest because they have reflective properties, and the corrugated design allows cooling air to flow underneath the tiles. Clay tiles come in a variety of shapes and colors, which can add character and interest to a home. They have no toxic runoff. If they outlast a house, they can often be removed and reused.

Clay tiles are expensive, but the roof never has to be replaced. Hail can shatter clay tile shingles, and they can break when they are walked on. Extra structural support is needed to support their weight.

Concrete

Concrete tiles are made from Portland cement and sand aggregate to look like clay tiles, slates, or cedar shakes, but cost much less. They have a high embodied energy but are very durable. The materials in concrete tile are biodegradable and renewable, and they do not have toxic runoff. Like clay tile, concrete tiles are fragile and can be fractured by hail.

Fiber-cement

Fiber-cement is made by adding finely ground sawdust to Portland cement to create tiles that are only half the weight of concrete or tile. Because of the lighter weight, they do not require extra structural support. Sawdust is often made from recycled wood, so fiber-cement tiles can be considered greener than concrete or clay tiles. Fiber-cement tiles are brittle and should be professionally installed.

Metal

Various types of metal roofing are becoming increasingly popular. Panels of corrosion-resistant steel, aluminum, or copper are stamped into various textures or are left smooth with ridges. The aluminum panels are made of almost 100 percent recycled content, and steel

Metal tiles are being installed on this new roof.

roofing can contain up to 50 percent recycled material. They come with various coatings and finishings, and in many colors. Metal roofing reflects more of the sun's radiation than it absorbs, keeping the attic cooler.

Many metal roofing products come in sheets that are easier to install than individual shingles or tiles. Metal roofing is the lightest type of roofing. It is fire-resistant and does not rot, crack, or support algae growth. It is designed to resist hurricane-force winds, and some home insurance companies give a discount for metal roofs. It requires little maintenance, but scratches in the finish must be painted over to avoid rusting. Care must be taken when walking on the roof not to dent the panels. Metal roofing, as with asphalt shingles, must be installed over a solid roof decking with a 15- or 30-pound felt underlayment. When installed in this way, it is as quiet during a rainstorm as any other type of roofing.

Avoid using copper or galvanized zinc roofing. Copper and zinc leach into rainwater draining from the roof and are toxic to aquatic life. Metal roofing that is not covered with stone granules can be recycled.

Slate

Slate roofs are expensive but attractive. Slate shingles are made by cutting or splitting rock, and are very durable. They can be removed from one building and used on another over and over. Installation requires a skilled professional. Slate is susceptible to degradation caused by acid rain, which is present in areas where coal-burning power plants give off sulfuric acid.

Polymer composites

Polymers combined with various products such as fiberglass, ground clay, or sawdust are used to create roofing materials that resemble shingles, tile, or slate. These products are flexible and durable and will not rot, split, or decay. They are guaranteed to last as long as 50 years and are highly resistant to fire, high winds, and strong impact. Some are made with special reflective cool colors that lower roof temperatures. Many are made with recycled materials and/or can be completely recycled when they eventually wear out. Many of these materials have not yet been tested to see if they leach any chemicals into rainwater.

EPDM roofing, or flat roofing

EPDM (ethylene propylene diene monomer) rubber single-ply roofing membrane has been used to cover flat and low-slope roofs for more than 40 years. According to the EPDM Roofing Association (ERA), every year

EPDM membrane is used for 1 billion square feet of new roofing on both commercial and residential buildings in the United States. EPDM is inexpensive and relatively easy to install. It does not give off odors or fumes during or after installation.

EPDM comes in a range of thicknesses. It can be installed using three different methods: fully adhering it to the substrate with a water or solvent-based adhesive; attaching it with manufacturer-approved mechanical fasteners; or laying it loosely and securing it with stone ballast. When properly installed, it lasts between 12 and 25 years, depending on the climate and how quickly the roof dries after a rain. EPDM should be coated with a light-colored or reflective sealant to deflect heat.

In 2006, ERA initiated a vigorous recycling program that picks up used EPDM from the job site and delivers it to a recycling center. In February 2010, ERA announced that more than 5 million square feet of EPDM had been recycled, an area exceeding any other type of recycled roofing product. ERA also emphasizes that the environmental "payback" time for EPDM is 15 to 20 years.

Prep for solar

Even if you are not yet ready to put in a solar hot water system or solar power system, installing solar mounts when you are putting a new roof on your house will save money and make it easy to install solar panels in the future. It is easy to find the rafters while the roof is exposed, and any openings can be sealed against leaks. Install two 1-inch insulated pipes and a 1¼ -inch conduit running from the roof to the utility room.

Cool roofs

During the summer, a dark shingle roof absorbs and retains the sun's radiation, reaching temperatures between 150 and 190 degrees F. Some of this heat transfers to the interior of the building, increasing the energy required to cool the building. Hot roofs heat up the air around them, creating **heat islands** — areas where the temperature is several degrees higher than surrounding rural lands. A roof material that strongly reflects solar radiation and efficiently emits the heat that it absorbs is known as a cool roof. Cool roofs are made of, or coated with, white or light-colored reflective materials. High-albedo (very reflective) coatings on roofing materials lower the absorption of solar energy and reduce surface temperatures. A cool roof reaches a maximum summer temperature of between 100 degrees F and 120 degrees F.

A study by the Heat Island Group, part of the Environmental Energy Technologies Division at the E.O. Lawrence Berkeley National Laboratory, found that buildings in Sacramento with lightly colored, more reflective roofs used up to 40 percent less energy for cooling than buildings with darker roofs. A similar study conducted by the Florida Solar Energy Center also showed cooling energy savings of up to 40 percent.

The **solar reflectance index** (SRI) measures the solar reflectance and infrared emittance of a roofing material on a scale of 1 to 100, where a completely black roof is 1 and a completely white roof is 100. The higher the SRI, the cooler the roof. Colored roofing materials with special reflective pigments or colors that have higher SRIs than similar dark-colored materials are called "cool colors."

Cool roof materials for flat or low-slope roofs include large pre-cut sheets of single-ply membrane that are fastened over an existing roof and coatings that are sprayed, brushed, or rolled onto a clean roof surface. Clay or concrete tiles with special reflective pigments are available for sloped roofs, and new products for residential construction regularly become available. The Cool Roof Rating Council (CRRC) has an online directory of cool roofing products (**www.coolroofs.org/products/search.php**). Roofing materials that meet specific SRI standards are given an ENERGY STAR label (**www.energystar.gov/index.cfm?c=roof_prods.pr_crit_roof_products**) and qualify for a federal tax credit of 30 percent of the cost of the roof, up to $500. Some local utilities offer incentives or rebates for cool roofs. The national model energy codes of the American Society of Heating Refrigerating and Air-Conditioning Engineers (ASHRAE) allow reductions in the amount of insulation required for cool roofs and the size of the HVAC system. California, Florida, and the city of Chicago have incorporated cool roof standards in their building codes. A cool roof also earns points for LEED certification.

Vegetated, or green, roofs

A vegetated roof is literally a green roof — the roof is covered with plants that thrive in local conditions. Vegetated roofs, also referred to as eco-roofs, green roofs, and living roofs, perform several func-

tions. Vegetated roofs help minimize heat absorption, reducing the amount of energy needed to cool the building. Vegetated roofs can also insulate up to 20 percent more efficiently than traditional roofs because the layers of plants, soil, and shrubbery serve as a natural retention system to keep heat, as well as cool air, inside the building. A vegetated roof is comprised of multiple layers of soil and plants that act as barriers to storm runoff. The plants serve as a natural filtration system that captures and cleans polluted storm water that would otherwise run off the building and circulate back into the water system via drains and sewers.

Urban heat islands (UHIs) in city environments can cause a higher than average temperature within a building. UHIs are a result of the solar radiation reflected, absorbed, and radiated by buildings, sidewalks, pavement, and rooftops. Vegetated roofs mitigate the heat island effect through evapotranspiration. Energy from the sun that plants absorb during evapotranspiration is not re-released into the building environment as heat. The result is an overall lower indoor air temperature, which reduces cooling needs.

> ### A Helpful Site
> 4specs.com (www.4specs.com/s/07/07-0870.html) lists green roofing companies, as well as building products and manufacturers.

A vegetated roof has several components that can vary significantly depending on the building's capacity. An intensive vegetated roof is an integrated system of soil, plants, trees, and other shrubbery and greens, essentially a mini-garden that becomes part of the outdoor environment. These roofs are referred to as intensive because they require a significant amount of maintenance, feeding, and irrigation in the absence of precipitation.

Intensive vegetated roofs are typically installed on a flat surface such as the roof of a garage or a lower story.

An intensive vegetated roof requires an irrigation system, a soil bed, and the structural ability of the building to hold the increased weight of the roof. The weight of a green roof varies significantly, but it can add as much as 150 pounds per square foot to the roof. A professional engineer should determine the weight capacity of an existing building's roof to see whether any additional structural support is needed. The engineering standards for green roofs are different from the requirements for traditional roofs. An intensive roof can cost upward of $30 per square foot and requires a significant flat, open space.

An extensive green roof, on the other hand, is typically less than 6 inches deep and requires less maintenance. Extensive green roofs are designed to be self-sustaining, intricate systems of native plants and shrubbery that need very little care and nurturing.

Cross Section (NTS)

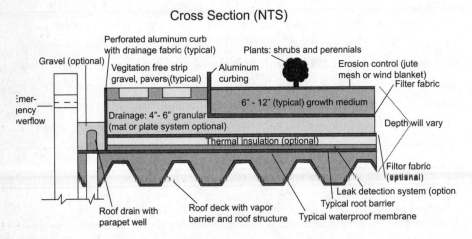

An intensive vegetative roof is like a rooftop garden. It is typically placed on a flat roof and may contain shrubs, small trees, paving stones, and other garden features.

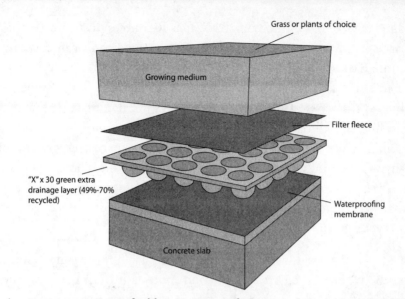

Grass or plants of choice

Growing medium

Filter fleece

"X" x 30 green extra drainage layer (49%-70% recycled)

Waterproofing membrane

Concrete slab

An extensive vegetative roof is like an extension of native vegetation – it contains native plants and shrubbery that grow almost without maintenance.

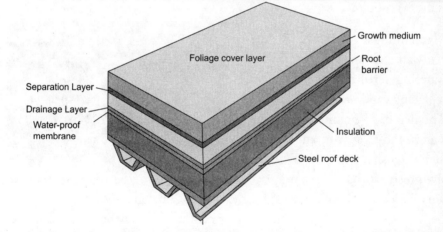

Growth medium

Foliage cover layer

Root barrier

Separation Layer

Drainage Layer

Water-proof membrane

Insulation

Steel roof deck

Another form of vegetated roof is a garden of plants placed in smaller sections around the roof instead of covering the entire roof. These are sometimes referred to as modular block vegetated roofs and are a good alternative if a fully vegetated roof is not practical.

Vegetated roofs require a waterproof membrane — hot rubberized asphalt is often used in green roofs — that deflects water and prevents the roof from absorbing the water. The industry term for the combination of plants, shrubbery, and greenery incorporated into a green roof is referred to as **growing media**.

According to the Environmental & Water Resources Institute (**http://email.asce.org/ewri/VegetatedRoof.html**), vegetated roofs can cost anywhere from $10 to upward of $24 per square foot, depending on the type of roof installed and the level of maintenance required. The cost varies according to the types of plants and the geographical climate. Plants that thrive in hot, dry climates, for instance, would be suitable for a building in Arizona but not for one in New York City. An experienced green roof company will be familiar with the types of plants and shrubbery that work best in different climates. Consider the climate in your geographical area and what plants are native to your area before incorporating a vegetated roof into your green building.

Vegetated roofs can last longer than traditional roofs if properly maintained. Because the vegetation covers the roof and protects it from harsh weather conditions and sunlight, a vegetated roof can last three times as long as a traditional roof. However, the long-term cost savings of a green roof make it more cost-effective.

Maintaining a green roof — especially an intensive one — involves watering, fertilizing, weeding, and replacing and re-soiling plants. The degree of maintenance varies significantly between an intensive and extensive green roof. Extensive green roofs are often only accessed a few times a year to perform maintenance work, which can be done by a professional green roofing company. Because the soil levels on intensive roofs tend to be anywhere from 4 inches to 8 feet deep and incorporate more plant and tree varieties, the maintenance is more demanding and costs more. Only professionals in green roofing should perform maintenance work on a vegetated roof. Many green roof companies offer maintenance services for roofs they install.

The USGBC recognizes vegetated roofs in the LEED system and gives points for optimizing energy performance, controlling storm water, reducing energy, incorporating water efficient landscaping, and reducing site disturbance.

Roof structure

The way in which the frame supporting the roof is designed and constructed contributes to the greenness of a building. Beams made of engineered wood, including laminated veneer lumber, I-joists, and glulams, are not only stronger than solid lumber, but also eliminate waste during manufacturing and can be delivered to the job site already pre-cut for easy assembly. Using I-joists or parallel-chord trusses instead of 2x10s or 2x12s avoids needing harvest lumber from old-growth trees.

The angles of the eaves in conventional roof trusses compress insulation so that it becomes ineffective, creating cold areas along the outer edges of the ceiling. Condensation that occurs when warm, moist air from inside the house encounters these cold areas acts as a catalyst for the growth of mold. During snowy weather, heat escaping along the edges of the roof trusses causes the snow to melt and re-freeze repeatedly, which builds up ice dams that push water back up under the shingles and into the house. It is important to specify that you want **raised-heel trusses** (trusses that have the edges raised a few inches to allow the insulation to expand to its full thickness all the way to edges of the walls).

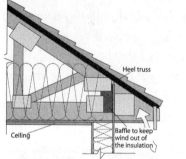

A raised heel truss maintains the loft (thickness) of the insulation.

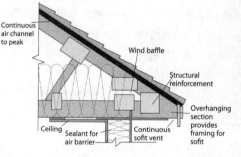

A cantilevered truss leaves space for the insulation to maintain its full loft.

Batt insulation jammed into the corners of a convention truss loses its R-value and the area may become moistened by condensation as warm air from the house hits cold spots at roof edges.

Other details of the roof construction are also important. Baffles or barriers must be installed to prevent air entering through soffit vents in the **eaves** (projecting roof edges) from flowing through the insulation in the attic. (**Soffit vents** are perforated panels or screens that allow air to flow in under the eaves.)

Moist air from inside the house must be prevented from leaking through the ceiling into the attic. Air leaks often occur where the walls join the ceiling, in corners, or where light fixtures or exhaust fans are recessed into the ceiling. The ceiling can be made airtight by installing 6-mil polyethylene sheeting over the ceiling and down behind the walls and sealing any seams or openings with tape. An air barrier can also be created using drywall and carefully taping the joints. Trusses and joists sometimes expand, contract, or warp, and drywall ceilings attached too close to them can crack from movement, creating an air leak. To avoid putting stress on the ceiling drywall, do not attach it close to the edges with screws — allow the walls to support its weight. Any gaps or cracks around openings for lighting fixtures, wiring, or vents should be sealed with expanding polyurethane foam.

Insulated attics

During a hot summer, the temperature of a roof can reach 190 degrees F, and in cold winter weather roof temperatures can drop well below freezing. Unless the underside of the roof is insulated, some of this heat or cold will be transferred to the interior of the house. Insulating the roof and the attic, as well as the ceiling, turns the attic into a semi-conditioned space that acts as a buffer between outdoor temperature extremes and the interior of the house.

Many modern homes have the air conditioning and heating ductwork running through the attic wrapped with R-4 to R-6 insulation. If the roof is not insulated, these ducts are carrying cooled or heated air for long distances through outdoor temperatures. It makes sense to make the attic part of the conditioned area of the house.

Roofs can be insulated using batting or spray-in foam insulation or with products that combine insulation with the roof decking. SIPs (structural insulated panels) have high R-values and can be used for roofs. Atlas Roofing Corporation® (**www.atlasroofing.com**) makes polyisocyanurate (polyiso) insulation attached to a sheet of oriented strand board (OSB) that can be used for roof decking. The insulation has air channels running through it to ventilate the roof. If insulation is installed directly under the roof decking, there must be a system for ventilating the shingles on the outside of the roof. Various types of rigid insulation panels can be attached to low-slope roofs.

Radiant barriers

A **radiant barrier** is a thin sheet or coating of a highly reflective material, usually aluminum, applied to one or both sides of a substrate material such as **kraft paper** (a high-strength paper made of softwood pulp processed with a sulfur solution), plastic films, cardboard, plywood sheathing, or air infiltration barrier material. While insulation stops heat transfer through convection by trapping still air, radiant barriers reduce heat transfer across open spaces by reflecting the heat back toward its source. Radiant barriers are primarily used in hot climates to reflect heat away from the house, thereby reducing the air conditioning load.

A radiant barrier can be laid on top of the insulation on the attic floor with the reflective side up or hung from the underside of the roof. Radiant barriers are available as sheets and membranes and also as panels that snap conveniently into the spaces between roof joists. In order to work properly, the reflective side of a radiant barrier must face an open space. Radiant barriers that are laid directly on top of insulation on the attic floor must allow water vapor to pass through them to prevent condensation from forming on the underside during cold weather.

Attic ventilation

Inadequate ventilation in your attic shortens the life of your roof, makes upstairs living spaces hot in the summer, and places heavier demands on your air conditioning system. Ventilation is necessary to promote the health of the wood frame and sheathing in the attic, and prolongs the life of roof coverings by lowering their temperature during the summer. (Roof color, however, has been found to have more of an impact on roof temperatures than attic ventilation.) In the winter, proper attic ventilation keeps the attic cold and protects your roof from structural damage from ice that forms when snow melts and refreezes on a warm roof.

Attic ventilation requirements are determined by factors such as roof color (black roofs are hotter than white), the amount of insulation in the attic floor, the existence of a vapor barrier, whether openings in the attic are covered by screens, and the amount of shade that falls on the roof. The basic standard is 1 square foot of cross-ventilation for every 300 feet of attic space.

Various types of vents are inserted to allow air to circulate in the attic:

- Soffit vents: Vents located around the eaves that draw cooler air up into the attic.
- Ridge vents: Openings along the highest part of the roof that allow heated air to escape.
- Gable vents: Vents in the vertical walls of gables.
- Off-ridge vents: Openings located at strategic places on the roof.
- Turbines: Openings with pipes topped by turbines that draw off hot air as the blades are turned by wind or convection currents.

Static ventilators such as fixed gable louvers or roof ridge vents work best in combination with vents located around the base of the attic. For example, soffit vents in the eaves allow cooler air to enter from below and escape as hotter air through the gable or ridge openings in the roof above. Make sure that vent openings are not obstructed by insulation.

Unventilated attics

As roof structures have become more complicated, with cathedral ceilings, gables, hip roofs, dormers, and multiple penetrations for lighting, skylights, and exhaust vents, it has become increasingly difficult to design proper attic ventilation, and to make ceilings airtight so that warm, moist air from the house does not enter the attic. This often results in moisture problems in the attic. One increasingly common solution is an unventilated attic. In this instance, insulation is installed under the roof and the roof also becomes the air barrier for the entire house, which makes the attic part of the building envelope and the conditioned space. There are no soffit vents, gable vents — no vents at all.

An unventilated attic has several advantages.

- An estimated 20 percent of the hot or cold air from an HVAC system leaks out through ductwork in the attic. Including the attic in the conditioned space reduces this kind of heat exchange and realizes energy savings of as much as 50 percent.
- In areas with high winds, wind-driven rain often penetrates vents. Vents can collapse during severe wind events, which causes pressure to build up in the house and blow out windows and contributes to roof uplift.
- Unvented attics perform better than ventilated attics during hurricanes.
- Unvented attics are also safer during wildfires.
- In coastal areas, salt spray entering the attic through vents often corrodes metal trusses and fasteners.

In climates where the monthly average temperature remains above 45 degrees F throughout the year and the relative humidity inside a home stays below 45 percent during the coldest part of the year, condensation on the roof deck is not a problem. In cold and/or humid climates, it is important to prevent the moisture from the warm air inside the house from condensing on the underside of the roof decking by doing one of the following: installing rigid foam insulation on top of the roof deck to keep it warm or installing an airtight barrier such as spray-in foam insulation on the underside of the roof decking. In some climates, open-cell foam insulation should be covered with a vapor retardant spray or membrane. This is not necessary for closed-cell foam insulation, which is itself a vapor retardant. In regions with heavy snowfall, warmth the snow blanket traps under the shingles may cause ice dams. A vented air space is needed between the rigid foam insulation and the shingles to dissipate this heat.

Shingles on roofs with unvented attics tend to be warmer by about 2 degrees F than on roofs with ventilated attics, and sheathing tends to be about 10 degrees F warmer. This reduces the life of the shingles by about 10 percent; however roof color has been found to have more impact on roof temperature than a ventilated or unventilated attic.

Attic fans

Powered attic ventilators (PAVs) are fans mounted on the rooftop or side-wall of the attic to move hot air out of attic spaces and lower the temperature under the roof. Solar-powered attic fans can be mounted as independent units.

A small PAV moves about 1,000 cubic feet of air per minute (cfm), and larger fans can move thousands. Extracting so much air creates a low pressure area in the attic that draws in replacement air from outside vents, as well as from any air leaks in ceilings and corners, around fixtures and cables, and in AC ducts. Unless the house is airtight, the fan is likely to be drawing off large quantities of cooler air from inside the house. This in turn creates lower air pressure inside the house that can draw in exhaust fumes from the garage or combustion gases from a hot water heater or chimney. Although an attic fan can help to lower temperatures in a ventilated attic, it should not be used unless the house is airtight.

Windows and Doors

Windows and doors are important architectural features that give character and visual appeal to a home, but they are historically problematic. Air leaks frequently occur around window and doorframes and around doors themselves. Until recently, most windows were single panes of glass that served as efficient heat transfer agents by letting cold into the house in the winter and out of the house in summer. Window frames and the spacers between panes of glass, made of metal or wood, also conduct heat. Windows account for 10 to 25 percent of a winter heating bill and make your cooling system work two to three times harder in summer. Window and door openings are often the source of water leaks as corners expand and contract in the heat and cold.

Over the last two decades, window technology has improved so much that some of today's windows have the insulation equivalent of an insulated two-by-four wall. They have insulated frames and spacers, low-emissive coatings, and high-performance glass. Good windows cost more, but they play an important role in energy conservation. Buy the best ones your budget allows. If you live in a cold climate, select gas-filled double-paned windows with low emissivity (low-e) coatings on the glass to reduce heat loss. In warmer climates, select windows with spectrally selective coatings to reduce heat gain. Selecting appropriate coatings for windows is an important element of passive solar heating.

Rating windows

The heat transfer resistance of windows is measured in U-values. A U-value is the inverse of an R-value (U=1/R). The lower the U-value, the less heat transfers through a window. Because the actual U-value of a glass window can be undermined by air leakage as well as the structure and materials of the window frame and spacers, the National Fenestration Rating Council (NFRC) (www.nfrc.org) was formed to standardize the evaluation of energy efficiency of windows. NFRC labels allow the consumer to compare one window product with another.

Insulated glass units (IGUs)

An insulated glass unit (IGU) is made of at least two pieces of annealed glass sandwiched together with a thermal spacer. The space between is then filled with either an argon or krypton gas. These odorless, nontoxic gases are denser than air and reduce the convection currents that would otherwise transfer heat from the warm side of the window to the cooler side.

Ordinary double-paned windows have an insulation value of R-2 if the space between the glass panes is ½ inch or more. A single pane glass window has an approximate R-value of 0.85, while a double pane glazed window has a value of 1.5 to 2.0, a low-e double pane glazed window has a 2.4 to 3.0 R-value, and a low-e double pane glazed window using an argon gas fill has a 2.7 to 3.6 R-value.

Low-emissive (low-e), or spectrally selective coatings

Infrared energy is found in the lower part of the light spectrum. Low-emissive coatings reflect infrared energy back toward the warm side of the glass while transmitting visible light from the higher part of the spectrum. Low-emissive glass is now standard for many manufacturers. There are many forms of low-e coating, including low-e squared (two coatings) and low-e cubed (three coatings). The most sophisticated allow visible light to pass through while blocking UV rays.

Heat Mirror® insulating glass

Heat Mirror® insulating glass incorporates a transparent Heat Mirror film produced by Southwall Technologies (**www.southwall.com**) that is suspended in the middle of an IGU to create multiple insulating cavities. This raises the R-value of the window to 7 and prevents excessive heat gain or loss.

Window frames

The window frames' material contributes to window's energy efficiency; heat conductivity of a window frame can compromise the heat resistance of high quality glass. Some materials, such as aluminum, are susceptible to thermal bridging and should only be used in the mildest climates.

Wood

The exteriors of modern wood window frames are clad with aluminum or vinyl to protect the wood from exposure to harsh weather and sunshine. These window frames are expensive, however, and many less costly alternatives are available.

Vinyl

Hard vinyl window frames and pipes do not emit the same toxic chemicals as soft PVC shower curtains and flooring, but manufacturing the windows does produce harmful byproducts. On the positive side, vinyl window frames are durable and have a similar energy efficiency to wood. Their lower prices make energy-efficient windows available to many homeowners who could not otherwise afford them.

Cutaway model of a vinyl window frame with insulation.

Plastic expands and contracts with temperature changes and requires two forms of weather stripping to compensate. Vinyl window frames are available in many architectural styles. Some vinyl frames are made with composite materials that make them stronger than straight PVC.

Fiberglass

Fiberglass window frames are especially suitable for extreme heat and cold because they expand and contract in the same way as the panes of glass they hold. Some Canadian models are hollow and filled with urethane foam to increase their R-values. Fiberglass window frames are inert and do not off-gas but during manufacturing workers are exposed to solvent-based resins.

Superwindows

Superwindows combine the best technologies and materials: insulated fiberglass frames, gas fillings, and double or triple panes of low-e glass. The result is a window that has almost the same R-value as the wall. Superwindows are an excellent choice if you can afford them (they cost almost twice as much as regular windows). On south-facing windows, however, triple-paned windows reduce solar gain. If you are relying on those windows for passive solar heat, you may need to use a different type of glass.

Doors

Doors are made from a wide variety of materials and are subject to the same green concerns as any other building material: sustainable source; no toxic finishes, glues, or offgassing; and disposal of the materials when you are finished with them. Because interior doors are protected from the elements and do not need to be insulated, your choice of doors for the interior of the house does not affect energy efficiency.

MDF doors may contain formaldehyde

Interior doors made of medium-density fiber (MDF) board look and feel like painted paneled wood doors. Conventional MDF doors contain urea-formaldehyde binders that negatively affect indoor air quality. Look for MDF doors made with another kind of binder.

In selecting exterior doors, it is important to consider air tightness, insulation value, and installation. Solid wood doors have an R-value of approximately R-1 per inch. Adding an exterior storm door can raise that to R-3, but the door still represents a big insulation gap in an R-24 wall. Insulated steel or fiberglass doors are significantly more energy efficient than wood doors. Fiberglass doors are made to look like wood grain and show less wear and tear than metal doors.

The problem with exterior doors is not only their lower insulating capacities, but also the air and moisture leaks around doorframes. Entry doors are opened and closed many times a day and subjected to a lot of wear-and-tear. In conventional buildings, doors are typically installed with the doorsill resting directly on the subfloor, sealed with caulk. Instead, an exterior door should be installed with a sill pan under the bottom, like a window, to prevent water from entering under the door during rainstorms. Expanding urethane foam can be used to make the spaces around the rough framing airtight before it is covered with decorative molding.

Every time a door opens and closes, it wafts hot or cold air in and out of the house. In cold climates, a mudroom — a small entryway sealed off from the rest of the house by a closed door — can act as an airlock by keeping the cold outside air from getting into the house. Sliding glass doors are similar to large windows except that they require a strong weather seal between the moving parts and the fixed frame. Choose durable frames and low-e glass.

Conclusion

An almost fanatical attention to the building envelope sets green building apart from conventional building practices. A green building strives to achieve maximum energy efficiency by insulating the entire conditioned space and controlling the entry and exit of air and heat wherever it occurs. At the same time, you must achieve balance with the construction budget and the availability of sustainable and nontoxic materials.

Although building construction has become a science taught at universities, most of the workers on a construction site have learned what they know by following the examples of other workers. It is important that the tradesmen putting your house together know how to install each component correctly, and that they pay attention to details. A building envelope is only as effective as its weakest elements, and many weaknesses occur because mistakes were made during construction.

Chapter 5

Heating, Ventilation and Air Conditioning (HVAC)

The heating, ventilation, and air conditioning (HVAC) system is one of the most expensive components of a house and also the one that consumes the most energy. Heating and cooling equipment allows homeowners to control the temperature and humidity inside a building and maintain it at a comfortable level regardless of the weather conditions outside. Natural heating and cooling is achieved through passive design, site orientation, and shading. Whether the heating and cooling system is mechanical or natural, ventilation is absolutely necessary in every house to maintain indoor air quality and control moisture levels. One of the problems with modern, airtight homes is that fumes, gases, and airborne particles accumulate in the air inside the house and are never flushed out. Accumulated moisture from daily activities inside the house eventually condenses somewhere inside the walls and causes mold. You can passively ventilate a house through natural ventilation or actively through mechanical distribution systems powered by fans.

Conventional building tends to use standard building models and standard HVAC systems without regard for individual differences from geographic location to location. In green building design, the mechanical HVAC system is designed after all the other energy-efficient design components are in place. Energy requirements are reduced and natural heating and cooling is maximized through site orientation, passive design, insulation, air barriers, and landscaping. Then the HVAC system is designed to provide supplementary heating, cooling, and ventilation where it is needed.

> ## Correct sizing of an HVAC system is crucial to energy efficiency
>
> A key to energy efficiency is installing an HVAC system that is the correct size for the cooling and heating needs of the house. A system that is too small will run heavily all the time to compensate. A system that is too large is also inefficient because it will be constantly turning on and off. An oversized system can also cause moisture condensation in the walls. Make sure your HVAC contractor is experienced with green design because many passive design features reduce the need for heating and air conditioning. A green home typically requires a smaller system.

Air Pressure and Air Barriers

Just by existing, a building creates currents of air that result in air pressure imbalances inside and outside the house and in different rooms and areas of the house. Three forces create low air pressure zones in and around a house. Wind blowing against a house creates positive pressure on the windward side and negative pressure at the corners and the more sheltered sides of the house. Temperature differences at the top and bottom of a house cause columns of air to travel upward (in a heated building in winter) or downward (in an air conditioned building in summer). This is called the stack effect. Mechanical fans in the HVAC system and exhaust fans in kitchens and bathrooms can cause low-pressure areas within the house or aggravate the stack effect.

Air being sucked into the house can bring pollutants with it, such as exhaust from the garage, radon from the basement, or sewer gas from drains. Moist or conditioned air exiting the house will cause condensation wherever it encounters a moisture barrier. The extra energy needed to heat and cool buildings when conditioned air escapes due to air pressure differences can be anywhere from 10 percent in cooling climates to 42 percent in heating climates. For these reasons, the building envelope should have an impenetrable air barrier to maintain a constant air pressure inside the house. A continuous air barrier is a combination of interconnected materials, flexible sealed joints, and components of the building envelope that separate conditioned and unconditioned spaces and make the building airtight. All the places where impermeable building components meet are tightly joined and sealed.

Forced Air Systems

The most common heating and cooling systems are forced air systems in which cooled or heated air is mechanically circulated around a house using fans and ducts. An HVAC contractor might not realize this, so it is essential that the contractor perform a heat-loss analysis using *Manual J* from the American Society of Heating, Refrigerating, and Air Conditioning Engineers (ASHRAE). A **heat-loss analysis** calculates room by room air conditioning loads for duct design purposes and whole house loads for equipment selection purposes.

Gas, oil, or electric heaters or heat pumps are used to heat the air, which then circulates through ductwork. In conventional homes, this ductwork often runs through a steaming hot attic or a freezing crawlspace or basement under the house. The design of the house should leave space for ductwork to run within the conditioned space of the house. There are three basic types of ducts:

- Sheet metal ducts are square and made of sheet metal, which does not contain contaminants and is easily recyclable.

- Flex ductwork is a thin sleeve fitted over a spiral wire frame. These are most effective when they run in straight lines. Ducts are typically insulated with fiberglass batting.

- New high-velocity ducts designed by a Canadian company move conditioned air at high speeds through small flexible pipes (3 to 4 inches in diameter).

Forced air cooling systems control both temperature (**sensible cooling**) and humidity (**latent cooling**). In humid climates, incoming air is dehumidified by condensing its moisture on a cold surface (such as a cooling coil), or by removing the moisture through absorption (**desiccant dehm-**

idification). In dry climates like the Southwest, air humidification may be required for comfort. Evaporative humidification also cools the air.

A modern HVAC system has sophisticated thermostat controls that maximize the efficient use of energy. HVAC systems are sized to meet heating and cooling loads during extreme weather conditions that historically occur only 0.4 percent to 2.5 percent of the time. Controls ensure that the HVAC systems perform properly, reliably, and efficiently during all of the conditions that occur 97.5 percent to 99.6 percent of the time.

Mechanical HVAC systems can be noisy and cause vibrations in the house. A good HVAC contractor knows how to reduce the noise level and anchor components so that there is little or no vibration.

Zoning

It is difficult to regulate the temperature inside a large home with a complex floor plan, high ceilings, and areas that are occupied only at certain times of the day. Many green builders employ zoning to reduce using mechanical HVAC systems. Instead of using a large HVAC unit to serve the entire house, it is divided into zones according to usage and structure, and a small HVAC unit serves each zone. Thermostats in each zone turn the units on and off as needed. When temperatures are moderate, a single small HVAC unit is often adequate to condition the whole house, and the other units never turn on at all. An alternative is to use a single HVAC unit with thermostats and regulators to control the flow of heated or cooled air into each zone.

High-velocity HVAC systems

High-velocity HVAC systems use special fan coil and air handling units that generate high-pressure air and force it out through small ducts in each room. Heated or cooled air is carried through the house by a main rectangular or round supply duct, from which flexible, sound-dampening, insulated, 2-inch diameter plastic feeder duct hoses branch off into each room. Air enters the room through strategically placed plastic 2-inch collars or slotted ducts. The ductwork requires only 1/10 of the space occupied by a conventional system, and the tiny ducts can easily be threaded down into walls and between joists. The HVAC units are insulated so that the system is almost soundless.

According to manufacturers, air is supplied at 440 to 1200 cubic feet per minute (CFM). The force with which the air enters a room automatically creates air circulation that quickly distributes the heated or cooled air throughout the room, so no area varies more than 2 degrees from the thermostat setting.

High-velocity systems remove 30 percent more humidity from the air than conventional HVAC units, which allows occupants to be comfortable at higher temperatures during the summer months. High-speed HVAC is especially suitable for renovations and retrofits because it does not require making large openings in walls or ceilings.

Radiant Heat

Instead of pumping heated air through ducts into the house, **radiant heat systems** give off heat from a masonry stove, radiator, or system of pipes. These systems take longer to warm up and cool down. Radiant heat is more comfortable than forced air because there are no currents of hot air circulating around the room. Radiant floor systems heat rooms by running heated water or fluid through tubing in the floor. They are practical for homes with high ceilings because the heat rises from the floor. The tubing takes a long time to start heating a room and must be kept running constantly to maintain heat in cold weather. These systems are also considerably more expensive than forced-air systems.

Radiant baseboards pump hot water through radiators located along the baseboard. The heat also rises from the floor upward. These can be used in places where only supplemental heating is needed. The house must be designed to allow for pipes and radiant baseboards in each room.

Geothermal Systems

Geothermal systems circulate water through pipes buried in the cool earth. The liquid is then run through a heat exchanger where heat is either removed from or transferred to a refrigerant in a sealed loop that is used to warm or cool the house. A supplementary HVAC unit then raises or lowers the temperature to the desired level. Geothermal units can be used with radiant distribution or forced-air systems. Geothermal systems use very little electricity to pump water, but they require considerable space to run the pipes underground. If you do not have a big backyard, you will have to install the pipes vertically in the ground, which can be very expensive. The type of soil on your property affects the efficiency of the system.

Geothermal units are expensive to install. The cost of a geothermal system for a typical home of 2,000 square feet averages between $14,000 and $18,000, almost double the cost of a conventional heating, cooling, and hot water system. Tax incentives are currently available for installing geothermal systems. For example, a U.S. federal income tax credit for 30 percent of the cost of a geothermal system is in effect until December 31, 2016. Many state and local governments offer tax exemptions or rebates to homeowners who install geothermal systems. Although they are more expensive to install, return on investment for geothermal heat pumps can typically be realized in as little as three years. According to the EPA, geothermal heat pumps are the most energy efficient and environmentally responsible heating and cooling systems available. Combined with energy from renewable resources such as wind, solar, or hydroelectric, the potential for savings in energy and costs is very significant.

Ventilation

Ventilation can be achieved with simple exhaust fans in the kitchen and bathrooms that draw out moist air and cooking residues. Fans should have a minimum capacity of 50 cubic feet, more for larger rooms. Fans can be noisy but quiet fans are available. The noise level of fans is measured by sone ratings. Look for a fan with a sone rating of 1 or less. Many forced air system have supply fans that introduce outside air through the heating and air conditioning ducts. A balanced system exhausts this air through a central duct located in the kitchen, bathroom, or hallway.

Heat Recovery Ventilators (HRVs) or Energy Recovery Ventilators (ERV)

Heat recovery ventilators (HRVs) or energy recovery ventilators (ERVs) are mechanical devices that admit a controlled and measured amount of fresh air into the house while also capturing and transferring the heat — or sensible energy — from the outgoing indoor air to the incoming air. This energy exchange preheats incoming air in the winter or "pre-cools" it (to a lesser extent) in the summer, which reduces the energy demand on the heating and cooling equipment.

To maintain optimum indoor air pressure, HRVs and ERVs are sized based on the square footage of the home and the unit's cubic feet per minute (cfm) rating, a calculation that roughly equates to 0.05 cfm per square foot of conditioned space. The industry standard of an ideal exchange rate for good ventilation is 0.35 air changes per hour. A greener standard would be 15 cfm per occupant of the house, which translates to between 0.5 and 0.6 changes per hour.

Natural Ventilation

Before air conditioning, homes were designed to take advantage of cooling breezes. Homes in climates with hot summers had shady porches or verandahs to cool the air around the house and also featured **breezeways** — halls that ran through the center of the house from the front door the back door. Green homes are designed to make the most of natural cooling. Windows are designed to open and close regularly to regulate natural ventilation. Windows placed to take advantage of prevailing breezes can be opened during warm weather to allow fresh air to circulate through the house. Natural ventilation works best if doors between adjoining rooms are opened, and if several windows are open at the same time.

Whole house fans

Whole house fans enhance natural ventilation by pulling air in through open windows and out through the attic. They are typically mounted in the attic with a vent in the ceiling. At night, when the outside air is cool, windows are opened and the fan draws the cool air into the house. In the morning, windows are closed to keep the cool air in the house. These fans are practical in areas that require air conditioning for only a few weeks during the summer. They can be controlled with a thermostat to shut off when the house becomes too cold.

On-demand Hot Water Systems

On-demand hot water systems — also referred to as tankless water heaters — work by heating water only as it is being used. When a hot water tap is turned on, cold water travels through a pipe into the unit, where it is heated by either a gas burner or an electric element before passing out through the tap. On-demand systems typically produce 2 to 5 gallons of hot water per minute and can be installed at each hot water site for optimal efficiency. (A typical showerhead uses less than 2.5 gallons per minute.)

On-demand hot water heaters prevent cold water from being wasted while people wait for hot water to reach the tap. They also eliminate using energy to heat and store hot water in a tank day and night while it is not being used. Although an on-demand system is more expensive to install than a conventional hot water heater, its life span is almost double that of a hot water tank. Tankless heaters can last up to 20 years, while conventional water heaters typically last less than ten.

Conclusion

Mechanical HVAC systems allow conventional homes to be comfortable even when they are located in extreme climates or are poorly designed. In a green home, a mechanical HVAC system is regarded as a backup to other energy-efficient design features. The HVAC system is not sized until the building envelope and passive solar features are fully designed and the true heating and cooling needs can be assessed. Each green home is unique and the HVAC system is fine-tuned to provide just the right amount of conditioning. The greatest energy savings attributed to green homes are realized when smaller, less complex HVAC systems result in energy bills that are just a fraction of those for a conventional home.

Chapter 6

Renewable Energy, Solar and Wind Power

reating an energy-efficient building that consumes as little energy as possible while maintaining the comfort of the occupants is a primary goal of green building. Another goal is sustainability. The coal, natural gas, and oil burned in power plants are nonrenewable energy sources that cannot be replaced when they are used up. While there is no way to accurately predict when the world's stores of coal, oil, and natural gas will be depleted, it is clear that consumers must quickly seek alternative sources of energy.

Solar energy and electricity generated by wind and moving water come from sources that are constantly replenished as long as the sun is shining, the wind is blowing, and water is flowing. Energy can also be produced by burning **biomass**: fuels derived from timber scrap, agriculture and food processing wastes, sewage sludge, and animal. Some biomass fuels are derived from trees, but because trees can regenerate, these fuels are considered renewable. Geothermal energy is also considered renewable. Depending on your geographical location and climate, all of these forms of renewable energy can be used in the home.

By maximizing energy efficiency, reducing energy consumption as much as possible, and installing a solar or wind system to supply all the electricity and heat used in a home, it is possible to build a **zero-energy home**

— a home that produces all the energy it consumes and leaves no carbon footprint. However, this is not always practical or affordable. One of the benefits to green building is the home uses only 50 percent of the energy used in a similar conventionally built home.

The Solar Patriot, a modular home displayed on the national mall in April, 2001 as part of the Solar Forum 2001, was permanently installed in northern Virginia. This "zero energy home" produces all the energy it needs using photovoltaic systems, passive solar designs, a geothermal heat pump, compact fluorescent lighting, and high efficiency appliances. It is connected to the electricity grid but has the capability to operate at least 24 hours without electricity from the utility.

The technologies discussed in this chapter can provide all or part of the energy needed in a home or supply energy for a specific purpose such as heating water. Electricity from a solar or wind system costs considerably more than electricity from a utility. These technologies involve a considerable initial investment in equipment that is recovered over time through savings on energy bills. To offset some of the initial cost, federal, state, and local governments offer tax credits, rebates, and incentives to homeowners who install renewable energy systems.

When solar or wind energy is incorporated in a new house, the additional expense becomes part of the mortgage and interest rates should be factored into any cost comparisons. The price tags for many renewable energy products are dropping as manufacturers increase production. If you do not choose to install a solar or wind system when you are building a house, you can still plan to add a system later by including space and mounts for solar panels on the roof or walls and running pipes and conduits to accommodate wiring.

Solar Heating

Considering that heating accounts for almost a third of the utility bill in a typical U.S. home, it may seem that using solar power to heat your home could result in big savings. The DOE, however, reports that in most cases it is not practical or cost effective for an active solar powering system to supply 100 percent of a home's heat. A system adequate to supply all of the heat for a home is very costly to install. At night and on cloudy days, you will need an additional source of heating. Whether homeowners feel they need it or not, most building codes and mortgage lenders require a home with solar heating to have a backup heating system, adding even more to the cost of using solar heating.

Check with your local building department before you contemplate a solar heating system or a solar air conditioning unit and get information about local building codes and special permits for homes in you area. Then check the requirements of your mortgage lender. If your lender requires you to have a conventional heating or cooling system, but will allow you to have a solar power system to supplement your conventional system, you can decide if you want to invest in solar. According to the DOE, an active solar heating system that provides 40 to 80 percent of your home's heating needs is most economical. Any less than 40 percent is not cost-effective because of the high initial costs and the additional need for another heating system as a backup.

Examine your home's heating needs carefully before you commit to a solar heating system. The effectiveness of solar heating depends on many factors, including your geographical location. In the South or Northwest where winters are usually milder, you require less heating than someone who lives in New England, and there is a greater possibility that a solar system can meet your needs.

Two basic types of systems are used to collect solar energy as heat. A **liquid-based system** heats either water or an anti-freeze solution in a liquid-based collector, and an **air-based system** heats air in an air collector. The liquid-based solar heating system can either supply hot water for radiant heating pipes, or supplement **a forced hot air heating system**, a conventional system that uses a furnace to heat air and circulates it through the home via ducts. The liquid-based system is mostly used when there is storage, such as a boiler or radiator, included in a heating system. Many homes have forced hot air heating systems. The incoming air passes over coils of heated liquid from the solar heater and is pre-heated before it goes into the furnace, so that less energy is required to raise its temperature to the desired level.

An air-based solar heating system uses air to absorb and transfer solar energy and can heat individual rooms in your home. It can supplement forced hot air heating systems. The heat collectors are usually integrated into roofs or walls. Wall installations should be on an exterior, south-facing wall. The sun heats a metal plate located on the collector, which heats the air in the collector. The air is then circulated into a room via ducts from roof-mounted collectors; in wall-mounted systems, electrically powered fans or blowers circulate the air.

Wall mounted solar system that heats one room (www.yoursolarhome.com/solarsheat.com/solarsheat/1500.html)

An example of an air-based system that can heat one room in your home is the SolarSheat 1500G, a wall-mounted unit with a solar-powered fan that costs about $1,900. The bottom of the collector draws air from inside your room. The air is heated in the collector using solar energy and blown back into the room through a duct in the top of the collector. The manufacturer claims it is capable of heating a room with an area of up to 1,000 square feet when the sun is shining. It does not need an electrical hookup because it is a self-powered collector. Because the air is immediately drawn from your room, heated, and then blown back into it via the solar-powered fan, a backup heating source may be required when the sun is not shining. This solar air collector is used to heat one room and is not recommended for an entire home.

Solar Water Heaters and Pool Heaters

Heating water for washing dishes, showers and baths, and laundry accounts for nearly 14 percent of a typical utility bill. Using solar energy to heat water is more practical than using solar energy to heat a home. The hot water is stored in an insulated tank rather than circulating through the whole house, so less energy is required. Also, hot water is not needed 24 hours a day; water can be heated and used during the day when the sun is shining and will retain heat in a tank for several hours after the sun sets.

According to the Interstate Renewable Energy Council (IREC), Hawaii has the most solar hot water installations because energy prices are high there and the state government offers tax credits and utility rebates as incentives to homeowners. Prior to 2006, about half of all solar water heaters sold in the United States were sold in Hawaii. As of 2007 Florida and California had the next-largest numbers of solar hot water heaters. Hot water heaters are less expensive to install in Hawaii because there is little likelihood that temperatures will ever drop below freezing there.

Solar water heaters hold water in pipes contained in panels on the roof of a building. When sunlight hits the panels and the pipes, the water inside is heated. Two main components of solar water heating systems are storage tanks and solar collectors. Three types of solar collectors are used for residential buildings:

- **Flat-plate collectors** usually consist of copper tubes fitted to absorber plates and are typically sized to heat 40 gallons of water. This is enough for a family of two, so you need to add an additional collector for each additional two people in your family.

- **Batch collectors**, also called integrated collector storage systems, heat water in dark tubes in an insulated box. They are not recommended for cold climates because the outdoor pipes can freeze. Water is stored in the tubes until it is used; the storage tank itself is the collector. Because the hot water is held in storage until it is used, it can become extremely hot. A tempering valve decreases the water's temperature before it reaches a faucet.

- The **evacuated tube solar collector** is considered one of the most efficient types of collectors. These collectors work well in very cold temperatures and have long, transparent glass tubes. Inside each tube is a pipe containing a heat-transferring fluid, covered with absorbent material that collects heat from the sun. These models are efficient but much more expensive than other types of collectors.

Three types of circulation systems are used to distribute hot water from the collectors for use in the home:

- In **direct circulation systems**, water is pumped through the collectors and into the homes. These systems work best in areas where it rarely freezes, such as southern Florida.

- **Indirect circulation systems** pump a non-freezing, heat-transferring fluid through the solar collectors. The liquid absorbs solar heat and then passes through a heat exchanger where the heat is transferred to the residence's water supply. These systems make sense in climates that are prone to freezing, such as areas in the Midwest.

- **Forced circulation systems** use electric pumps, controllers, or valves to move the water from the collector to the storage tank.

Solar water heating systems almost always require a backup water heating system as there will be cloudy days and days when you need more hot water than your solar water heating system can provide. A conventional water heater can serve as a backup and be turned on only when it is needed.

A solar hot water heater can eliminate a substantial portion of your utility bill. Conventional water heaters generally have to be replaced after 15 years. If you have to replace your old water heater, which would cost you about $1,500, you could invest an additional $1,500 to install a solar water heater.

This is a water heater in a zero energy house that combines active and passive solar technologies and a freon-based geothermal heat pump. The thermal panels on a garage roof provide energy for this water heater. If more hot water is needed during a prolonged dark spell, the geothermal heat pump can heat the water.

Heating your pool

Solar thermal energy can also be used to heat a swimming pool. If you do not use your pool heater very often, and if the cost of operating it is not high, you may not recoup your investment in a solar pool heater for many years. There are more cost-efficient ways to reduce the amount of energy you use to heat your pool.

Solar pool covers resembling oversized sheets of bubble wrap collect the sun's heat and transfer it to the pool water. These covers are much less expensive than installing solar panels just to heat your pool. A 24- by 40-foot rectangular cover can be purchased for about $200, while solar panels could cost approximately $5,000.

Solar Power

Solar power is radiation from the sun converted into electricity through the use of photovoltaics (solar panels). The term "PV system" refers to the photovoltaic technology and equipment used to convert the sun's light into electricity. Systems that convert the sun's energy into electricity or heat do not consume fuel as other traditional energy sources do. They also do not create pollution, produce noise, or use any moving parts. Solar power is a clean, environmentally friendly method of producing energy for your home.

According to the Solar Energy Industries Association (SEIA), U.S. homes with rooftop solar panels produced 156 megawatts of electricity in 2009, more than double the 78 megawatts produced in 2008. Growth was fueled by U.S. government tax incentives allowing homeowners to deduct 30 percent of the total cost of a solar panel installation from their taxable income, and by a drop of more than 40 percent in the price of PV modules.

Many national and state governments are devoting significant resources to promote using solar energy to produce electricity both in power plants and in individual businesses and residences. They regard using solar energy as crucial to reducing greenhouse gas emissions. They also hope to defuse a looming energy crisis by decreasing individual consumers' demand for electricity delivered by utilities. Solar energy still provides less than 1

Home with solar panels built into the roof.

percent of U.S. electricity. The United States ranks fourth, behind Germany, Italy, and Japan, for the number of solar installations. California has the most solar-electric installations of any state in the United States, followed by New Jersey, Florida, Arizona, and Colorado.

A number of factors, including your budget, your geographical location, and your energy requirements, will determine whether solar energy is practical for your home and what kind of PV system you choose. You might decide on a full-scale off-grid PV installation, a grid-tie system that supplies part of your electricity needs, or a PV array that runs a specific appliance. You can start small and add more solar panels as money becomes available.

Photovoltaic energy

Passive solar heating and solar water heaters collect and store the sun's energy as heat. Sunlight can also produce electricity when it strikes certain types of materials. This phenomenon is called the photovoltaic effect. Photovoltaic cells (PV cells) are small units that convert sunlight into electricity.

Each PV cell produces only a small amount of electricity, but groups of PV cells are connected electronically and placed in support structures or frames to form PV modules designed to produce electricity at a certain voltage, such as 12 volts. The actual voltage produced depends on the amount of sunlight striking the module. These modules are mounted in sturdy frames with positive and negative terminals, called solar panels. Solar panels are wired together to form arrays large enough to supply the voltage needed to run an appliance or supply an entire building with electricity.

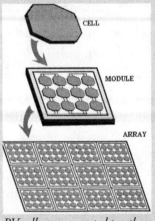

The first practical solar cells that used the photovoltaic effect to convert energy from the sun were developed in the mid-1950s by Bell Labs. With its silicon solar cells, Bell Labs was able to achieve nearly 6 percent efficiency and its cells were demonstrated at a National Academy of Science meeting in 1954. The satellite Vanguard I, launched in 1958 in collaboration

PV cells are connected together in PV modules and arranged in PV panels

with the U.S. Signal Corps, carried a small (less than 1 watt) PV array to power its radios and operated for eight years. Three more satellites launched the same year, Explorer III, Vanguard II, and Sputnik-3, carried PV power systems. Though efforts to commercialize silicon solar cells faltered during the 1950s and 1960s, PV-powered systems became the accepted energy source for space applications.

During the 1970s, Dr. Elliott Berman, working with Exxon corporation, designed a solar cell that brought the price of producing electricity down from $100 a watt to $20 a watt. Solar cells were used to power navigation warning lights and horns on offshore gas and oil rigs, lighthouses, and railroad crossings. They came to be regarded as a sensible alternative in remote areas that could not be connected to a power grid.

In 1973, the University of Delaware built one of the world's first PV powered residences, named "Solar One." The system was a PV/thermal hybrid, with roof-integrated arrays that acted as flat-plate thermal collectors. Fans blew the warm air above the array into phase-change heat-storage bins. During the day the arrays fed excess power to a utility through a special meter, and at night the system purchased electricity from the utility.

The first PV systems providing power for entire villages were established in Schuchuli, Arizona, and Tangaye, Upper Volta, in 1979. By 1982, worldwide PV production exceeded 9.3 megawatts. Solar power units proved more cost-effective for supplying power to remote locations and villages than the installation of electrical cables to bring electricity from faraway electric power plants.

In 1999, according to the U.S. Department of Energy, the amount of PV installed worldwide reached 1,000 megawatts, and that amount reached 15 gigawatts by the end of 2008. Solar panels are still made of silicon today but are much more efficient than in the past, with some achieving more than 19 percent efficiency. Power plants that generate electricity using solar energy are being built all over the United States. In April 2010, Florida Power & Light (FPL) opened the Space Coast Next Generation Solar Energy in Cape Canaveral to provide electricity to Florida homes. The 10-megawatt solar plant, featuring approximately 35,000 highly efficient solar photovoltaic panels on 60 acres at NASA's Kennedy Space Center, will generate energy for more than 1,000 homes and reduce annual carbon dioxide emissions by more than 227,000 tons.

In June, 1997, the U.S. Department of Energy (DOE) announced the Million Solar Roofs Initiative (MSR), with a goal of having 1 million solar roofs in place in the U.S. by 2010. The DOE partnered with hundreds of state and local governments, industries, universities, and community organizations to pioneer using photovoltaic energy by individual homes and businesses. By 2006, the equivalent of more than 377,000 solar water heating, photovoltaic (PV) systems, and solar pool heating systems had been installed in the United States. MSR was replaced in 2006 by the Solar America Initiative (SAI), which aims to achieve cost parity with conventional electricity generation by 2015. These initiatives helped to increase the acceptance of solar technology, stimulate research and development, and expand the market for PV applications. In 2001, Home Depot began selling residential solar power systems in some of its home improvement stores.

Today, hundreds of companies produce, market, and install PV systems. Whether you decide to install a system yourself or hire a contractor, you will have a wide range of products and applications from which to choose.

Photovoltaic Energy for Your Home

Experts agree that installing a complete stand-alone PV system to supply all of the electricity for your home does not make economic sense unless you live in an isolated location far from the power grid. It is even more costly and impractical if you do not live in a sunny climate because you will need extensive battery storage and backup generators. Most of the PV systems used on homes today supplement electricity supplied by a utility company. They are tied to the power grid so they can draw power at night and at other times when the PV panels do not produce enough current. There are also many ways to use photovoltaic energy to power individual appliances or replace environmentally unfriendly acid batteries. If you are not yet ready to install PV panels to power your home, there are still a number of smaller projects using solar energy that can reduce your dependence on the power grid and cut down your utility bills. Tiny PV cells have been used for decades in solar-powered calculators. You may already using small-scale PV technologies in solar-powered flashlights, emergency radios, and portable phone chargers.

Stand-alone, or off-grid, systems

Stand-alone systems are completely independent of the power grid. While the sun is shining, PV panels generate electricity that is stored in batteries to be used when it is needed. A backup generator fueled by fossil fuels may be needed to supply additional energy

Photovoltaic power used to pump water for livestock.

during times of the year when there is not enough sunlight. Stand-alone systems are an economical choice for homeowners living in remote rural areas who might have to pay thousands of dollars to connect to the electrical grid. They are also economical for vacation cabins and work sites.

Stand-alone systems can also be used for smaller projects, such as supplying power for outdoor lighting and security systems, running a pump to water livestock, or providing a backup power supply for a business office. You might have seen stand-alone PV units powering train signals and call boxes along highways.

Grid-tie, or on-grid, systems

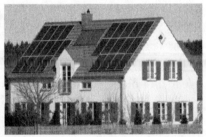

The most common systems installed on residential buildings are grid-tie PV systems. These systems allow you to use the electricity your PV system generates while the sun is shining and buy electricity from a utility at night, on cloudy days, or at times when your energy needs exceed the capacity of your system. If your PV system generates

Photovoltaic panels installed on the roof of a home.

more electricity than you need, the excess is directed back to the power grid and bought by the utility company through **net metering** — a program in which the utility company deducts the amount of outgoing power from the amount of power flowing in through your electricity meter.

Many states and counties offer subsidies and tax incentives to homeowners who purchase on-grid PV systems because they relieve some of the demand on overburdened utilities.

Grid-tie works well in hot sunny climates where the use of air conditioning causes peak demand during the hours when the sun is shining.

On-grid system with batteries

One drawback is that in most grid-tie systems, the power from your PV system will also be shut off when the grid experiences a power outage. A grid-tie system with backup, or grid failover system, includes a bank of batteries that provide electricity during a power outage. Backup batteries are an expensive component of a PV system, and have to be replaced every few years, so unless your area experiences frequent power outages the extra expense may not be justified. Grid failover systems are useful in areas where the supply of electricity is unreliable, or when an uninterrupted supply of electricity is needed — for example, to refrigerate lab supplies, keep computers operating, or run medical equipment.

Grid fallback systems

In a **grid fallback system**, the power your solar array generates is stored in a bank of batteries. The electricity to run your home is drawn from these batteries until they are depleted, then you switch over to the grid until your batteries are recharged. Grid fallback systems are cheaper than grid-tie systems for small household PV installations because both solar panels and batteries are low voltage units (12v, 24v, or 48v). Grid-tie systems typically require generating several kilowatts of electricity, which means that a larger number of solar panels must be linked together to produce a voltage of several hundred volts. A grid-fallback system that powers one or two electric circuits in your house can be built for several hundred dollars, while the least expensive grid-tie system costs thousands of dollars. If your solar array generates less than 1 kWh, a grid fallback system is probably cheaper. If your array generates more than 1 kWh, a grid-tie system may be more cost-effective.

A grid fallback system can be easily expanded as more funds become available; it is difficult to expand a high-voltage system unless the expansion was part of the original design. Grid fallback systems do not sell excess energy to a utility — it is stored in batteries for your use. One advantage of a grid fallback system is that you are using your own solar power even at night as long as your batteries are not depleted.

More than 170,000 U.S. homes are equipped with solar panels

According to the ASES, in 2009, residential-grid-connected photovoltaic installations in the United States grew 40 percent to 435 megawatts (MWs). The typical size for a residential installation is about 2.5 kilowatts. Divide that into 435 MW and the result is 170,000 homes now equipped with solar arrays.

Location and Climate

Solar heating and electricity systems function best and provide the greatest return on investment in climates with plenty of clear, sunny days. Your geographical location determines not only the amount of sunlight available to produce electricity, but also how much electricity and heat you need at various times of the year and how efficiently your PV system converts solar radiation to electricity (conversion efficiency). For example, if your home is in central Pennsylvania, you will receive less than 2 kWh of radiation per square meter in January, a very cold month when you need extra electricity to heat your home. In August, Phoenix will receive between 5 and 6 kWh of radiation per square meter, during the time period when air conditioners are needed night and day. The conversion efficiency of PV panels diminishes, however, in extreme heat.

The two maps below show the difference in the amount of radiation received in different parts of the United States in January and August. A grid-tie system will buy electricity from a utility when the solar panels cannot produce enough. An off-grid system will have to be large enough to produce the required amount of electricity, and have adequate battery storage or a backup generator to supply electricity when there is not enough radiation from the sun.

You can estimate how much electricity a solar panel on your home can be expected to generate by looking up the solar irradiance data for your area. The amount of solar energy — number of hours of sunlight combined with the strength of the sunlight — falling on one square meter (9.9 square feet) is known as the **insolation** of a particular location on the globe. Insolation is expressed as average solar irradiance — ultraviolet, visible, and infrared radiation — falling on a square meter in kilowatt hours per day (kWh/m2/day). You must look at the solar irradiance for each month of the year. The maps below are from the Renewable Resource Data Center of the National Renewable Energy Laboratory (NREL) (**http://rredc.nrel.gov/solar/old_data/nsrdb/redbook/atlas**). They show the average monthly irradiance of the U.S. for the months of January and August.

U.S. Solar Radiation Maps

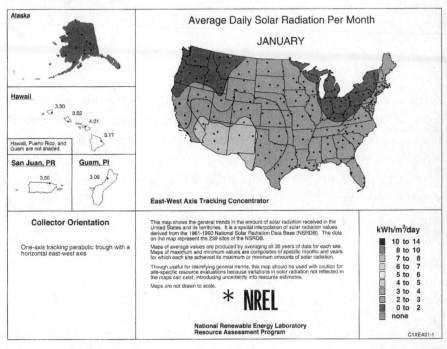

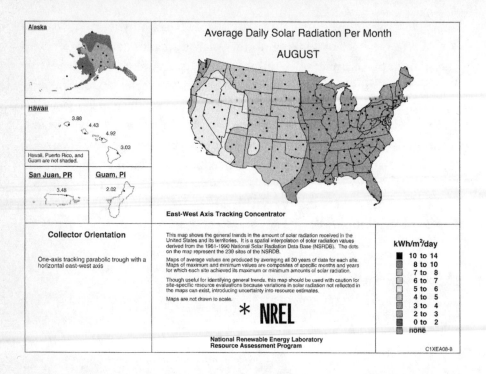

Every solar panel bears a label stating its wattage — the number of watts it can be expected to generate based on a solar irradiance of 1,000 watts (1 kilowatt) per hour. To get a rough idea of how much electricity you can expect a solar panel to produce each day, you can multiply the average daily solar irradiance times the stated wattage of the panel. For example, a 20 watt solar panel could be expected to produce 40 to 60 Wh (Watt hours) in central California in January, and 100 to 120 Wh in August. These calculations are only approximate because the solar irradiance of your particular location will be affected by local weather conditions, the angle and location of your solar panels, and whether obstacles such as tall buildings or mountains block sunlight at any time of the year.

To get an accurate idea of what to expect from a solar power system, you must also look at the maximum and minimum amounts of irradiance for various times of the year. For example, during a prolonged winter blizzard or a period of cloudy days in summer, your solar panels would receive much less than the average amount of radiation. You would either need a backup power source to meet your energy requirements, or you would have to install a system large enough to generate enough electricity even on those days.

If you live in the city with the most sunny days, Yuma, Arizona, you can expect to have 242 sunny days in a year. Phoenix, Arizona comes in second with 211 sunny days, and Las Vegas, Nevada, comes in third with 210 sunny days. Using a PV system to supply electricity for a home would be much less practical in locations with few sunny days per year such as Cold Bay, Alaska (20 sunny days), and Hilo, Hawaii (36). Regions at high latitudes experience only a few hours of sunlight on winter days, and exceptionally long summer days.

You must also look at the highest and lowest temperatures recorded in your area because your equipment must be able to withstand these extremes. If you live in a region subject to hurricanes, heavy winds, or ice storms, you need insurance adequate to cover possible damage to your solar panels.

Recycling expired solar panels is an important component of clean energy.

Most solar panels are guaranteed to function efficiently for 20 to 25 years, and many of the earliest panels are still in use after 30 years. Eventually solar panels will need to be replaced. If solar power systems come into widespread use, as anticipated, discarded solar panels will create serious waste management problems.

First Solar (www.firstsolar.com/en/recycle_program.php), the largest manufacturer of thin film solar modules, has established the solar industry's first comprehensive, prefunded module collection and recycling program, designed to minimize the environmental impact of producing PV systems. As each module is sold, First Solar sets aside funds for the estimated future cost of collection and recycling in custodial trustee accounts. The site of each module installation is registered with First Solar, and labels on each module contain contact information and instructions for returning the product free of charge. When the customer is ready to discard a module, First Solar provides free packaging and transportation to a recycling center, where valuable materials are recovered and almost 90 percent of each collected First Solar PV Module is recycled into new products.

Evaluating your Energy Consumption

To determine your energy needs for a new home or to calculate the pay-off from using a PV system, you have to look at your current electricity consumption. A solar contractor knows how to evaluate your household energy use and determine the size, type, and number of solar panels and other components you will need for your solar system. It is important to do this during the design stage, so that the house plans include enough space for the solar panels and other components. Special windows, roof tiles, and other architectural features can serve as solar panels. The house can be designed so that solar panels are placed where they receive the most exposure to sunlight, adequate ventilation, and protection from hazardous winds.

Understanding your electricity bill

Energy is measured in British thermal units (Btus). A Btu is equal to 250 calories, the amount of energy required to raise the temperature of a pound of water by 1 degree Fahrenheit. This is approximately the amount of heat produced by lighting a match. A Btu is such a tiny unit of energy that larger quantities of energy are measured in quads — a quad is one quadrillion Btus. According to the DOE, an average U.S. household consumed 4.7 quads of electricity in 2009.

Electric power is measured in watts. Your utility company bills you for the number of kilowatt-hours (kWh) of electricity you use in a month. One kilowatt-hour (kWh) is one hour of using electricity at a rate of 1,000 watts. When you want to compare the cost of electricity produced by a solar system to the cost of electricity from your utility, you must look at the cost per kWh. Gather your electricity bills from the past year and add up the total number of kWh for the year. Divide the total amount you paid for electricity by the total number of kWh. This will tell you how much you paid per kWh for your electricity.

The table below, using data from the DOE, shows how much the average customer paid per kWh for electricity provided by utilities in June 2009 and 2010. In some states, electricity is several cents cheaper than in others; this is determined by the type and cost of fuel and the type of power plant used to generate the electricity, how the plant is financed and managed, and the distance that the electricity has to travel to reach consumers.

Average cost of electricity per kWh (in cents) in June 2009 and June 2010 for U.S. residences by region and state

Census Division and State	June-10	June-09		Census Division and State	June-10	June-09
New England	**16.3**	**18.19**		**East South Central**	**9.73**	**9.88**
Connecticut	19.47	21.07		Alabama	10.84	11.1
Maine	15.37	15.26		Kentucky	8.38	8.43
Massachusetts	14.62	18.03		Mississippi	10.21	10.46
New Hampshire	16.19	16.62		Tennessee	9.45	9.48
Rhode Island	16.53	16.2		**West South Central**	**11.12**	**11.42**
Vermont	15.71	15.13		Arkansas	9.56	9.41
Middle Atlantic	**16.29**	**15.74**		Louisiana	8.93	7.76
New Jersey	16.86	16.91		Oklahoma	9.36	8.33
New York	19.12	18.51		Texas	12.13	12.96
Pennsylvania	13.33	12.45		**Mountain**	**11.26**	**10.61**
East North Central	**11.89**	**11.37**		Arizona	11.75	11.28
Illinois	12.6	11.39		Colorado	11.95	9.95
Indiana	9.19	9.59		Idaho	8.21	8.3
Michigan	12.87	12.56		Montana	9.34	9.4
Ohio	12	11.32		Nevada	12.42	12.02
Wisconsin	12.83	12.46		New Mexico	11.34	10.38
West North Central	**10.27**	**10.02**		Utah	9.16	9.06
Iowa	10.56	10.58		Wyoming	9.08	9.23
Kansas	10.26	10.08		**Pacific Contiguous**	**13**	**12.78**
Minnesota	10.68	10.4		California	15.51	15.02
Missouri	10.13	9.79		Oregon	9.13	9.01
Nebraska	9.98	9.83		Washington	8.26	7.9
North Dakota	9.38	8.87		**Pacific Non-contiguous**	**24.18**	**20.62**
South Dakota	9.76	9.26		Alaska	16.92	17.72

South Atlantic	11.3	11.45		Hawaii	28.36	22.2
Delaware	14.51	14.88				
District of Columbia	14.33	13.91				
Florida	11.65	12.14				
Georgia	10.86	10.72				
Maryland	15.22	15.95				
North Carolina	10.13	9.9				
South Carolina	10.58	10.31				
Virginia	10.77	11.15				
West Virginia	8.62	7.95				
U.S. Total					11.92	11.85

TIP: It takes almost 3kWh of energy to deliver 1 kWh of electricity to you.

Here is another good reason to go solar: According to the DOE, in 2005, an average power plant required 10,210 Btu of energy, the equivalent of almost 3kWh, to generate and deliver 1 kWh of electricity to an end user. In other words, we are paying a high price in energy for our electricity.

How you use electricity in your home

If you calculate the cost of your electricity per kWh month by month, you will probably find that the cost is higher during the months when you use greater amounts of electricity for heating or air conditioning. Your electricity consumption during the months when you are not running an air conditioner or a heater is called your **baseline usage**. By comparing your baseline usage to your consumption during winter and summer months, you can see how much electricity you are using for heating and cooling. You can also divide your total annual amount of kWh by 365 (or 366) days to see how your average daily usage compares to the American average of 20 kWh per household.

In the U.S. and Canada, homes are wired for appliances that require voltages of 110 V or 220 V. Most household appliances use 110 V, but appliances that generate lots of heat such as clothes driers and kitchen stoves use 220 V. Because too much electricity is lost when low voltages travel through cables for long distances, the 12,000 V to 25,000 V coming from generators in a power plant passes through a step-up transformer that increases the voltage to about 138,000 V. The electricity then travels through high-voltage transmission lines to local stations and substations with step-down transformers that deliver the electricity to homes as 220 V.

The electricity enters your home through three wires, two carrying 110 V each and one neutral ground wire. Every house has a main power panel that distributes electricity to various parts of the house. If you look inside your home's fuse box, you will see that each circuit breaker is labeled for a specific appliance or specific part of the house. The wires going from the panel to most of your power outlets connect one of the 110 V wires with the neutral wire to form a circuit that delivers 110 V. The wires going to outlets for your clothes dryer and stove connect both 110 V wires with the neutral wire to deliver 220 V.

Looking at how much electricity you use for various purposes around the house can give you an idea of how much you can reduce your electricity bill by switching to solar energy or by upgrading to more energy-efficient appliances. For example, installing a solar water heater could reduce your water heating bill by 50 to 80 percent.

Today the majority of solar power systems are grid-tie systems that draw backup electricity from your utility when your solar panels are not producing enough, and "sell" excess electricity to your utility when your solar panels produce more power than you need. The climate where you live will have a significant impact on the energy savings you can achieve with a solar system. According to the chart above, space cooling makes up 17 percent of the average household's electricity consumption. If you live in a hot climate where you use air conditioning 24 hours a day for several months during the summer, a grid-tie system could significantly reduce your utility bills because it would be operating at maximum capacity during the hours when air conditioning is needed most. (Remember that heat can diminish the efficiency of PV panels, so maximum production can be sustained only if the panels are kept below a certain temperature.)

The calculations you have made using your electricity bills and average usage data are only rough estimates of how much you can save on utility bills by installing a solar system. Appendix A explains how to do a detailed "load analysis" of your home by adding up the amount of electricity used by each of your appliances. You need this information to design a PV system that meets your energy needs.

Future price of electricity from the grid

The cost of electricity from the grid is based on the price of the fuel used to produce it. If unforeseen political or geophysical events suddenly raise the price of coal or oil, utility prices could double within a few years, making your solar power system a much better financial investment.

Solarbuzz, an international solar energy research and consulting company, posts a monthly global solar energy price index on its website (**www.solarbuzz.com**). It surveys solar power installation companies all over the world. In June 2010, the average price for a standard grid-tie 2 kilowatt peak system with a battery backup, mounted on the roof of an existing home, was $16,400. This price included full system integration and installation costs. It allowed for a 5 percent interest charge on financing, but did not deduct rebates or tax incentives. At this price, the cost of electricity per kWh in a sunny climate (such as the sun belt of the U.S., Africa, Australia, and Asia) was $24.38 and in a cloudy climate (such as northern Japan or Germany), $75.41.

A 1 kilowatt peak small-scale solar energy system that provides only a fraction of an average home's energy requirements costs $10,000-$15,000. A 5 kW system that can provide all the energy requirements of most conventional homes costs between $35,000 and $45,000.

Doing a load analysis

The first step in designing a PV system is finding out exactly how much power you need. For a PV system that will power only one or two appliances, such as a well pump and a light, you need to know how much voltage those appliances require. To design a standard grid-tie PV system for an existing home, you need only a 12-month energy usage report. The optimal size for your grid-tie system will depend on the average hours of sunlight per day in your geographical location.

If you are designing an off-grid PV system or a PV system for a new home, you will need to do a complete load analysis for your home. This involves making an itemized list of each appliance that will use electricity in your home, including digital clocks, cell phone and camera chargers, and smoke alarms, and calculating the amount of power needed to operate each one. You will have to calculate how much electricity the HVAC system, lighting, and appliances will use. *Use the worksheet in Appendix A to do a load analysis.* It will take some time but is easy to do.

Price of a PV system

A study conducted by the Lawrence Berkeley National Laboratory found that installation costs of PV systems vary widely across the states. Average costs range from a low of $7.6 per watt in Arizona to a high of $10.6 per watt in Maryland. The study suggests that the variation in average installation costs is a result of differences in the size and maturity of PV markets. Greater demand creates more competition, resulting in increased efficiency and possibly reducing the cost of the PV system components. The two largest PV markets in the United States — California and New Jersey — have some of the lowest average costs.

Your cost may be determined by local competition between solar contractors in your area. Tell each contractor that you are shopping around for the best rates. The contractor, who wants your business, might lower his or her price to make the sale.

The national average cost to install a 1 kW photovoltaic system varies, but can range $9,000 to $12,000 per kilowatt, meaning a 3-kilowatt system could cost up to $36,000. In 2010, the average cost across the U.S. for a grid-tie system was $8 to $9 per watt for a system installed by a professional contractor. An off-grid system or one with backup batteries cost 20 to 30 percent more, or about $10. If you installed the system yourself, the cost was around $6 to $8 per watt. You might expect a smaller system to cost much less, but that is not always the case. Smaller systems cost more per watt than large systems because both systems require the same basic equipment and have the same fixed costs. Whether small or large, a system entails costs for setup, permits, and paperwork — as well as equipment and installation — so there might not be much of a price reduction for a smaller system.

Be as specific as possible when asking a contractor to bid on a solar project. The contractor cannot calculate costs accurately without knowing exactly what components you will need. Most contractors will help you create detailed specifications for your solar systems. The contractor should be able to tell you the size and number of solar panels you will need, how much money you will save on your energy bills, and the environmental benefits of your system. Ask for a bid that shows the total installed cost with an itemized breakdown for equipment, labor, permits, taxes, and other costs, as well as deductions for any available rebates or tax credits.

When comparing bids, look carefully to see what is included in each bid:

- The quantity, make, and model of the PV panels and equipment
- The system's maximum generating capacity and estimated annual energy production
- Warranty information
- What components will be installed where
- Hardware
- Connection to the grid (if applicable)
- Permitting and inspection fees
- Sales tax
- Travel and transportation
- When the system will be ready for use
- Clean-up

The bid you get from a contractor for a solar water heating system should contain an estimate of the amount energy the system will save annually in kilowatt hours or therms. A bid for a solar electric system should state system size in watts or kilowatts, and estimate the annual amount of electricity the system will produce. Ask the contractors to outline the PV system output in AC watts, indicating the capacity of the system in either watts or kilowatts.

The lowest bid is not necessarily the one you should accept. Consider everything you know about each contractor: years of experience, craftsmanship, customer service, warranty policy, ability to qualify you for rebates and incentives, recommendations from references, and when he or she will be available to do the work. The lowest bid may omit certain expenses or services. Your system could end up costing more money if you accept the lowest bid and then have to pay to fix problems caused by mistakes or poor craftsmanship. A well-established company is more likely to be around several years from now to honor warranties and service your system.

Use a sun chart to do a site survey

If you are concerned that surrounding trees and obstructions may create problems for your solar array, you can do a more detailed survey using a sun chart — a graph of the sun's elevation and azimuth (the measurement of the angle where a straight line drawn along the ground at your location and a line drawn through the sun intersect) throughout the day. The Solar Radiation Monitoring Laboratory at the University of Oregon provides offers a free program that creates printable sun charts for any location on its website, http://solardat.uoregon.edu/SunChartProgram.html, and instructions for using a sun chart to do a site survey. You will need a compass and a clinometer — an instrument that measures elevations (your protractor and pencil are a simple clinometer). You will be able to plot obstacles on the sun chart and see whether they present a serious difficulty.

Is access to sunlight a legal right?

As more homeowners install solar arrays on suburban roofs, the question of legal protection for solar access must inevitably arise. It takes a homeowner as long as 20 years to recoup the cost of a solar installation. To operate effectively, solar panels must have unrestricted access to sunlight, but the path of the sun's rays often passes through a neighbor's airspace. Many homeowners are reluctant to invest in a solar system because they fear their neighbors might plant trees or construct buildings that would obstruct the sunlight from their solar array. State and local governments are very interested in promoting solar energy and are looking for ways to protect solar access.

Many states passed solar access laws during the energy crisis of the 1970s. Currently, 34 states and approximately a dozen municipalities have some form of solar access law. In 2008, the issue of solar access made headlines when a family in California was forced by the court to cut down two red-wood trees that shaded a neighbor's solar panels. The judgment was based on the Solar Shade Act (AB 2321), which California passed in 1978.

In October 2008, the U.S. Department of Energy's Solar America Board for Codes and Standards released a model solar access statute intended to encourage dialogue on the issue. As of March 2009, most of the 25 major U.S. cities enrolled in the Department of Energy's Solar America Cities program were reviewing their solar access laws.

Components of a Solar Power System

Depending on the type of system you are designing, it will include these components:

- Solar panels
- Mounts, frames, and hardware
- Cables
- Batteries
- Controller
- Inverter
- Racks and wire cages to house the batteries
- Junction and distribution boxes
- Fuses, circuit breakers, safety disconnects
- Lightning protection
- Grounding circuit to protect the system and the people using it
- Meters and monitors
- Tracking devices to arrays facing the sun
- Wind turbine
- Backup generator

Solar panels

Three basic types of solar panels are currently used for residential installations: amorphous, polycrystalline, and monocrystalline solar panels.

Amorphous solar panels, also known as "thin film solar panels" are the cheapest to manufacture but have only 6 percent conversion efficiency. (**Conversion efficiency** is the percentage of solar radiation that is converted into electricity.) As a result, they are large and can only be used where there is no size restriction for the solar array, or for a system with low power requirements (up to 200 watts). Larger systems would require so many panels that the additional expense of mounting and wiring them would make them impractical. Amorphous panels can produce electricity in hazy and overcast conditions, and sometime even in bright moonlight. The cost of manufacturing amorphous panels and solar films is dropping every year, and they are the main focus in developing cost-effective PV systems.

Polycrystalline solar panels are made from solar cells with a conversion efficiency of 12 percent to 16 percent, and a 12 volt polycrystalline panel is about 1/3 the size of an equivalent amorphous panel. Their guaranteed life expectancy is longer, about 25 years. The cost of manufacturing polycrystalline panels makes them about 50 percent more expensive than amorphous panels, but their prices are also dropping from year to year.

Monocrystalline solar panels are the most efficient panels available, with a conversion efficiency of 14 percent to 22 percent. They are the smallest and the most expensive solar panels, costing 20 percent to 30 percent more than polycrystalline panels.

String-ribbon is a relatively new manufacturing technology that combines thin film with crystalline manufacturing techniques to double the number of solar cells per pound of silicon. Its conversion efficiency (13 -17 percent) rivals monocrystalline solar panels at a lower cost.

Carbon footprints of solar panels

Clean energy has a carbon footprint just like fossil fuels. The carbon footprint of a solar panel mostly results from the manufacturing process and from its disposal. The carbon footprint of solar panels is expressed as grams of CO_2 equivalent per kilowatt hour of electricity generated (g CO_2eq/kWh). **Carbon payback** is the amount of time a solar panel must operate to compensate for its carbon footprint. Because a solar panel must generate a certain amount of energy to replace the energy used to create it, carbon payback is shorter in climates with many hours of sunlight than in cloudy areas.

A recent study conducted by the Institute of Science in Society (ISIS) of solar panels in northern and southern Europe estimated the carbon paybacks of the three types of solar panels as:

Amorphous solar panels: .9 - 1.5 years
Polycrystalline solar panels: 1.3 -2.9 years
Monocrystalline solar panels: 2.1 - 3.6 years
String-ribbon panels - Less than one year

Solar panels with higher conversion efficiency typically cost more than panels with lower efficiencies because the manufacturing process is more complex and expensive. A high conversion efficiency gives you more power per square foot. If you have ample space for your solar array, there is no reason why less efficient (and less expensive) solar panels cannot do the job — you just need to cover more square feet with them. An exception would be when very high power needs require you to install large numbers of the less efficient panels — then the cost of mounting and wiring them might outweigh the price difference.

The most common solar panels are rectangular configurations of solar cells mounted in aluminum frames and covered with glass or plastic. These come in various sizes — for a small solar application a single rectangular solar panel might supply all the power you need. Less conventional shapes tend to cost more but may fit more accurately into available space

Blue solar panel

or be more aesthetically pleasing. You can find triangular solar panels, and panels that are integrated into architectural features such as shingles, roof tiles, and windows. Solar panels can also be installed as awnings or shades over a walkway or patio. Some panels incorporate gutters and flashing so that they can blend in with the rest of a roof. Flexible solar panels come in rolls that can be spread across a flat roof. These are not as efficient as other types of solar panels, but are inexpensive if you have enough space and do not require mounts.

Typical solar panels are blue or black. A large solar array spread over a roof can be incongruous with a carefully planned architectural design. If your solar array will be prominently visible, consider its appearance when choosing your solar panels. Architects designing new energy-efficient homes incorporate the location and "look" of the solar panels in the overall design concept.

Secondhand solar panels can reduce the cost of a PV system

Secondhand solar panels can be purchased very inexpensively from some solar product dealers and are sometimes listed for sale on sites such as Craigslist (www.craiglist.org) and eBay (www.ebay.com). Used solar panels typically become available when businesses or homeowners upgrade their systems. Some solar panel manufacturers and dealers sell returned panels, discontinued models, display panels, and "blemished" panels at a discount. Although secondhand panels can make your system much more affordable, there are some considerations:

- Used solar panels typically do not come with a warranty.

- Most rebate programs and incentives require the professional installation of new panels with warranties.

- It is difficult to predict the life of a used solar panel. The output of new solar panels from the factory is usually 10 percent greater than the output printed on their labels. Though the output decreases over time as panels deteriorate in the sunlight, the output from an old panel can still be close to its labeled output. Solar panels that have been in storage do not deteriorate.

- Though new solar panels are guaranteed for 20 to 25 years, they often continue to function well long after that. Some panels are still used after 40 years.

- Older panels are larger than their modern counterparts and may not be practical if space is a problem.

- Used solar panels may be damaged. Do not buy panels that are scratched, cracked or have moisture or condensation under the glass. Other common problems are loose connections and burned-out bypass diodes. A knowledgeable person can fix these problems, but it is extra effort that may not turn out well.

- The hard surface of some used panels may have turned brown over time. Check the output of these panels — they may still be operative and will not degrade any faster than clear panels.

- Test the output of used solar panels before buying. Test a panel by setting your voltmeter to DC volts and measuring across the + and - terminals of the panel while it is exposed to sunlight. A 12 volt panel should show about 21 volts in full sun. Panels designed to be connected in sets of four (four panels in series) will show 4 to 5 volts. To determine how much current you can expect from the panels, set the voltmeter to DC amperes (high range) and connect it between the + and - terminals in full sun. Multiply the current of a 12-volt panel by 17 volts to get the output in watts.

Mounting systems

Solar panels can be mounted on the roof, on the walls, on poles, or on the ground. They can also be incorporated in architectural features such as shingles and awnings. A fixed mount on a roof is the least expensive option. A ground mount is more expensive because it requires a concrete base and a specially constructed rack, but it may be the only option if your roof cannot support the weight of a large solar array. Mounts and frames made of metal created to withstand outdoor conditions are a better choice because even the best wood frames will not last as long as the solar panels they hold.

Roof mounting

Your climate and roof type will determine the best mounts for your solar panels. Your solar array will remain in place for at least the next 25 years and the mounting system should be able to withstand the most extreme weather conditions in your area. Ideally, your panels should be mounted at the angle that will expose them to the optimum amount of sunlight. Most solar panel manufacturers sell mounts designed specifically for their products. A mount typically consist of fixtures that screw into the rafters underneath the roof and an adjustable rack that attaches to the fixtures and holds the panels. Installations on composition shingle roofs are the easiest and least expensive. Tile roofs are the most difficult and most expensive because the tiles break easily. Tile roofs are also prone to leaks after solar panels have been installed.

Four types of roof mounts are common:

- **Rack mounts** hold multiple solar panels fixed to the roof. Rack mounts are typically parallel to the roof surface and have the same angle of tilt.

- **Stand-off mounts** are adjustable frames that support the panels above the roof. The angle of the solar panels can be adjusted so that it is different from the roof angle. Stand-off mounts are often used when a house has a sunny northern exposure and too much shade on its south side. The solar panels on the northern side can be angled up so that they face south. Stand-off mounts sticking several feet up from a roof can be eyesores but they provide maximum exposure for the solar panels.

- **Direct mount panels** are attached directly to the roof. There is no space between the solar panel and the roof where air can circulate and cool the panels. This type of mount is cheaper because you do not have to buy racks. Flexible solar panels can be rolled across a flat roof.

- Building Integrated PV (BIPV) solar panels are incorporated in shingles that are attached directly to the rafters, or in other architectural features such as windows or awnings.

A flat roof or a south-facing roof is an optimal location for a solar array. If the roof does not slope directly to the south, you can use angled supports to face the array directly into the sunlight. If you are building a new home, plan your landscape carefully. For the south side of your home, select trees and shrubs that will not grow tall enough to obstruct your solar array.

Roof panels have to be installed where there are no shadows during the day. Because this house has no south-sloping roof, this 2.5 kilowatt system is installed on an east-sloping roof with an additional tilt toward the south.

If you are mounting solar panels on an existing roof, you must check under your roof to see if it is strong enough to support a solar array. Individual solar panels weigh about 30 to 40 pounds, and the weight can add up. Determine what kind of hardware and mounting fixtures will be needed to attach the array to the roof. Consult an architect or a builder if you are uncertain. Roof mounting kits are sold by solar panel manufacturers, and you can also build your own.

Solar arrays need to be cleaned off occasionally because dust, grime, and snow all block sunlight and make the solar panels inefficient. Consider how you will clean solar panels mounted on your roof without too much difficulty. Mounting

them on the lower edge of the roof makes them easier to reach with a ladder instead of having to climb around your roof.

Wall mounting

Solar panels can also be mounted on a wall if they can be angled in the right direction without protruding too far from the wall. Make sure no overhanging eaves or architectural features will interfere with sunlight falling on the panels.

Ground mounting

A solar array can be mounted on a frame on the ground, where it is easy to clean and you can manually change the angle of the array throughout the year. A ground mount requires adequate open space in your yard or garden. Take note of any obstacles that might cast shade on your installation. Solar suppliers sell a variety of ground frames or you can build your own. Depending on ground conditions, you might have to lay a foundation to support the frame.

Mounting on a shed or patio

A solar array can be located atop a specially constructed storage shed or patio awning. PV panels incorporated in building materials and components can take the place of traditional panels. You will need to calculate the cost of building the shed or patio in addition to your solar installation.

Pole mounting

Smaller arrays of up to 600 watts can be mounted atop a pole. You will need a heavyweight pole and a substantial foundation to withstand heavy winds. Pole mounts help to keep the solar array cool in a hot climate. Solar suppliers sell poles and hardware.

Solar trackers

A **solar tracker** is a mechanical device that changes the angle of the solar panels to follow the path of the sun so your solar array is always at the optimum angle. It can increase the capacity of your system by 30 percent. Commercial solar trackers are expensive, so it is usually less expensive to buy a slightly larger solar panel array that will generate more power.

Solar trackers are typically created to be pole mounted or ground mounted. If you are using a solar tracker, you must be especially aware of obstructions to the east or west, because the panels will face in those directions in the mornings and afternoons when the angle of the sun is low.

Inverters

Inverters step up the DC voltage coming from your solar panels or batteries to the 120v AC voltage used for most household appliances. You will not need an inverter for an off-grid system if all your appliances run on 12/24 volts. You will need an inverter for a grid-tie or grid fallback system, or to run 120v appliances on an off-grid system. Inverters make up about 25 percent of the cost of an off-grid system and about 10 percent of the cost of a grid-tie system. The type and size of the inverter you need depends on the size and purpose of your PV system.

Modern inverters operate quietly and require almost no maintenance. Your solar contractor will recommend an appropriate inverter for your system. Grid-tie inverters are more expensive than inverters for off-grid systems because they are more complex. A grid-tie inverter allows you to feed AC from your PV system into the grid, and to draw power from the grid when your solar panels are not producing enough. Some inverters include battery charge controllers that manage batteries and charge them from the grid when enough solar power is not available. For grid-tie systems, your utility may require you to use a specific inverter, and for inverters to have certain certifications or ratings.

Cables and wiring

It is essential to use the right cables and wires to connect your system. Electric current always encounters some resistance when flowing through a cable, but you can reduce resistance by using a larger cable. If the cable you use to connect your solar array to a battery controller or inverter is too small, you will lose a large percentage of the power your solar panels generate. It is a good idea to use a cable that has a slightly larger capacity than you need in case you expand your system later on.

Solar equipment suppliers sell specially made cables in different lengths that have connectors already attached to the ends. These make the installation process faster and ensure that the connection is sealed against moisture. You can also purchase cabling and connectors separately and make your own cables. When designing your own system, always try to keep your system components as close together as possible to reduce the length of the cables that connect them.

In designing a PV system, you will need to use three types of cables:

Solar array cables: Solar array cables connect solar panels to each other and your solar array to the junction or connector box. These cables are called "array interconnects" and can be bought in specified lengths. They are used outdoors, so they must be resistant to UV rays, moisture, and temperature extremes. The National Electric Code (NEC) requires that these connector cables be located outside the building until they are near the entrance to the connector box.

Battery cables: Battery cables connect the batteries in your battery bank together and connect your batteries to the controller and to the inverter. You can purchase ready-made battery interconnect cables from battery suppliers. If you make up your own battery cables, be sure to use the correct battery connectors to attach them to the battery terminals.

Appliance wiring: A grid-connect system uses conventional electrical wiring. You will also use standard wiring if you are using an inverter and running your appliances on a 120v system. If you are running your household appliances on 12v or 24v, you must use larger cables to wire your house.

> ## Resistance is higher when wires and cables are hot.
>
> As wires heat up, resistance increases and more power is lost. This is not a problem over short distances but can be significant for longer cables. If you live in a climate with very hot summers, your cables are insulated in a conduit or ganged with other cables so heat cannot dissipate easily, or a cable runs for more than 100 feet, use one wire size higher.

Ground Fault Protection Devices

Section 690.5 of the *2008 NEC (National Electrical Code)* requires a PV ground-fault protection device (PVGFPD) as part of almost every PV system. Because solar panels are active any time they are exposed to light, a short circuit or malfunction in a roof-mounted solar array could continue for hours without being detected, and could result in a dangerous house fire. Ground fault protection devices detect ground faults (malfunctions or short circuits) in PV arrays, interrupt the fault current, disconnect the malfunctioning part of the PV array, and signal the homeowner that a fault has occurred. Some inverters have built-in GFPDs. Otherwise you must purchase and install a GFPD near the inverter. PVGFPDS typically cost $180 to $300 and must be large enough to accommodate your PV system. If you plan to expand your system later, buy a larger GFPD.

A PVGFPD does not eliminate the need for branch circuit protection — each module in your solar array still needs its own fuse/breaker/disconnect to protect the wiring.

Batteries

Off-grid and grid fallback systems require batteries to store excess electricity and provide power when the sun is not shining. The cost of batteries accounts for anywhere from 10 to 50 percent of the total cost of a PV system. The batteries used for PV systems are deep-cycle batteries, meaning that they can discharge 80 percent of their power and be recharged again hundreds of times. A variety of options are available for battery backups. The batteries used for PV systems are typically 12-volt lead acid batteries.

Your solar contractor will recommend batteries appropriate for your system. Your batteries supply power at night and at times when your PV system is not supplying enough power, such as stormy winter days. Depending on your climate, your battery bank should be large enough to hold enough power to supply your system for three to five days. Multiply your daily energy requirement by the number of days for which you need to store backup power to get the number of watt hours you need and determine the size and type of batteries to purchase.

Types of batteries

There are three basic types of lead acid batteries:

Wet, or "flooded," batteries

Wet batteries, also called "traction batteries," are less expensive, last longer, and perform better than sealed batteries, but they require monitoring and must be topped up with distilled water every three to six months. If you tip a wet battery, the electrolyte will spill out, which creates a risk of injury or damage from the corrosive acid.

The least expensive wet batteries are golf cart batteries, which cost around $75 each and are suitable for small systems of up to 800 watts. They have a life of three to five years. Marine batteries can also be used but have a shorter life (two to three years) and can only be used in banks of up to four batteries. L16s were originally designed for use in floor sweepers and can be used for systems up to 1600 watts. They cost around $250 each but last five to eight years. The most expensive wet batteries cost about $700 each and last for ten to 12 years. They can be used for systems up to 6,000 watts. Wet batteries give off small amounts of explosive gases when charging, so they need to be placed in a ventilated area.

Absorbed Glass Mat (AGM) batteries

Also called "sealed regulated valve," "dry cell," "starved electrolyte," "non spillable," and "Valve Regulated Lead Acid" batteries, AGM batteries have the electrolyte fully contained in a fine fiber boron-silicate glass mat. They withstand shock and vibration better than other types of batteries because the plates inside the battery are tightly packed and firmly mounted. AGM batteries do not require maintenance, will not spill corrosive liquids, and do not give off explosive gases. They have a life of four to ten years and perform best if they are not allowed to discharge more than 50 percent of their capacity before being recharged. AGM batteries do not tolerate overcharging. Leaving them unused for long periods does not diminish their performance, which makes them suitable for vacation homes.

Gel batteries (gel cells)

The electrolyte in a gel battery is a gel rather than a liquid, so the batteries do not have to be kept upright. Gel batteries do not give off explosive gases and require little maintenance. They are easily damaged by overcharging. Their lifespan is typically three to four years, and they are not suitable for systems with a power drain larger than 400 watt-hours.

NiCad batteries

Non lead-based batteries such as nickel-cadmium (NiCad) batteries are more expensive but can last a long time if they are not discharged too deeply. A new type of nickel-cadmium battery, fiber-nickel-cadmium, has outstanding longevity if it is regularly discharged only 25 percent before being recharged by the solar panels. Nickel-cadmium batteries cannot be monitored in the same way as lead batteries. Because a NiCad battery has a constant output right up to the last moments before it is completely discharged, it is difficult to measure the depth of discharge. Read manufacturer's directions for maintenance of NiCad batteries.

Battery cycle life

Your batteries will feed power to the PV system when it is needed and recharge whenever there is sunlight. Each time a battery is discharged and recharged, it is cycled. After being recharged a certain number of times, a battery becomes chemically depleted and has to be replaced. The number of times a battery can be "cycled" depends on the degree to which it is discharged each time (depth of discharge, or DOD). A battery that is 80 percent discharged in each cycle can be recharged fewer times than a battery that is only 40 percent discharged. The battery manufacturer will typically supply an estimate for the number of cycles at each level of discharge that looks something like this:

Cycle life of a battery

% Depth of Discharge	No. of Cycles
10%	3200
25%	1200
50%	500
75%	250
100%	**200**

Your batteries will last longer if your battery bank is big enough so it does not get heavily discharged during ordinary use. This will also give you extra backup power when something unexpected happens, such as severe winter weather that lasts several days.

Getting the most out of your batteries

Batteries are sensitive to extreme heat and cold and will deteriorate if they are not properly maintained. When designing your solar system, you can do several things to keep your batteries performing optimally for as long as possible.

Do not put more than four strings of batteries in parallel. If you need a battery bank with a large capacity, it is better to buy larger batteries than to wire together too many smaller ones. Too many batteries wired in parallel begin to drain power from each other.

Do not mix new batteries with old ones. If you combine new batteries with second-hand batteries that are more than six months old, the new batteries will be discharged more frequently than the old ones. The performance of the new batteries will be dragged down to the level of the old ones.

Keep the batteries at a comfortable temperature. Most batteries perform best at about 77 degrees, so it is best to locate them indoors and insulate them from extreme temperatures. Try to keep the batteries between 55 and 80 degrees F. Batteries can be kept outside but should be insulated from extreme temperatures and protected from moisture.

Temperature's affect on batteries

Battery capacity is reduced when temperature goes down, and increases as temperature goes up. If your batteries will be spending several months out in the cold, you must take the reduced capacity into account when sizing your system batteries. Battery capacity is typically rated for about 77 degrees F. At freezing, battery capacity is reduced by 20 percent, and at 22 degrees F, it has only half its rated capacity. At 122 degrees F, battery capacity would be about 12 percent higher than the standard rating.

Batteries in the utility room of the Zero Energy House in Loudoun County, Virginia

Battery voltage also varies with temperature, varying from about 2.74 volts per cell (16.4 volts) at -40 degrees F (-40 degrees C) to 2.3 volts per cell (13.8 volts) at 122 degrees F (50 degrees C). If your batteries will experience extreme temperature variations, your controller should have temperature compensation. Even a controller with temperature compensation will not function accurately if it is located inside at a different temperature from batteries outside or if you have a large insulated battery bank. The inside temperature of a large battery bank may vary only 10 degrees over 24 hours while the external temperature fluctuates 50 degrees. When installing external temperature sensors, attach them to one of the positive plate terminals and wrap them with insulation so they maintain a temperature close to that of the battery interior.

Though high temperatures increase battery capacity, they shorten battery life. For every 15 degrees over 77 degrees F (25 degrees C), battery life is cut in half.

Controllers

A **controller** is a device that manages the power going into and coming out of your batteries. It stops them from being overcharged by your solar array and cuts off power to your appliances before the batteries become completely discharged. Controllers also shut off the circuit to your solar array at night when it is inactive to prevent "reverse flow" of current into your solar panels.

Controllers with on/off control regulate the flow of energy to the batteries by switching the current fully on or fully off. Controllers with pulse width modulation (PWM) reduce the current gradually. Either method works well when set correctly for your type of battery. A PWM controller with two-stage regulation first holds the voltage to a safe maximum until the battery is fully charged, then drops the voltage lower to sustain a "finish" or "trickle" charge that tops up the battery when needed. If your system will only be used intermittently, such as for a vacation cottage that is sometimes unoccupied for days at a time, two-stage regulating is the best choice because it maintains a full charge in the batteries while minimizing water loss and stress.

The voltage levels at which the controller switches on or off or changes the charge rate are called **set points**. Some controllers allow you to adjust the set points manually; others do not. Correct set points are determined according to the type of battery and anticipated patterns of usage.

A battery's storage capacity varies with temperature, so the set points should be adjusted if your system experiences significant seasonal temperature changes. A "temperature compensation" feature on some controllers raises the set points when it senses a low battery temperature. Compensation is essential if your batteries are exposed to temperature fluctuations greater than about 30 degrees F (17 degrees C),. A controller with a built in temperature sensor should be mounted very near to the batteries where it experiences the same temperatures. Some higher-end controllers have a remote temperature probe that attaches directly to a battery and reports its temperature to the controller.

Controllers manage the charge in each battery and ensure each battery becomes recharged. As batteries age, their capacities and discharge rates begin to vary. A controller can detect these variations and balance the batteries as it charges them to lengthen battery life.

Controllers have a variety of tracking displays ranging from colored lights to digital displays. Most controllers have an LCD screen that shows you how much power your solar array is generating and how much charge is stored in your batteries. More sophisticated controllers allow you to compare your day-to-day usage and power generation. If you want a detailed record of your energy usage, you can purchase a separate tracking device that includes an amp-hour meter for about $200. In that case, you do not need a controller with sophisticated tracking functions.

Lease a solar system

SolarCity (www.solarcity.com), a major U.S. solar provider, now offers SolarLease™, a program that allows homeowners to lease instead of purchase a PV system. In place of an initial outlay of $20,000 to $35,000, customers pay a regular monthly fee, which is less than the amount of a utility bill. SolarLease contracts also include warranties and service, replacement of defective panels, and free pick up of the solar panels when the lease expires. At the end of the lease, the customer can opt to replace the old panels with the  newest equipment, or continue leasing the system in five-year increments. When the home is sold, the owner either transfers the lease to the new owner, or prepays it and adds it to the price of the home. SolarCity currently serves more than 1,500 communities in Arizona, California, Colorado, Maryland, Oregon, Texas, and Washington, D.C.

In some states and utility districts, the leasing plan is known as PurePower. A PV unit is installed on a home and the homeowner pays SolarCity the same amount for the electricity generated by the solar panels as for electricity from the utility. When utility prices go up, however, the homeowner continues to pay the lower original rate for solar energy. Utility companies partner with SolarCity to offer these plans because the solar panels relieve some of the demand for electricity from the grid, and customers are satisfied because they know they are using cleaner energy and locking in lower prices.

Wind Turbines

Wind turbines convert the kinetic energy in wind into mechanical power that runs a generator to produce clean electricity. The blades of a wind turbine are aero¬dynamically designed to capture the maximum energy from the wind. The blades spin a shaft connected to a generator that makes electricity. A wind turbine that produces all the electricity needed by an average household requires an acre or more of property. If you have this much space, and live in a rural area where there is enough wind and where local regulations allow tall towers on private property, an off-grid, wind-powered system is an option. Wind turbines can also supplement a home's power supply in a grid-tie system.

Evaluating your site's potential for wind energy

Wind turbines typically do not begin generating power until the wind speed reaches 10 miles per hour. If your area does not regularly experience winds of at least 10 to 12 mph, a wind turbine is impractical. The DOE Wind & Water Power Program website (**www.windpoweringamerica. gov/wind_maps.asp**) has wind maps showing wind data for each state in the United States. The wind resource estimates on these maps generally apply to terrain features that are well exposed to the wind, such as plains, hilltops, and ridge crests. Local terrain features may cause the wind resource at a specific site to differ considerably from these estimates. More detailed wind resource information, including the Wind Energy Resource Atlas of the United States, published by the U.S. Department of Energy (DOE), can be found at the National Wind Technology Center website (**www. nrel.gov/wind**) and the DOE Wind Powering America website (**www. windpoweringamerica.gov**). You can obtain detailed information about average wind speeds in your area from a local airport, but the physical conditions on your building site might not be the same as at the airport. If someone else in your neighborhood has a wind turbine, you can also get useful information from them.

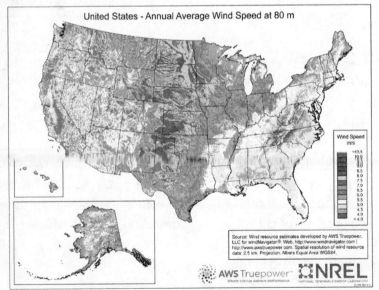

This map from the U.S. Department of Energy. This 80-meter high-resolution wind map can be used as a guide to identify regions for commercial wind development. Estimates of the wind resource potential that would be possible from development of the available windy land areas (after excluding areas unlikely to be developed) are provided in tables and charts.

The best way to evaluate the potential of wind energy for your site is to monitor the wind directly with a wind resource measuring system. A wind energy contractor will probably have this equipment. Measurements should be taken at the height where your rotor will be located. You may have different wind speeds on different areas of your building site. Experts can even judge wind speed by looking at the shapes of the vegetation and trees on the site. Geologic obstacles such as hills and gullies, vegetation, buildings, and trees can all affect wind speed, both now and in the future.

A turbine should be placed upwind from buildings and trees and should be at least 30 feet above any obstacle within 300 feet. Remember to account for the future growth of vegetation and any future construction. There should be enough space for guy wires that will anchor the tower to the ground, and to allow the tower to be raised and lowered conveniently for maintenance.

Components of a Wind System

A wind turbine system consist of the following components:

- Rotor
- Generator or alternator mounted on a frame
- Tail (usually)
- Tower
- Wiring
- Controller
- Inverter
- Batteries

Rotor

Most rotors have two or three blades, usually made of a composite material such as fiberglass. The amount of power a turbine will produce is determined primarily by the diameter of its rotor, which defines its swept area, or the quantity of wind intercepted by the turbine.

Tail and frame

The rotor and generator are mounted on a frame with a tail at the opposite end from the rotor. The tail keeps the rotor facing into the wind.

Tower

The turbine is mounted on a tower. Wind speeds increase with height, so the higher the tower, the more power the wind system can produce. The tower also raises the turbine above the air turbulence caused by obstructions such as hills, buildings, and trees close to the ground.

The wind turbine should be installed on a tower with the bottom of the rotor blades at least 30 feet above any obstacle that is within 300 feet of the tower. Relatively small investments in increased tower height can yield very high rates of return in power production.

There are two basic types of towers, self-supporting (free standing) and guyed. Most home wind power systems use a guyed tower. **Guyed towers,** which are less expensive and easier to install than self-supporting towers, consist of lattice sections, pipe, or tubing (depending on the design), and supporting guy wires. However, because the radius of the guy wires must be one-half to three-quarters of the tower height, guyed towers require enough space to accommodate them. Tilt-down towers can be tilted over and lowered to the ground during hurricanes. Though they are more expensive, they make it easy to perform maintenance on smaller, lightweight turbines (5 kW or less). Aluminum towers are not recommended because they crack easily under stress. Manufacturers of wind turbines usually provide wind towers as part of their wind system packages.

Mounting turbines on rooftops is not recommended

All wind turbines vibrate and transmit the vibration to the structure on which they are mounted. This can lead to noise and structural problems with the building, and the rooftop can cause excessive turbulence that shortens the life of the turbine.

Generator

The generator or alternator is the component that converts mechanical energy from the rotors into electricity and accounts for about one-third of the cost of a wind system. It is typically mounted on the top of the tower directly behind the rotor. A gearbox between the rotors and the generator increases the speed at which the generator turns. The generator must be sized for your particular rotor and wind speeds.

Inverters, batteries, and controllers

The inverters, batteries, and controllers of a wind turbine system are similar to those used with a solar system. The manufacturer typically supplies packages containing the components needed for different purposes.

Cost of a Wind Energy System

A small turbine can cost anywhere from $3,000 to $50,000 installed, depending on size, application, manufacturers' service agreements, and the connection fees of local utilities. According to the American Wind Energy Association (AWEA), a typical home wind system costs approximately $32,000 (10 kW); a comparable photovoltaic solar system would cost more than $80,000. Wind energy becomes more cost effective.

The length of the payback period depends on the system you choose, the wind resource on your site, electricity costs in your area, how you use your wind system, and whether you receive any rebates or tax incentives. You can analyze the economics of a small wind electric system using the Wind Energy Payback Period Workbook (**www.nrel.gov/wind/docs/spread_sheet_Final.xls**), a downloadable spreadsheet tool that calculates the payback period.

Insurance

Wind-generated electricity, like electricity generated by a PV system, can be sold back to your utility through a net-metering agreement. *See the following net metering section for more information.* Some utilities require small wind turbine owners to maintain liability insurance in amounts of $1 million or more to protect them from liability for facilities they do not own and have no control over. Seven states (California, Georgia, Maryland, Nevada, Oklahoma, Oregon, and Washington) have regulations prohibiting utilities from requiring liability insurance, and Idaho and Virginia limit the amount of insurance that can be required.

The National Renewable Energy Laboratory has produced Small Wind Electric Systems Consumer's Guides for numerous states to help homeowners, ranchers, and small businesses. You can download these guides from its website (**www.windpoweringamerica.gov/small_wind.asp**).

Hybrid Systems

Wind turbines added to a PV system can charge batteries any time a breeze is blowing. The small wind turbine industry estimates that 60 percent of the United States has enough wind resources for small turbine use. In Alaska, where winter days have only a few hours of sunlight but strong winds, standard PV installations often include a wind turbine. A micro wind turbine can be installed on a pole attached to your roof or the side of your house, or on a stand-alone pole or tower. If your home is located near a creek or river, you might also be able to use a water turbine turned by the current to generate extra electricity.

A wind turbine is added to your PV system calculation in a similar way to solar panels. Manufacturer's specifications tell you the output of a turbine under various wind conditions. Hybrid controllers regulate the charge coming in to your batteries from both the wind turbine and the PV system. A solar contractor can tell you whether a wind turbine is viable in your area, and the types of turbines in use for similar PV installations.

Backup Generator

A backup generator can run on gasoline, biodiesel, diesel, liquid propane, or natural gas and can be set up to turn on automatically when your batteries are discharged to a certain level, your utility grid fails, or your PV system is not generating the power you need. You can also turn it on manually to recharge your batteries when needed. A generator can charge your batteries during the time that a heavy load such as a heater or air conditioner is drawing power from your system, and then shut off so that smaller loads like lights and clocks run off battery power. It is a waste of fuel to keep a generator running just to operate a few small loads.

Residential generators are available with outputs from 6 to 150kW. Generators can be controlled through an inverter. In a well-planned PV system, a generator will only be used 50 to 200 hours per year.

Have a generator in a grid-tie system installed by a licensed electrician

Any interaction between an active utility line and a generator can be dangerous. Have a licensed electrician install the generator to ensure it is done safely and correctly. During a grid power outage, a running generator could back-feed electricity into the utility power lines and injure anyone servicing those lines. If your running generator is not isolated from the utility lines, serious damage to your generator and your appliances could result when the power comes back on.

Selling Power to Your Utility

The Federal Public Utility Regulatory Policy Act of 1978 (PURPA) allows businesses and individuals to sell excess electricity generated by solar or wind systems to their local utilities at avoided cost. **Avoided cost** is the utility's wholesale cost to produce electricity and is about one-fourth of the retail price. Utilities that buy excess electricity at wholesale prices install a second meter at your home to measure the outgoing power. Net metering is now offered in more than 35 states.

Net metering

Your electricity meter literally runs backward in net metering. When the sun is shining brightly and your PV system produces more power than you are using, the excess electricity is fed to your utility grid. This excess electricity offsets the electricity you use from the grid when your PV system is not generating enough power, so you end up selling electricity for the same price you would pay for it. With net metering, you will recoup the cost of installing a PV system much more rapidly.

Time of Use (TOU) price structures charge more for electricity used during peak hours. In the summer, solar systems typically produce the most electricity during peak hours, the hottest time when air conditioners are running in nearly every building. If your utility has TOU, you will earn even more credit because you will be buying at the lower off-peak prices and selling your electricity at higher peak-hour prices.

Net metering gives you an added financial bonus.

The retail price your utility charges for electricity incorporates not only the fuel used to generate the electricity, but also the cost of building power plants, administration, lines and substations, and operation and maintenance costs. When you sell your electricity to your utility at retail price, you are being paid more than your electricity is really worth. You could say that your utility is indirectly paying part of the cost of buying PV equipment.

You can find detailed information about net metering in your area by contacting your local utility company or looking at the DSIRE online database (**www.dsireusa.org**). Your utility will ask you to sign a contract, called a Net Metering (NEM) Agreement, spelling out the details of the arrangement. Your electrical contractor will probably also be required to sign. You will be asked to submit the specifications of your PV system and a wiring diagram, and the date when your system will be ready to begin operating. You may be asked to choose between monthly billing and a single annual utility bill. The contract will cover liability and insurance, maintenance, and what happens during power outages.

You will connect to your utility grid through your inverter. All utilities require UL 1741 certification for grid-tie inverters. *See the following UL Certification section for more information.* Each state has utility interconnection standards that dictate the requirements for your grid connection. Your solar contractor or electrician will be familiar with these standards. You will also be required to submit proof that you have all the necessary permits and that your installation conforms to local building codes.

The utility company will inspect your installation to confirm that it conforms with the NEC, the connections are wired correctly, and the workmanship meets certain standards. It will install a new meter and connect it to your inverter.

UL Certification

Underwriters Laboratories® (UL) (www.ul.com/global/eng/pages) is a global independent safety science company that has been researching product safety and setting global safety standards since 1894. The UL Mark on a product means that UL has tested and evaluated representative samples of that product and determined that they meet UL requirements. Under a variety of programs products are periodically checked by UL at the manufacturing facility to make sure they continue to meet UL requirements.

Renewable Energy Credits and Green Power

The energy you produce with your PV, wind, or biomass system has two kinds of value: the electric power you produce, and the fact that it is clean, renewable energy. Recent climate change legislation mandates that utilities, manufacturing plants, state and local governments, and certain industries reduce their carbon emissions and their fossil fuel consumption by using renewable energy sources for a certain percentage of their energy needs. In addition, some manufacturers, industries, and organizations want to reduce air pollution and to publicize themselves as green industries selling green products.

To help in meeting these goals, a system of Renewable Energy Certificates (RECs) has been developed to track the source of energy and to differentiate between renewable energy and energy produced with fossil fuels. One REC represents 1,000 kilowatt hours of clean, renewable energy. RECs can be bought and sold separately from the electricity they represent and are a sort of energy currency. A utility or industry that does not have access to clean, renewable energy can still meet its goals or declare itself green by purchasing RECs from an individual or utility that produces renewable energy. The electricity represented by RECs is known as **green power**. RECs are registered, numbered, and tracked by regional tracking systems and any sale of RECs is accompanied by an affidavit that no one else can claim that energy as green.

An REC can be used only once. After a buyer has made an environmental claim based on a REC, that REC is considered permanently retired. Buyers can also have their RECs retired in their name by their supplier to ensure that no other entity can lay claim to the same environmental benefits.

You own the RECs for the energy produced by your PV system. Some utilities will enter into a separate agreement to buy your RECs, which they can then sell to customers who specifically want "green power." If you sell RECs for electricity generated by your PV system that you use in your own home, you can no longer claim to be using green power.

In Minnesota, Xcel Energy's Solar*Rewards program gives customers a one-time payment of $2.25 per installed watt of generating capacity in exchange for ownership of the RECs produced by the systems for 20 years.

Solar-powered Appliances

If you are planning an off-grid PV system, particularly for a seasonal vacation cabin or a remote location, you can use appliances that are designed to run on solar power sources. A variety of 12v/24v appliances are on the market. A solar-powered refrigerator is smaller and more expensive, but it avoids needing to purchase

Solar-powered refrigerator

extra solar panels and battery storage to provide electricity for a conventional refrigerator. SunDanzer offers a model 46 inches wide by 34.5 inches high that retails for about $1,200. (**www.sundanzer.com/Home.html**).

Conclusion

Many green homes incorporate solar or wind energy to supply at least part of their energy needs. Solar radiation can be used to heat the home or provide hot water, and to generate electricity with photovoltaic panels. Wind turbines convert the kinetic energy of wind into electricity.

Solar systems are widely used in California, Florida, and the Southwest, areas where there are a large number of clear, sunny days. In areas with less sunshine, a larger PV system is required to produce the same amount of energy. Wind turbines are used mostly in rural areas because a typical wind turbine requires at least 1 acre of open space. Federal law requires utilities to buy excess power generated by residential solar and wind systems through a net metering system.

Although a PV or wind system can reduce energy bills by 50 percent, the initial cost of equipment is high and it may be a decade or more before the energy savings pay for the cost of the system. Federal, state, and local governments offer tax credits and rebates to lower the initial cost of installing an alternative energy system. A solar or wind system is economical for a remote building site that has not been connected to the power grid because it can cost thousands of dollars to have power lines laid. Solar and wind systems are also practical for vacation cottages with relatively low energy needs and for smaller applications such as water pumps and lighting systems.

Chapter 7

Water

Worldwide demand for water tripled over the past century, and is currently doubling every 21 years. Scientists predict that by 2025, one-third of all humans will face severe and chronic water shortages. It is environmentally responsible to use water sparingly and efficiently. Systems that minimize a building's water use and waste are a key element of green building. Effective water efficiency planning seeks to use less water without sacrificing comfort or performance. There are a variety of ways to integrate water efficiency in your home, from installing a storm water management system that captures and cleans rainwater to installing low-flow faucet fixtures to reduce water pressure.

Water Efficiency

CalRecycle (**www.calrecycle.ca.gov**) recommends these measures for efficient use of water in a building:

- Install a dual plumbing system that uses recycled water for flushing toilets.
- Use a gray water system to recover nonpotable water for landscape irrigation.
- Use ultra low-flow fixtures to reduce waste and conserve water.
- Use a re-circulated or point-of-use hot water system to provide hot water for sinks, dishwashers, and showers.
- Use a low-pressure micro-irrigation system to supply water to exterior areas of the building.

- Install a separate meter system for the landscape.
- Control water usage from hoses, sprinklers, and other water distribution systems with irrigation controllers.

Many building codes in urban and suburban areas do not allow gray water systems, but that could change in the near future, especially in areas experiencing water shortages. If you are building a new home in an area with a dry climate, you might decide to install the plumbing for a gray water system while the house is being built, to be used later when local zoning authorities approve it.

Dual plumbing/gray water systems

A dual plumbing or gray water system has two sets of pipes — one that provides clean water for drinking and washing, and another that collects wastewater from sinks and showers, known as **gray water**, and recycles it for purposes like flushing a toilet or irrigating landscape. The system stores and treats gray water, often in a tank underground, and then makes it available for use.

Many states, like New York, offer tax credits for incorporating gray water systems into a building or residence, while other states such as Colorado only allow gray water to be used for cleaning and irrigation.

Just So You Know...

Toilet wastewater is referred to as black water; it is not used in gray water systems because it is not sanitary.

Public health concerns have generated controversy over using gray water systems, particularly in highly populated urban areas. Officials are concerned that gray water might mix with black water in a plumbing system, leading to the spread of disease-causing bacteria. Gray water also contains bacteria that can multiply when it is stored in a tank. It should not be used to water edible plants in a garden.

Separating gray water from black water generally involves a parallel wastewater system. Space must be available for larger components such as a holding tank or some filters, which can be located in a basement, shed, or possibly outside.

Gray water systems are more common in rural farmland areas. Gray water systems have many advantages, including:

- Conserving fresh water by using recycled water for land irrigation and watering. This is particularly beneficial in hot, arid areas of the country where fresh water supplies are severely limited.
- Less wear and tear on a septic tank from non-toilet wastewater, which translate to lower maintenance costs.
- Recycling natural nutrients such as food particles from this wastewater that would otherwise be wasted, which enriches the quality of the soil in your landscape.

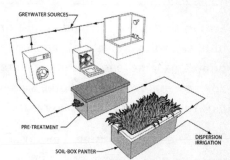

The cost of gray water and dual plumbing systems varies depending on the size. A system is generally either a gravity system or a packaged system. The more simple gravity system treats and delivers

In a gray water system, a second set of pipes carries water from kitchen and bathroom sink and shower drains through a tank (something like a septic tank) that settles out impurities, then into a storage and filtration system.

gray water without using electricity; the more advanced and efficient package systems require electric pumps and cost significantly more. In a typical residential household, a simple gray water system can save anywhere from 10,000 to 50,000 gallons of water a year, which yields less than $200 a year in savings.

Low-flow fixtures

In 1994, the government required that toilets use no more than 1.6 gallons per flush compared to 3.5 gallons per flush for toilets manufactured prior to that year. Since this guide was established, using low-flow fixtures for other water sources has become increasingly popular as a method of water conservation.

Low-flow fixtures reduce the amount of water flowing from water fixtures such as showerheads, faucets, and toilets without lowering the water pressure. They use much less water than conventional fixtures. **Aerators**, low-flow fixtures that mix air with water to slow down the water flow without affecting the pressure, can be attached to sinks and showerheads to significantly reduce water use by 30 to 70 percent.

What Does Low-Flow Mean?

Low-flow is defined as:

1.6 gallons per flush for toilets
2.5 gallons per minute or less for faucets and showers
These are just minimums, however. It is possible to incorporate fixtures that use even less than these amounts of water.

Sensors that control the amount of time water flows through a faucet and turn water off automatically are another low-cost way to reduce water consumption. Some sensors require that the user physically hold the water knob down to produce flow, and others allow water to flow through the faucet for 5 or 10 seconds at a time. Sensors can also be used for outdoor landscaping.

Toilet and urinal flushing typically account for nearly one-third of a building's total water consumption. Dual flush toilets, which have different flush volumes for liquid and solid waste, greatly reduce water usage for flushing toilets. Ultra-low flush (ULF) toilets use an efficient bowl design and increased flushing velocities to remove waste, instead of large amounts of water. There are two main varieties of low-flush toilets: gravity flow and pressurized tank systems. The gravity flow technology is the same as that found in conventional toilets except the rim wash on some models comes through an open slot rather than through little holes. The toilet bowl may have steep sides and a narrower trapway to strengthen the siphon action that pulls the waste out. The pressurized flush employs pressure from the house water line to increase the velocity of the water going into the bowl. Incoming water presses against a rubber diaphragm that compresses a pocket of air inside the toilet tank. The water is released by pushing the flush valve.

Waterless urinals are coming into increasing use. A waterless urinal is coated with a slippery surface and contains a mechanical trap or a U-shaped cartridge that blocks odors as urine passes through to the sewage system. Some of these odor blocks contain naturally occurring microbes that break down the uric scales and reduce stains and clogged drains. A waterless urinal in a home can save 3,000 gallons of water per year. Some local building codes have not been updated to allow waterless urinals.

Your Water Budget

Part of the building design process should be creating a water budget detailing your building's expected water use. Indoor and outdoor water budgets calculate the amount of water a household requires based on the size of the family, number and types of fixtures and appliances, and landscape needs. Water budgets are calculated using the flow rates of fixtures such as toilets, faucets and showerheads, and appliances such as dishwashers and washing machines, and the expected usage of each. An outdoor water budget is calculated based on the size of the lawn and the types of grass and plants used for landscaping.

When the building is occupied, water consumption should be monitored. If your water usage later exceeds your water budget by more than 10 percent, it is a sign that the water system is not performing as it should be. There could be a leak or faulty connection, or the designers could have miscalculated when they anticipated the behavior of the building occupants.

Water-saving Appliances

An estimated 22 percent of water use in a home goes into the washing machine. High efficiency washing machines use only 23 gallons per load, almost half of the 40 gallons used by conventional washing machines. Front-loading washing machines are typically more efficient, though some top-loading machines also conserve water. Front loading washing machines also cause less wear and tear on your clothes, so that they do not have to be replaced as often.

Waterless washing machines

Soon you will be able to purchase washing machines that use almost no water at all. Researchers at Leeds University in the U.K. have developed a new technology that employs reusable nylon polymer beads that become absorbent under humid conditions. The beads, which have an inherent polarity that attracts stains, are added to the wash along with as little as a cup of water and a drop of detergent. The water dissolves the stains, and the beads soak up the water along with the dirt, which is absorbed into the center of the beads. The machine automatically removes the beads at the end of the wash cycle. The clothes come out almost dry, so there is no need for an electric dryer. The beads do not require cleaning and can be reused for 100 loads of laundry (about six months of laundry in an average family). The machine uses just 2 percent of the energy a conventional washing machine consumes because it does not require a spin or a rinse cycle. The researchers have established a company, Xeros Ltd., (**www.xerosltd.com**) to market the technology.

Engineers at Electrolux (**www.electroluxusa.com**) have designed a prototype KaionWAVE washing system that uses ultraviolet-C light to clean nano-coated fabric, a durable and stain resistant fabric that many predict will be used to make the clothing of the future. Ultraviolet-C light and free radical oxygen are used to clean the nano-coated fabrics. The ultraviolet-C light penetrates through the fabric to kill bacteria and viruses, while the free radical oxygen acts as a powerful oxidizing agent to break down dirt into carbon dioxide and water. The KaionWAVE washing system functions as both washer and dryer.

Dishwashers

Dishwashers with the ENERGY STAR label save on both energy and water. Using any ENERGY STAR-qualified dishwasher instead of washing your dishes by hand saves 5,000 gallons of water, $40 in utility costs, and 230 hours of labor annually. A dishwasher manufactured before 1994 wastes more than 10 gallons of water per cycle compared to a new ENERGY STAR model. Older dishwashers also consume more energy because they use larger amounts of hot water. Newer models use finer, more targeted streams for hot water. Currently, 695 dishwasher models across 52 brands qualify for the ENERGY STAR label.

Conclusion

People living in desert environments have always been conscious of the need to use water sparingly. Today, even those who live where water is plentiful are becoming aware that it is a precious and expendable resource. Conventional buildings often waste water by using more than is necessary for daily activities and by irrigating landscaping. Green building strives to minimize water use while maintaining a comfortable lifestyle, through water-efficient fixtures, recycling, and carefully measuring the water used for each purpose.

Chapter 8

Green Landscaping

Landscaping, just like every other aspect of a green building, should be part of the initial design process. Look at the vegetation growing on the site and identify trees and plants that you want to save. Large trees take decades to grow and provide shade to help cool the house and the yard. Established vegetation provides storm water drainage and protects soil from erosion. The plants already growing on your site are resistant to local insect pests and will not require insecticides and fertilizers.

Creating a sustainable landscape in your outdoor space will contribute significantly to your building's greenness. Green landscape planning and design incorporates a multitude of factors, including climate, erosion control, maintenance, water usage, and the natural habitats in the surrounding area. Instead of intruding on any natural habitats or ecosystems, the objective is to landscape with plants, flowers, grass, and shrubbery that enhance the indigenous surroundings. You will also want to consider how you will use this outdoor space and what types of shady and sunny areas you want to create.

A properly designed landscape also helps control the building's temperature and provides a natural barrier to outdoor weather. Landscapes can be designed, for instance, to create breezes in certain areas and to direct wind. This helps to lower the overall thermal temperature of the building and reduces the need for forced air systems like air conditioning.

Protecting the Building Site

It is a practice of green building to disturb the site as little as possible during construction. Once construction work begins, heavy trucks and equipment will tear up the vegetation and compact the soil. Cordon off the areas that will not be paved later on, and designate spaces for delivery and storage of building materials, parking, and activities such as mixing concrete and cutting framing.

If site work is being done in an area that will later be part of the garden, remove the top 6 inches of soil and stockpile it in an area that is designated for paving. The soil can be replaced when the construction work is finished. Natural topsoil contains nutrients and air and reduces the need to use fertilizer.

Trees

Shading and evapotranspiration from trees can reduce surrounding air temperatures as much as 9 degrees F (5 degrees C). The U.S. Department of Environmental Protection estimates that trees and vegetation planted around a  home can reduce cooling costs by 25 percent and heating bills by between 25 percent and 40 percent. Because cool air settles near the ground, air temperatures directly under trees can be as much as 25 degrees F cooler than air temperatures above nearby blacktop. A mature stand of deciduous trees reduces surrounding air temperatures by 15 degrees F. Shading an air conditioning unit with a tree reduces cooling costs by as much as 10 percent.

Trees and shrubbery also help reduce air pollution by absorbing carbon dioxide and releasing oxygen back into the air.

Trees also provide a buffer against winds during storms, channel breezes to help cool and ventilate a house, and protect solar panels and collectors from dust or snow. Proper placement of trees is crucial to energy efficiency. A tree that shades a home in winter can increase heating needs, and even a small amount of shade falling on a solar panel dramatically decreases its production of electricity. Planting deciduous bushes about 4 feet from the east and west windows of a house reduces heat buildup from sun slanting in through the windows in the mornings and evenings. Bushes also deflect rain and snow away from the building foundation. Dense pine trees to the north and west of a home deflect winds during winter storms. Shade during the summer is very important. Deciduous trees on the south side of a home provide shade during the summer and allow solar gain in the winter when their leaves fall off. They should not be planted too close to the south side of the house, though, or their trunks and branches could reduce solar gain by half.

Lawns

Nearly 50,000 square miles of America are covered in lawn, and Americans collectively spend about $40 billion annually on seed, sod, and chemicals. Every year 70 million tons of fertilizer and 70 million pounds of pesticides, or about ten times the amount of pesticides per acre used on crops, are spread on American lawns. The 35 million lawn mowers in the U.S. use 580 million gallons of gasoline per year, and watering lawns uses about 13 percent of residential water use or between 15 and 20 gallons per day per household. The average U.S. homeowner spends 40 hours and $500 a year to send grass clippings amounting to 21 percent of municipal solid waste to the local landfill. According to the EPA, 90 million lawn and garden machines emit 6 million tons of pollutants — 5 percent of total annual emissions — including hydrocarbons, particulates, nitrogen oxides, carbon monoxide, and carbon dioxide.

Although lawns do absorb carbon dioxide from the atmosphere, recent studies indicate that nitrous oxide emissions from fertilization offset 10 percent to 30 percent of the carbon sequestered and that the fossil fuels consumed by lawn mowers, blowers, and other equipment used for lawn maintenance emit more carbon than the grass absorbs. Pesticides used on lawns are harmful to beneficial insects such as bees and toxic to aquatic life. Pets and children playing barefoot on lawns are directly exposed to these chemical substances. Pesticides and fertilizers are washed by rain into storm water systems and waterways. Many homeowners do not know how to use them correctly. When fertilizer is improperly applied, more than half of its nitrogen content washes away. Excess nitrogen in lakes and streams causes algae blooms and excess vegetation that suffocate aquatic life. Lawns also replace natural habitat, eliminating the plants that support native animals, birds, and insects, leading to a loss of biodiversity.

If grass is part of your landscaping, choose varieties that thrive in local conditions, do not succumb to local insect pests, and do not require excess watering or fertilizer. Follow local guidelines for watering and fertilizer application. Compost lawn clippings or leave them on the grass.

Consider omitting lawns altogether and landscaping with native plants instead. A landscape of native plants requires relatively little upkeep. Your yard becomes an extension of the surrounding natural environment and replaces some of the native habitat that has been lost to development. Some homeowner associations object to native gardens because they do not conform to the aesthetic standards of a neighborhood, but if you communicate and explain what you are doing, you may be able to get approval. A 2009 Florida law states that any landscape that follows Florida *Yards and Neighborhood Guidelines* promoting the nine principles of Florida-friendly landscaping "supersedes and takes precedence over all other municipal, county and homeowner association rules, ordinances or laws." Native plant gardens are given this status because "the use of Florida-friendly landscaping and other water use and pollution prevention measures to conserve or protect the state's water resources serves a compelling public interest."

Nine Principle of Florida-Friendly Landscaping™ of the Southwest Florida Water Management District

These principles apply to environmentally friendly landscaping in any area:

- Use the right plant in the right place.
- Water efficiently.
- Fertilize appropriately.
- Mulch.
- Attract wildlife.
- Manage yard pests responsibly.
- Recycle.
- Reduce storm water runoff.
- Protect the waterfront.

Create a Certified Wildlife Habitat

Landscaping that creates or maintains wildlife habitat earns points in the LEED and NAHB National Green Building Certification programs. Using native plants on your site and adding features such as a water supply and ground cover helps to preserve biodiversity. You and your family can enjoy watching the birds, butterflies, and small animals that visit your yard.

The National Wildlife Federation's Certified Wildlife Habitat™ program has certified more than 136,000 sites across the country. Your garden can qualify for certification if it contains the following elements:

- **Food Sources** - Example: Native plants, seeds, fruits, nuts, berries, nectar
- **Water Sources** - Example: Birdbath, pond, water garden, stream
- **Places for Cover** - Example: Thicket, rockpile, birdhouse
- **Places to Raise Young** - Example: Dense shrubs, vegetation, nesting box, pond
- **Sustainable Gardening** - Example: Mulch, compost, rain garden, chemical-free fertilizer

Instructions for getting certified can be found at the NWF website (**www.nwf. org/gardenforwildlife/certify.cfm**). When your application is approved, you can purchase an official sign to place in your yard.

Native Plants

It is always best to choose vegetation that is native to your local area. This is beneficial not only because it reduces the distance that plants must be transported to your building site, but also because these plants, flowers, grass, and shrubbery have adapted to the geographic climate and the soil in your area and will flourish with minimum irrigation, pesticides, and fertilizers. Besides just looking good, native vegetation can help to control and treat storm water by absorption and cleaning, just as a green roof would. Even plants that are suitable for your climate zone may not thrive in your garden if soil or water conditions are not conducive. A landscape architect can help you to evaluate the soils on your building site and select appropriate plants.

In general, your landscape should complement your building and help achieve your overall green goals. Consult a landscape designer who has experience with native vegetation in your area as well as green design. The PlantNative.org website (**www.plantnative.org/pro_dir_main.htm**) has a directory of native plant nurseries and landscapers. Many states have programs to certify master gardeners and specialists in native plants.

Avoiding Using Invasive Plants

Beautiful, unusual, exceptionally hardy, drought-tolerant, or fast-growing plants are sought by gardeners the world over. Unfortunately, those resilient qualities allow some non-native species to adapt quickly to new environments and propagate rapidly, which causes serious ecological disturbances. Some invasive plants such as mile-a-minute, purple loosestrife, and kudzu ruthlessly choke out other plant life and put extreme pressure on native plants and animals. Ultimately, invasive plants alter habitats and reduce biodiversity. Plants selected for their aesthetic value may be hard to banish from your garden even after their invasive tendencies are revealed and may spread to neighboring yards and into natural areas.

Invasive Plants:
- Produce large numbers of new plants each season.
- Tolerate many soil types and weather conditions.
- Spread easily and efficiently, usually by wind, water, or animals.
- Grow rapidly, which allowes them to displace slower growing plants.
- Spread rampantly when they are free of the natural checks and balances found in their native range.

Before purchasing plants for your garden, check to see whether they are invasive. Enature.com has compiled a guide to invasive garden plants in each state, available through its website (**www.enature.com/native_invasive/invasives.asp**). If you discover invasive plants in your yard, remove and destroy them.

Xeriscaping

The word xeriscape is derived from the Greek words "xeros" meaning "dry," and "scape," meaning a kind of view or scene. **Xeriscaping** means to landscape with slow-growing, drought tolerant plants that can thrive without regular maintenance in the climate conditions where they will be used. Although indigenous plants are a natural choice for water and waste efficient landscapes, xeriscaping is not restricted to native plants. Plants from areas with similar climates can also thrive in a xeriscape.

The ideal xeriscape needs little or no irrigation and very little trimming or maintenance. Xeriscapes require less fertilizer and fewer pest control measures than traditional landscapes, which reduces the release of excess nutrients and pesticides into local water systems. All of these benefits translate into additional cost savings. Using native plants for your landscaping creates habitat for wildlife and makes your yard part of the natural environment.

Advanced Irrigation Systems

Traditional sprinkler systems are very wasteful; about one-third of the water evaporates, and the water falls on the leaves of plants rather than around the roots where it is needed. Advanced irrigation systems deliver the water to where it is required more efficiently than traditional water sprinklers. Drip lines directly water the roots of plants, or target each plant with a micro-spray. Rain sensors turn off the irrigation systems when the soil is already wet or a certain amount of rainwater is detected.

Turning off sprinklers for a single rainy day can save 500 gallons of water. After a heavy rain, it is not necessary to irrigate again for several days.

A rainwater collection system can replace some of the potable water used for irrigation. It can be as simple as a gutter spout emptying into a rain barrel, or it can include filtration and storage tanks. Using rainwater for irrigation filters out impurities washed from the roof before the water enters the water table.

Landscaping for More Energy Conservation

You can reduce the amount of energy needed to heat and cool your house by strategically placing trees and shrubs.

Windbreaks

A windbreak can lower the wind chill near your home during cold winter months. Wind chill occurs when wind speed lowers the outside temperature. To plant an effective windbreak, you need to know which plants grow best in your region and what direction the wind comes from around your house. Trees and shrubs with low crowns work best because they block wind close to the ground. Trees, bushes, and shrubs are often planted together to create a wind barrier from the ground up. The most common type of windbreak consists of dense evergreen trees and shrubs planted to the north and northwest of a home, the direction from which most cold winter winds blow in the Northern Hemisphere. Evergreen trees combined with a wall, fence, or man-made earth berm can deflect or lift the wind over the home.

A windbreak will reduce wind speed for a distance of as much as 30 times the windbreak's height. For maximum protection, your windbreak should be planted at a distance from your home of two to five times the mature height of the trees. Be careful not to plant the trees too close to the house where they will block the winter sunlight or cast shade on your solar panels.

Summer winds can have a cooling effect, especially at night. However, if summer winds are hot and you live in a climate where you use air conditioning all summer, you may want to block the winds from circulating near your home.

Insulation

Planting shrubs, bushes, and vines next to your house creates dead air spaces that insulate your home in both winter and summer. Place plants so that there will be at least at least 1 foot of space between them and the wall when they are fully grown.

Shading

To use shade effectively, you must know the size, shape, and location of the shadows your trees and plants cast as the sun moves across the sky during the day. You can find trees with the

appropriate size, density, and shape for almost any shading application. You must also know which trees work well in your region. Deciduous trees block solar heat in summer but let sunlight through in winter when they lose their leaves. Evergreen trees provide shade year-round. Homes in cooler climates may not need shade at all. Trees, shrubs, vines, and groundcover plants can reduce heat radiation and cool the air by shading the ground and pavement around your home. A patio or driveway can be shaded with a large bush or row of shrubs, a hedge, or vines on a trellis.

Solar energy absorbed through your roof and windows increases the heat inside your home during the summer, but shade on your roof may interfere with the operation of your solar panels. Locate trees where they will not block sunlight falling on your solar array. Even the shadows of bare branches of deciduous trees can affect the efficiency of your solar panels.

Living Walls

A **living wall** is essentially the same concept as a vegetated roof, except it integrates plants on a vertical wall instead of a horizontal roof. Living walls, which can be used either outside the building or inside, clean and irrigate storm water, and they also help significantly with air filtration.

Living walls that help with air circulation inside a building are often referred to as active living walls. Living walls are placed so they receive adequate sunlight from windows or open spaces. These walls give off oxygen inside a space and absorb carbon dioxide, improving the air quality. Active living walls are typically incorporated into the building's air conditioning and filtration system and are used to clean and de-pollute the indoor air.

Inactive or passive living walls do not contribute to air filtration and are typically not hooked up to the building's air filtration system.

Living walls provide insulation for the building, and they also help to control excessive temperatures. In urban areas where heat-absorbing surfaces

Living ivy wall at Princeton University.

are dense, heat becomes trapped in the building envelope, which causes interior temperatures to rise. Living walls reduce heat absorption through the walls.

What to Grow in a Living Wall

Some plants that are particularly efficient at filtering toxins out of the air are bamboo palms, chrysanthemums, spider plants, and certain variations of ivy.

Buildings in cities or areas where space is limited can greatly benefit from living walls, as they allow the vertical integration of plants and vegetation and do not require any additional square footage. Using a living wall inside a home improves air quality and helps to create a more wholesome indoor environment. Some living walls include waterfalls, which add to the overall aesthetic and acoustical benefits and help drown out distracting noises and outdoor noise pollutants.

Permeable Pavement

Permeable pavement is a method of paving roads, walkways, driveways, and other outdoor spaces to enable storm water to drain properly. If you cannot incorporate a full storm water control system to capture, treat, and reuse rain water, this is an excellent, less expensive option. Installing permeable pavement involves using a pervious material such as concrete to create a design that enables water from storm runoff to drain through and between the concrete pavers to be absorbed into the soil beneath them. The concrete used in permeable pavement — pervious concrete — is carefully manufactured to allow water to pass through it and down into the soil. This is mostly achieved through the absence of sand in the concrete mixture for the pavers.

In addition to the environmental benefit of storm water control and management, permeable pavement is made primarily of recyclable materials. Permeable pavement is also cooler and helps to control heat islands. Using permeable pavement can earn LEED points for its eco-friendly potential.

Porches, Decks, and Fences

Porches, verandahs, and decks add outdoor living space to a home and are popular in all climates. Decks are open to the sky, while porches have roofs, but both are exposed to the weather and tend to deteriorate more rapidly than the rest of the house. The materials used when constructing these areas should be chosen for their durability and resistance to rot.

Many of the woods traditionally used for constructing decks and fences are not sustainably harvested. Some materials cost less initially but deteriorate much sooner than more expensive materials and have to be replaced more often, creating more waste. Wood is now being replaced with a variety of other materials, including plastics and composites. In evaluating these products, it is important to know what percentage of their contents is recycled. If a company manufactures eco-friendly products, this information is included in its sales literature and on the product packaging, as well as posted on the company website.

Decks and porches that are not attached correctly to the walls of the house may cause moisture leaks and deterioration, compromising the durability of the whole building. The weight of a deck puts an additional structural load on the wall. Gaps and openings may trap water where it does not dry out quickly.

Wood

In the past, most decks were made of redwood or cedar because of its beauty, durability, and resistance to insects. However, the most durable cedar and redwood come from the heartwood of old growth trees; younger sapwood does not have the same properties. FSC-certified cedar and redwood are available from certified forests along the west coasts of the U.S. and Canada, but they are increasingly expensive.

Tropical wood species such as Ipé, Meranti (from Malaysia, the Philippines, and Southeast Asia), and Cambara are hard and durable. Because many of these woods grow in rainforests, it is important that they be FSC-certified. Ask the supplier for chain-of-custody documentation showing the wood's origin. Because tropical woods do not grow in the U.S., the energy used to transport them to your building site must be taken into consideration.

Treated lumber

Pressure-treated lumber is a more affordable alternative. Southern yellow pine and some western softwoods are pressure-treated with chemicals to make them resistant to insects and rot. The two most common chemicals used to treat lumber are alkaline copper quaternary (ACQ) and copper azole (CA). Both contain high levels of copper oxide and pressure-treated lumber should not be handled like untreated wood. Manufacturers recommend wearing gloves and a dust mask when cutting and handling the wood, washing work clothes separately from other laundry, and washing hands well before eating. Because the copper is corrosive to aluminum or steel, only stainless steel or galvanized (G185) fasteners should be used to construct the deck.

Treated lumber is rated according to the amount of chemical that remains in the wood, expressed as pounds of chemical per cubic foot of wood. Lumber that is in contact with the ground should have a retention level of 0.40, while lumber used aboveground, a level of 0.25.

Nontoxic treated lumber products have recently appeared on the market. TimberSil® (**www.timbersilwood.com**) is infused with sodium silicate, a melted mix of sand and soda ash that is baked in kilns to permanently encase its fibers with a flexible layer of innocuous glass. It is sold dry and ready to paint or stain. ES+Wood™ (**www.eswoodtreatment.com**) is pressure treated with DOT Borates (Disodium Octaborate Tetrahydrate), a natural preservative, and EnviroSafe Plus®, a colorless, polymer system. It does not off-gas and can be used inside as well as outside a house.

Treated lumber should never be burned

Never dispose of old treated lumber or scraps by burning them because the smoke can be toxic if inhaled. Lumber treated with chromated copper arsenic (CCA) was withdrawn from the market in 2003 because of its potential toxicity. One tablespoon of ash left from burning CCA-treated lumber contains enough arsenic to kill a person.

Composite decking

Composite decking made from wood waste and recycled plastic is a popular green alternative to wood. It comes in various textures and colors and, though it does not exactly resemble wood, is very attractive. It lasts longer than wooden decking and can be painted and stained. It comes shaped like boards or tongue-and-groove planks and is not strong enough to for structural framing, so it must be used with a wood or metal framework.

The first composite was Trex®, but similar products are now available from a number of companies. Because they contain cellulose, composites are vulnerable to mold and must be cleaned regularly.

Plastics

Decking and fencing is manufactured from polystyrene, high-density polyethylene, polypropylene, and polyvinyl chloride (PVC). Cel-

lular PVC decking is made by adding a foaming agent to PVC and is manufactured to resemble wood. Plastic decking expands and contracts more than wood or composites and must also be used with a wood or metal structural framework. Plastic fence panels make effective noise barriers. Plastic requires almost no maintenance and is typically manufactured in pre-formed units for easy assembly. Plastic lumber is available in dimensions from 5/4 decking to 12x12 posts.

Plastic decking and fencing made with recycled plastic is considered green. Some products, however, are manufactured from virgin plastic. Manufacturers of recycled plastic products include Bedford Technology (**www.plasticboards.com**) and Renew Plastics (Trimax Structural Lumber) (**www.trimaxbp.com**). PVC is difficult to recycle, releases dioxin and other contaminants when burned, and its manufacture produces hazardous by-products.

GREEN PRODUCT SPOTLIGHT

Perhaps one of the most environmentally friendly building materials for a fence is recycled materials. SimTek Fence (**www.simtekfence. com**) offers homeowners fences made from recycled and recyclable polyethylene plastic. The fence, which comes in six colors and blocks 98 percent of direct sound, boasts a lifetime warranty and will never need staining or painting, nor will it crack, fade, or warp. The fences are made from linear low density polyethylene plastic and are reinforced using galvanized steel, which allows them to withstand winds up to 110 mph. Aside from their superior strength, these fences also resist most impacts and baseballs, rocks, and golf balls bounce off the walls without damaging them.

These fences can be an environmentally friendly addition to a new or existing home because not only are they made from recycled materials, but they also will need to be replaced less often than a conventional fence.

An example of a SimTek Fence

Powder-coated aluminum

Powder-coated aluminum is coated with a fine powder veneer that protects it from rust and corrosion. It is very strong and resistant to fire and insects, as well as stains and dirt. Powdered aluminum can be painted but comes in many permanent colors. It is not intended to look like wood. It is used for decking, fencing, roofing, and lawn furniture. Powdered aluminum decking and fencing is more expensive than other types of decking. Aluminum is 100 percent recyclable.

Attaching a deck or a porch to a house

Decks are often attached to a house using a ledger — a framing member attached to the outside of the house that supports one end of the deck's floor joists. Often water running down a wall seeps between the ledger and the wall and remains trapped there, which encourages mold and decay. Eventually the structural framework of the house is attacked by decay. The same problem can occur where the roof a porch is attached to the wall of the house.

The ideal solution is not to connect the deck to the house at all. A free-standing deck is more difficult to build, but it does not cut into the wall of the house. No ledger is used; the deck stands alongside the house and is completely self-supported by concrete piers and a wood frame. Building codes typically do not allow load-bearing attachments on masonry or stucco walls anyway.

When a ledger is used, it should be attached after the house wrap and/or drainage plane have been installed. A layer of self-adhering membrane applied to the sheathing before the ledger is installed helps prevent water intrusion. The ledger should be attached to the rim joist or studs using bolts or lag screws. Flashing should be then be molded over the top of the ledger, extending about 4 inches up the wall of the house and tucked under the house felt to direct water away from the space between the ledger and wall. Some builders insert blocks or spacers between the ledger and the wall to create ½ inch of space so moisture can drain away.

Rot and decay will occur in any area where water can enter a small gap or space, such as the joints between timbers. Most decks are built with wooden posts supported by concrete piers. The wooden post should not come directly into contact with the cement because water can enter the space between them. Instead, the post is attached to the concrete pier with a galvanized steel post connector that leaves an airspace, called a capillary break, between the bottom of the post and the concrete.

Conclusion

Many conventional building projects end when the equipment and debris is removed and the lot is covered with sod or seeded with grass. Green building includes landscaping in the original design process and regards the exterior of the home as an opportunity to enhance the energy efficiency, the interior air quality, and the home's aesthetics. Plants provide shade and beauty, help to manage storm water run off, and may even purify gray water. Green landscaping practices include protecting the site from damage during construction, conserving water, preserving existing vegetation, and impacting the natural environment as little as possible.

Chapter 9

Selecting Green Materials and Products

One of the ongoing challenges of the green building movement is how to determine the relative greenness of a particular product or building material and how using it will affect the environment. Green building materials are basic materials that have low environmental impacts compared to conventional building materials. Green building products are building components whose characteristics convey some kind of environmental benefit and make them preferable in some way to other building components with similar functions. A green building product could be an energy-saving device that does not contain any green materials.

There are many ways in which using a particular product might impact the environment — beginning with the energy used to produce it and the disturbance to the environment caused by extracting and moving raw materials. A product might use up an inequitable amount of resources, create harmful substances as byproducts during manufacturing, consume energy, emit toxins, generate waste, and end up occupying space in a landfill or leaching toxins into the soil or water table. In addition, there is no universal agreement on environmental priorities. One school of thought emphasizes recycling materials and keeping them in productive use, even if some additional energy must be expended to do so. Another viewpoint considers global warming as the greatest threat and uses energy consumption as the primary criteria in selecting green materials – if more energy is required to recycle a product than to use virgin materials, it should not be recycled.

Use materials available from local manufacturers

Although bamboo is an environmentally friendly alternative to wood flooring from clear-cut forests, most bamboo flooring is manufactured in Asia. Having bamboo flooring shipped from Asia not only increases the cost to you, but also contributes to carbon emissions from the trucks, ships, and cargo planes that transport the product. You might be able to source wood flooring materials at a lower cost from a reclaimed wood manufacturer 1 mile from your construction site, which would eliminate the need for long-distance transportation and reduce your impact on the environment.

A product that greatly increases the energy efficiency of a building and reduces overall carbon emissions may be made of materials that cannot be recycled. An example is the energy recovery ventilators (ERVs) or heat recovery ventilators (HRVs) that are often used to meet LEED ventilation requirements. As heated air leaves the building, ERVs can transfer as much as 80 percent of its heat to the incoming outside air, heat that would otherwise have been continually lost and replaced by the heating system. However, the components of ERVs cannot be easily re-used or recycled.

Even green building materials may have a harmful environmental impact. For example, wood certified by the FSC comes from a sustainably managed forest that protects the biodiversity of local ecosystems. However, harvesting that wood, processing it, and transporting it to the building site consumes large amounts of water and energy.

Selecting materials for a green building project typically involves a trade-off. There is no one rule for deciding which product, material, or technology is best. Choices must be made based on the building owner's priorities, the site location, the availability of products and materials, and the project budget.

Social Responsibility is Green

The standard of sustainability protects not only the physical environment, but also the well-being of the people who live in it. If workers are exposed to toxic chemicals or hazardous conditions during the manufacture or processing of a product, that product should not be considered green. Products imported from outside the United States may have been manufactured by underpaid laborers working and living in terrible conditions or produced by a factory that contaminates surrounding neighborhoods and waterways with pollutants. In many countries, labor and business laws are not properly enforced. Most organizations providing third-party certification for green products seek to verify that workers' rights are protected and that the laws of the country where the product is manufactured are observed. For example, the principles of the Forestry Stewardship Council (FSC) include:

- Compliance with all applicable laws and international treaties.
- Demonstrated and uncontested, clearly defined, long-term land tenure and use rights.
- Recognition and respect of indigenous peoples' rights.
- Maintenance or enhancement of long-term social and economic well-being of forest workers and local communities and respect of worker's rights in compliance with International Labour Organization (ILO) conventions
- Equitable use and sharing of benefits derived from the forest.
- Identification and appropriate management of areas that need special protection (such as cultural or sacred sites, habitat of endangered animals or plants).

Green Construction Materials

The CalRecycle (www.calrecycle.gov) website for California's recycling and green building initiatives gives the following resource efficiency criteria for building materials:

- **Recycled content:** Products with identifiable recycled content, including postindustrial content with a preference for postconsumer content.

- **Natural, plentiful, or renewable:** Materials harvested from sustainably managed sources and preferably have an independent certification (certified wood) and are certified by an independent third party.

- **Resource efficient manufacturing process:** Products manufactured with resource-efficient processes including reducing energy consumption, minimizing waste (recycled, recyclable, or source reduced product packaging), and reducing greenhouse gases.

- **Locally available:** Building materials, components, and systems found locally or regionally, which saves energy and resources in transportation to the project site.

- **Salvaged, refurbished, or remanufactured:** Includes saving a material from disposal and renovating, repairing, restoring, or generally improving the appearance, performance, quality, functionality, or value of a product.

- **Reusable or recyclable:** Select materials that can be easily dismantled and reused or recycled at the end of their useful life.

- **Recycled or recyclable product packaging:** Products enclosed in recycled content or recyclable packaging.

- **Durable:** Materials that are longer lasting or are comparable to conventional products with long life expectancies.

Selecting Materials for the Interior of a Building

The materials and fixtures used inside a building are just as important as the materials used for the foundation and structure. Cost-effective and manageable alternatives to many conventional building materials contribute significantly to the greenness of a building. Low-flow toilets, faucets, and showerheads conserve water. Lighting fixtures with CFLs or LEDs use only a fraction of the electricity traditional lighting consumes. Durable materials that do not have to be replaced for many years are preferable to materials that deteriorate quickly. Low-maintenance products that are easy to clean use up fewer resources over time and contribute to the quality of life of the home's occupants. Aesthetic beauty is also important because the materials used inside the home will be seen and handled every day.

CFL light

A primary objective of green building is a high indoor environmental quality (IEQ) achieved through appropriate lighting, efficient temperature control, access to daylight and outdoor views, and good indoor air quality (IAQ). This objective serves as a guide for selecting materials for the inside of a building, alongside consideration of the possible impact of each material or product on the environment.

> ## Look for bargains at local Habitat for Humanity and contractor liquidation stores
>
> Habitat for Humanity (**www.habitat.org**) sells excess and donated building materials in its thrift stores. You may not find enough of the same material to complete a large project, but you might find enough tile, for instance, to use for your bathroom. Liquidation stores also sell salvaged or leftover construction materials, fixtures, and appliances at deeply discounted prices.

Woods

When it is responsibly harvested and not treated with chemical sealants, wood is a very green product. For wood flooring, cabinetry, and furniture, always choose products that are certified by a reputable third party, such as the Forest Stewardship Council (FSC) or the Sustainable Forestry Initiative (SFI). Certified wood should be accompanied by a certificate that provides detailed information on the wood's origin and processing. Always ensure that any finishing material applied to the wood is formaldehyde-free. For more information on wood guidelines, visit the FSC (**www.fsc.org**) and SFI (**www.sfiprogram.org**) websites.

Although wood from newly cut old-growth trees is not green, reclaimed wood flooring made with old-growth wood salvaged from old buildings and barns is green and beautiful. Manufacturers of reclaimed wood flooring can be found all over the U.S.

> ## EPA Recommends 'Exterior-Grade' Pressed Wood Products
>
> According to the U.S. National Institute of Health, "the EPA recommends the use of 'exterior-grade' pressed-wood products to limit formaldehyde exposure in the home. Before purchasing pressed-wood products, including building materials, cabinetry, and furniture, buyers should ask about the formaldehyde content of these products. Formaldehyde levels in homes can also be reduced by ensuring adequate ventilation, moderate temperatures, and reduced humidity levels through the use of air conditioners and dehumidifiers."

The chemical sealants and floor finishes used to coat some wood products often contain dangerous VOCs that emit toxins throughout their lifetime, not just when they are initially applied to the wood. Wood is sometimes soaked in formaldehyde. Many wood cabinets and other pressed wood products such as plywood, particleboard, and paneling also use glue that contains formaldehyde.

Engineered wood, which is made out of smaller pieces of wood glued together, sometimes uses dangerous adhesives. The glue often contains formaldehyde. Examples of engineered wood include I-joists, plywood, fiberboard, glued laminated timber, insulation board, and cement board. If the packaging label of a product does not include information about formaldehyde content, as to see the Material Safety Data Sheet for that particular product. It should be on file at the store selling the wood product, or available directly from the manufacturer.

Bamboo

Flooring, cabinetry, and furniture made of bamboo and bamboo veneer is becoming increasingly popular as an alternative to wood. Bamboo is considered a renewable resource because it is a grass that grows quickly and does not require pesticides. Bamboo can be harvested every three to five years, compared to 20 years for trees. Bamboo plantations help reduce rainwater runoff and control erosion on hills and slopes. The bamboo is not killed off when it is harvested but left in place to regenerate Bamboo comes in natural, light colors and darker amber shades achieved by steaming it (the darker color is 10 percent softer than the natural color). Other colors are due to dyes that may contain heavy metals or other toxins.

Confirm that bamboo veneers do not contain urea formaldehyde, and that adhesives used to install bamboo flooring do not contain VOCs. Much of the bamboo sold in the U.S. is harvested and processed in China and comes from natural groves and plantations (some originates in Vietnam). There is concern that large man-made bamboo plantations are a threat to bio-diversity. Bamboo certified to the standards of the Forest Stewardship Council meets criteria for environmental sustainability and social responsibility. Chinese manufacturers of bamboo products have been known to use potentially toxic binders, finishes, and other chemicals, create quantities of solid waste, and run unsafe equipment. Several distributors of bamboo products require the manufacturers they work with to be registered under International Organization for Standardization (ISO) standards 9001 for quality control and 14001 for environmental management systems EMS.

Another concern is the carbon emitted while transporting the bamboo products from China to the U.S. However, ocean freighters are more energy efficient than the trucks used to transport wood domestically and the impact of bamboo flooring is comparable to that of wood flooring.

Cabinets

Many of the cabinets sold today are made of particleboard, which contains a urea formaldehyde that can emit harmful chemicals for years. Nontoxic alternatives are available if you look for them. Columbia Forest Products has replaced formaldehyde with a soy-based protein binder in its plywood. FSC-certified plywood comes from a sustainably harvested source. Particleboard and medium density fiberboard (MDF) cabinets cost less than plywood, but are more fragile and may crumble when exposed to water. Some use recycled fiber. Sierra Pine (**www.sierrapine.com**) manufactures Medite® II, a formaldehyde-free particleboard. Roseburg SkyBlend particleboard (**http://roseburg.com**) is made with 100 percent recycled wood fiber particleboard and contains no urea formaldehyde.

Cabinet doors are subject to a lot of wear-and-tear and should be made either of FSC-certified hardwood or a hardwood frame with a veneer panel. Lyptus® hardwood products (**www.lyptus.com**) are made from fast growing eucalyptus trees grown on plantations and take a wide range of stains and finishes. Beautiful cabinet doors are made with bamboo veneer. German beech, a light hardwood native to Europe with qualities similar to maple, is extremely sustainable because of forest management practices implemented 200 years ago in European forests. When ordering cabinets, specify that you want formaldehyde-free and FSC-certified wood.

Counters

Almost any countertop material can be considered green. Because counters are expected to come into contact with food, they do not contain toxic chemicals. Some materials are less green because they must be transported long distances or because they are laid over a substrate that does contain harmful sealants. Durability and ease of maintenance are also considerations. Linoleum, made of linseed oil, wood dust, and pine resin, makes a durable countertop if installed with a low-VOC adhesive. Plastic laminates are also an inexpensive material if the substrate is toxin-free.

Many solid surface countertops are made with recycled content. Paper-Stone® (**www.paperstoneproducts.com**) is made from 100 percent post-consumer recycled paper saturated with phenolic resins. The resin-saturated sheets are stacked and fused together under heat and pressure. PaperStone®'s nonporous surface is stain resistant and absorbs virtually no water. Surface cuts or mars may be sanded or rubbed out with an abrasive pad. Richlite (**www.richlite.com**) materials are  made either with FSC-certified wood pulp or postconsumer recycled paper using an innovative WE™ (Waste-to-Energy) manufacturing system that captures toxins and recirculates heat to minimize fuel consumption, pollution, and carbon emissions.

Stainless steel is durable and easy to clean but more expensive than many other materials. Tile, especially tile made with recycled content, is a very green material and is available in a wide variety of sizes and colors. The grout on tile countertops should be resealed every three to six months to keep out bacteria. Wood with a nontoxic finish is a good choice if the finish is maintained. Maple butcher block countertops are often made from recycled or scrap material from furniture or flooring manufacturers.

Stone is a popular material for countertops. Porous types of stone must be regularly resealed to prevent them from absorbing moisture and bacteria. Granite is mined in many countries and may have to be transported a long distance to your kitchen; look for a stone that is more locally available.

Some granite countertops emit high levels of radon gas

The popularity of granite countertops has grown rapidly in the U.S. over the last decade. Most granite contains tiny amounts of uranium, which can emit radiation as it degrades. In July 2008, several newspaper articles revealed that while most are harmless, some granite countertops had been found to emit high levels of radon gas. The Marble Institute of America (**www.marble-institute.com/industryresources/consumerradonbrochure. pdf**) denies that granite countertops pose any danger to consumers but recommends having your home tested for radon levels if you have any concerns.

Concrete countertops are durable and heat resistant and can be made into almost any shape and colored with pigments or decorated with inlays. Concrete requires some maintenance; it must be resealed from time to time.

Recycled glass countertops use 85 to 100 percent recycled glass and concrete. Based on the centuries-old technique of terrazzo, chips of discarded glass from bottles, windows, windshields, and old traffic lights are embedded in concrete and given a polished finish. Recycled glass countertops require minimal maintenance.

Carpeting and Flooring

Traditional carpeting has very high levels of VOCs. Some carpets introduce as many as 100 chemicals into a home. These chemicals come mostly from the adhesives used in the carpet backing and other glues and materials to hold the carpet together. Most conventional carpeting, particularly very inexpensive carpeting, is made from synthetic materials that incorporate vinyl, another dangerous compound. Other harmful chemicals, compounds, and products in carpets include:

- Antistatic sprays
- Petroleum byproducts
- Artificial dyes
- Urethane

Some people report symptoms including skin irritation, dizziness, headaches, and nausea after a new carpet is installed. Carpets attract dust mites, mold, mildew, and other allergens that are difficult to control and can sick-en building occupants who suffer from allergies. Carpeting is also highly unrecyclable, and about 4 billion pounds of carpet are wasted each year in the United States, which makes conventional carpeting one of the biggest offenders against sustainability. Carpets also collect dust, pet dander, and chemicals tracked in from outdoors and absorb gases from other products.

In the early 1990s, the Carpet and Rug Institute (CRI) launched its Green Label program to certify carpeting and other upholstery material. Their more recent Green Label Plus program certifies carpeting materials as low-emitting (under 50 grams per liter). For more information on green carpeting, standards, and guidelines, visit **www.carpet-rug.org/index.cfm**.

Instead of carpeting, many green homes have bare concrete floors, bamboo, linoleum, cork, or even recycled rubber flooring. Cork flooring is made from the cork leftover after manufacturing cork bottle stoppers and has natural antibacterial properties. The bark of a cork oak can be harvested every 25 years without harming the tree. Recycled rubber is attractive but offgasses during most of its life and should only be used in well-ventilated areas or outdoors.

Cradle-to-Cradle

The concept "cradle-to-cradle" was introduced by William McDonough, an architect, and Michael Braungart, a chemist. Cradle-to-cradle refers to a method for evaluating the impact of a product on both human life and the environment, from the product's inception through the manufacturing process, use, demolition, recycling, and ultimately after it is no longer in use. The method assesses the use of every synthetic and natural material and process associated with the product, such as the storm water discharge during the manufacturing process, the potential reuse of the product, and the toxicity that each material in the product exudes to the environment.

Sealers and Adhesives

Traditional sealers have high levels of VOCs and other toxic chemicals. A variety of sealant products that are low-emitting and contain low levels of VOCs and chemicals are available. Green building website Green Building Supply (**www.greenbuildingsupply.com/Public/Non-ToxicFinishes/Sealers/index.cfm**) provides an extensive list of green alternatives to traditional sealers for cement, wood, stucco, stone, grout, and caulk.

Solvent-based wood finishes are extremely toxic, especially for children and asthma-sufferers. Several companies manufacture water-based finishes that are safe to use, though they do not produce the same effect. Solvent-based adhesives are even more toxic than wood finishes. Toluene, xylene, and petrochemicals found in adhesives are known carcinogens and cause damage to the brain, nerves, and kidneys. Urethane-based adhesives are much safer. Look for the VOC listing on the label and avoid products that contain more than 150 grams per liter or contain petrochemicals. There is an environmentally friendly alternative for almost every application.

Paints

Paint is one of the most common finishing products used throughout a home. Traditional paints contain high amounts of VOCs. The regulation of VOC amounts in common materials such as paint varies by state, and some states do not have specific regulations. The nationwide limit on VOCs in paint is 250 grams per liter, but even at this concentration they can be harmful. Paint manufacturers including Behr, Sherwin-Williams, and Benjamin Moore have started making low-VOC paints that have less than 50 grams per liter.

A good way to ensure a specific type of paint is low-VOC is to review a product's material safety data sheet (MSDS), which provides information on chemicals used in the product. Ask for the MSDS wherever you purchase your paint and supplies; many are available online. Look for VOC levels in the section that breaks down the characteristics of the paint. Constantly changing government regulations require companies to prepare a MSDS to provide information on any potential harm or side effects that each chemical in a product could cause, as well as an emergency course of action to take if someone is exposed to the chemical. The U.S Occupational Safety and Health Administration (OSHA) began requiring MSDS documentation for all hazardous substances in May 1986. The documentation includes instruction for the correct use and handling of products, health risks and side effects, substance evaluations, storage recommendations, and what should take place in an emergency arising from use of the products.

Material safety data sheets are used worldwide, but each country has its own laws regulating them. In the United States, a hazard communication regulation requires MSDS usage in any workplace where potentially hazardous substances are being handled. OSHA enforces these laws. Although consumer products, including household chemicals, are not required to carry MSDSs at this time, the documentation is available online for many products. For more specific information, check the manufacturer's website.

One alternative is not to use paint at all. Tinted stucco requires almost no maintenance. BioLime, a manufacturer using a technique that originated in Italy centuries ago, produces all-natural lime-based paints, plasters, stuccos, and thermal coatings. The coatings breathe naturally and allow moisture to evaporate. When applied, the lime goes through a chemical reaction in which it reabsorbs the CO_2 it lost during the manufacturing process. It bonds naturally with the substrate and any cracks that form heal by themselves.

Cleaning products

Cleaning products can have the most direct impact on the indoor air quality of your home and also on your family's health. Disinfectants, bathtub scrubbers, and dishwashing liquids contain chemicals that are harmful. In 1989, the EPA estimated that the fumes produced by common household cleaners were three times more likely to cause cancer than other air pollutants. According to a 2007 study published in the *The American Journal of Respiratory and Critical Care Medicine,* exposure to cleaning products accounts for 15 percent of all asthma cases. When bleach is mixed with many common toilet-bowl cleaners, it produces toxic chlorine gas. Bleach and ammonia combine to produce chloramines gases, which cause eye and respiratory irritation. Bleach mingled with certain naturally occurring compounds forms carcinogenic organochlorines.

Toxic Ingredients in Common Household Products	
Ingredient	**Use and Harmful Effects**
2-butoxyethanol	Also known as ethylene glycol butyl ether. Used as a solvent in carpet cleaners and specialty cleaners. Can be inhaled or absorbed through the skin and may cause blood disorders, as well as liver and kidney damage. According to the New Jersey Department of Health and Senior Services, long-term exposure may also cause reproductive damage.

Ingredient	Use and Harmful Effects
Ethoxylated nonyl phenols (NPEs)	A group of endocrine-disrupting chemicals used in cleaning products. Known as "gender-benders," nonyl phenols can induce female characteristics in male fish, for example. The European Union has banned them from all cleaning products manufactured or used in the EU.
Methylene chloride	Used alone or as an ingredient in paint strippers. Listed as a possible human carcinogen (Group 2B) by the International Agency for Research on Cancer (IARC). The U.S. Consumer Product Safety Commission estimates that since regulators in the U.S. compelled manufacturers to put warning labels on products containing methylene chloride in 1987, there has been a 55% reduction in the number of cancers that would have been caused by these products.
Naphthalene	Naphthalene, and another chemical called paradichlorobenzene, are used in moth balls and moth crystals. Naphthalene is listed by California's Office of Environmental Health Hazards Assessment as a substance "know to the state to cause cancer," while paradichlorobenzene is listed by IARC as a possible human carcinogen. A garment bag or a box with a tight fitting lid is more effective against moths than the odors of mothballs.
Silica	Silica, a finely ground quartz, is carcinogenic when it occurs as fine respirable dust. Some abrasive cleansers that are regularly used around the home contain silica dust. Replace abrasive cleansers with a cream cleanser or a similar product that does not contain silica.
Toluene	A potent reproductive toxin, used as a solvent in numerous products, including paints. Listed by California's Office of Environmental Health Hazard Assessment as a reproductive toxin that may cause harm to the developing fetus. Pregnant women should avoid products containing toluene.
Trisodium nitrilotri-acetate (NTA)	Used as a builder in laundry detergents. NTA is listed as a possible human carcinogen (IARC 2B) by IARC. It can impede the elimination of metals in wastewater treatment plants, causing metals that have already settled out to re-enter the liquid waste stream.
Xylene	Often found in graffiti and scuff removers, spray paints and some adhesives. A suspected reproductive toxin that has shown reproductive harm in laboratory experiments. Also a neurotoxicant that can cause memory loss on repeated exposure.

Ingredient	Use and Harmful Effects
Bleach (Sodium hypochlorite)	Reacts with acids (typically found in toilet bowl cleaners) to form chlorine gas. Mixed with ammonia, it can create chloramine gas, another toxic substance. In the environment, sodium hypochlorite is acutely toxic to fish. Chlorine in bleach also binds with organic material in the marine environment to form organochlorines, toxic compounds that persist in the environment.
Phosphates	Phosphates cause eutrophication, an excess of nutrients that causes streams and lakes to become choked with aquatic plants and algae. Manufacturers have reduced or even eliminated phosphates from laundry products, but most dishwasher detergents available from major manufacturers contain 30% – 40% phosphates. Some also contain high levels of chlorine-based sanitizing ingredients.

Many cleaning products do not list their ingredients on their labels, which makes it difficult to select products that do not contain dangerous chemicals. Many product labels now bear terms like "environmentally friendly," "organic," or "green," but there is no guarantee that this is true. In 1992, the Environmental Protection Agency (EPA) introduced its "Design for the Environment," or "DfE" label for household and commercial products, such as cleaners and detergents, that meet stringent criteria for human and environmental health. A full list of DfE products can be found on the Design for the Environment website (**www.epa.gov/dfe/pubs/projects/formulat/formpart.htm**). Green Seal certifies that products bearing its Green Seal label are non-toxic and non-corrosive, free from carcinogens (according to the standards of five major agencies) and mutagens (as determined by the United Nations), and truly biodegradable (according to the Organization for Economic Co-Operation and Development). You can search for Green Seal products at **www.greenseal.org/FindGreenSealProductsAndServices.aspx**. Smaller alternative manufacturers of green household products, such as Method, Ecover, Nature Clean, Simple Green, and Seventh Generation, promise transparency on their labels and environmentally safe products. These companies do not necessarily seek EPA or Green Seal certification, but their labels speak for themselves.

Soaps, detergents, toilet cleaners, and bleaches not only degrade indoor air quality. They all go down the drain and end up in wastewater systems and waterways, where their ingredients harm aquatic and marine life and may even enter the food chain. Manufacturing cleaning products also has an impact on the environment. In addition to greenhouse gas emissions and waste products, there is concern about the source of ingredients. The essential oils used in many cleaning products are often produced using unsound agricultural practices such as monocropping, in which the same plant is grown on the same soil year after year, instead of rotating among several species.

Another concern is the containers in which cleaning products are packaged. In 2009, sales of bottled body washes in the U.S. surpassed sales of bar soaps for the first time, partly because of soap manufacturers' ad campaigns. The magazine Advertising Age reports that sales of bar soaps in the U.S. have fallen 40 percent since body washes were introduced. If they are not recycled, the empty plastic body wash bottles represent much more waste in landfills than the paper and cardboard wrappers of bar soaps. Plastic bottles that have contained toxic cleaning products present an environmental hazard when they go into a landfill.

A simple green alternative is to make your own cleaning products from simple ingredients such as white vinegar, baking soda, and lemon juice. Many recipes and cleaning suggestions can be found online and in magazines and books.

Third Party Certification

The best way to ensure the materials you are using meet the low-emitting standards of green building is to choose certified products and materials. Institutes like the FSC and the CRI have their own guidelines and certification processes to ensure products in their industry are sustainable. Several other third-party organizations and watchdogs do the same thing for a variety of products and materials. These include Green Seal™ and BIFMA (Business and Institutional Furniture Manufacturers' Association).

Green Seal™

Green Seal is a nonprofit organization created to ensure that standards of environmental sustainability are uniformly monitored for cleaning services claiming to be green. The organization maintains strict standards for its Green Seal stamp of approval. They consider the Green Seal as an indicator of environmental responsibility for products and services.

The group was founded in 1989 and maintains specific environmental standards for products and consumers. They first implemented product certifications in the early 1990s. Now, according to the Green Seal website, 20 categories of products are certified by the organization, including:

- Home products and services
- Personal care and consumer packaged goods
- Construction materials, equipment, and systems
- Facility operations, maintenance, and services
- Hospitality, lodging, and food service
- Transportation and utilities

Green Seal tests and evaluates products based on their contents, how the materials were obtained, how the products are manufactured, what they are contained in and how they will be used, and what methods will be necessary for product and container disposal. If a product has been approved by the Green Seal organization, the Green Seal logo will appear on the product's label. When researching and interviewing cleaning services, you can ask if their business and their products have received the Green Seal stamp of approval. Information is also available on the Green Seal website.

If you wish to have a service or product certified, you can follow the evaluation procedure outlined on the Green Seal website (**www.greenseal.org**). The organization institutes standards based on requirements determined by the International Organization for Standardization (ISO).

Standards for Standards

Just because a manufacturer declares that its product is green or organic does not make it so. When you are spending extra money for a green home, or selecting one product over another because it is certified to be green, you want to know exactly what you are buying. The green movement is relatively new, and the many emerging green certification programs are challenged to create standards that can be universally recognized. The ISO (International Organization for Standardization) is a network of the national standards institutes of 163 countries, coordinated by a Central Secretariat in Geneva, Switzerland. Its members include both governmental bodies and private institutes created by industry associations. Third-party certification programs such as LEED certification and Green Seal follow ISO guidelines in setting the standards that determine whether a particular product or practice is green.

The ISEAL Alliance (**http://community.isealalliance.org**) is the global association for social and environmental standards. ISEAL works with established and emerging voluntary standard systems and supports the use of voluntary standards by companies, nonprofits, and governments. The ISEAL Standard-Setting Code sets the rules for legitimate and effective standard-setting processes. It applies to all standards that promote improvement in social and environmental practices.

Finding Green Manufacturers and Retailers

You can search online for green manufacturers and retailers in your state. There is almost always a green(er) alternative. Here are some websites with information on green building materials:

- **Building Research Establishment Environmental Assessment Method (BREEAM) ECD and the Building Research Establishment (BRE). (www.breeam.org)** The original green construction assessment program.

- **Green Manufacturer (www.greenmanufacturer.net/directory):** An online directory of green manufacturers around the U.S. It also has an abundance of other information on green building.

- **Green Builder (www.greenbuilder.com/general/greendbs. html):** This website lists sustainable sources as well as other green building information. The website also has an extensive green building and design database.

Several trade shows and conferences around the country are excellent sources for finding green manufacturers and retailers, as well as for learning more about the green building industry. These include the Green Manufacturing Expo (**www.canontradeshows.com/expo/gmx10**) that takes place around the country each year; Greenbuild (**www.greenbuildexpo.org**), an annual international expo and conference sponsored in part by the USGBC; and more regional conferences such as the Lean to Green manufacturing conference (**www.sme.org/cgi-bin/get-event.pl?--001981-000007-home--SME**) in Columbus, Ohio.

Resources to Assist in Assessing Building Materials

The Athena Institute (www.athenasmi.org/about/index.html). Using software including the ATHENA v.2.0, the institute helps professional architects, engineers, and builders assess the life cycle of different products.

The Environmental Resource Guide by the American Institute of Architects and the EPA. This guide helps professionals assess the life cycle of different building products and materials, which determines what each product's impact is on the environment. The guide is a good resource for an introduction on green building materials and can be purchased at www.wiley.com/WileyCDA/WileyTitle/productCd-0471183768.html.

Conclusion

Deciding whether one building material is greener than another can be difficult because green priorities sometimes contradict each other. Individual homeowners also have different priorities: some put carbon emissions and energy efficiency above all else; others are concerned about protecting biodiversity and human rights; still others are primarily concerned about clean air and exposure to environmental toxins. Financial resources are also a concern because a green product is sometimes considerably more expensive than a conventional one.

Builders and homeowners who want to make educated choices are increasingly relying on certification programs implemented by third-party organizations and agencies. Nearly every industry now has some sort of green certification program. Manufacturers are responding to the demand for green materials by developing new products and implementing their own environmental standards, which they can then use as part of their marketing campaigns. For consumers, the words "green" and "eco-friendly" are synonymous with health and well-being.

Chapter 10

Green Interior Design

Green interior design embodies two important objectives of green building — excellent interior air quality and the comfort and well-being of the occupants. Many conventional homes built with standard house plans include rooms that are rarely used, such as tiny formal parlors near a front entrance, or rooms that are too small or too large for their purposes. A giant master bathroom with multiple sinks, tubs, and showers to accommodate two people might impress a prospective homebuyer but is not practical. It must be heated, cooled, lit, cleaned, and maintained, and the extra fixtures and fittings add considerably to the cost of building the home. Lights are often placed squarely in the center of a ceiling instead of where they will be needed during daily activities. At the beginning of the design process, a green architect interviews the homeowner to find out what kind of spaces are needed and how the occupants spend their time and then creates a layout that naturally accommodates the activities of the occupants. One homeowner might require a large area for formal entertaining and a secluded, quiet space for a home office, while another might need play areas with plenty of storage for small children, or a studio with an inspiring view.

Green architects and interior designers also consider how the function of a home might change over the years and plan so that the interior of the home can be altered without a great deal of expense and disruption. For example, as children grow up, a play area might become a living room, or an artist's studio might become a bedroom when the house is sold.

Interior decorating is part of the overall design of a green home because many interior elements of the home serve multiple functions. For example, stone, concrete, or tile floors that absorb solar radiation falling through the windows are part of a passive heating system. Additional thermal mass may be added in the form of stand-alone planters or stone or brick wall facings or by setting dark heat-absorbent tiles into the floor. Shades, shutters, and curtains are not only decorative, but also help to insulate the windows and shield them from unwanted glare. Built-in masonry stoves may be used for heating. Indoor plants can be part of a ventilation system. Strategically placed walls and arches help to shelter certain spaces from glare or excess sunlight.

Green homes make the most of natural light, and outdoor scenery and views of garden plants are taken into consideration when window placement is decided. The exterior views become features of the interior design, creating balance and harmony between the inside and the outside of the building.

Biophilic Design

In his 1993 book, *The Biophilia Hypothesis*, Harvard entomologist E. O. Wilson theorized that human beings have a genetically based need to interact with nature. The co-editor of that book, Stephen Kellert, published *Biophilic Design: The Theory, Science and Practice of Bringing Buildings to Life* in 2008, identifying some attributes of biophilic design, including environmental features such as natural materials and plants; natural shapes and forms; and relationships between humans and nature such as the ability to see distant objects (prospect) and the ability of an environment to provide security (refuge).

Numerous scientific studies have demonstrated that people experience less stress when they connect to nature in some way, whether real or symbolic. Although it is diffcult to measure the degree to which exposure to nature affects workers in an office building, people of all ages are healthier, more productive, and more content when they have access, even at a distance, to daylight and outside views. In one study, children exposed to daylight in their classrooms appeared to score better on examinations. Studies in hospitals showed that patients experienced positive effects, such as less pain and faster recoveries, when they were exposed to sights and sounds of nature, either directly or through photos, videos and floral patterns on walls and ceilings. The American Institute of Architects' minimum code for design and construction of health care facilities now requires window views of nature, natural light and natural gardens.

Though sustainable design currently gives priority to reducing human impact on nature though energy efficiency and new technologies, there is increasing interest in the impact of nature on human beings.

Materials for the finishes and furnishings in a green home are carefully selected according to several criteria. First, they must be nontoxic and should not emit fumes, odors, or VOCs into the living space. All-natural materials are a first choice, if available. Secondly, recycled or recyclable materials are used wherever possible. Durability is also a consideration because a product that requires high maintenance or frequent replacement wastes resources. Finally, the environmental impact and embodied energy of a material is considered — whether its contents come from a sustainable source, how much energy is used for its manufacture, and how far the material must be transported to the building site.

Drywall

Drywall, used for finishing walls and ceilings, is the most common indoor building material in the United States. It is inexpensive and widely available. The gypsum-based drywall manufacturing process produces 51 million tons of greenhouse gases and consumes almost 1 percent of all the energy used in the U.S. annually. The energy used to make a standard sheet of drywall is 100,000 BTUs or more per 4x8 sheet. The kraft paper outer layers of drywall are made of recycled material.

Drywall with cores of gypsum made of recycled residue from air scrubbers at coal-fired plants is denser and more durable than standard drywall. It adds thermal mass to the interior walls. It costs more than standard drywall; you can save money by installing it only on the walls and using standard drywall for the ceilings.

New types of drywall are quickly becoming available. EcoRock® is made without calcination through a process in which a foamer added to a mixture of ingredients causes them to heat up and then cool into a board of drywall. EcoRock® can be recycled to make new board. Though EcoRock® is now being used in small quantities in California, its manufacturer, Serious Materials, delayed going into mass production when the Great Recession slowed construction of new homes.

Micronal® PCM SmartBoard™, made by BASF, incorporates tiny spheres of wax in its gypsum core that melt and solidify at temperatures close to the interior temperatures of a building. When the wax melts it absorbs heat, which it gives off as it cools and solidifies. A thin sheet of Micronal® PCM SmartBoard ™ gives the same heating effect as a heavy brick or stone wall.

Magnum Board® (Magnesium Oxide Board or MgO Board) is completely mineral-based and can be used in almost any application. It is nontoxic and resists moisture, mold, rot, insects, and fire. Unlike gypsum board, the manufacturing process does not require high temperatures. One side of the board is paperless and can take many kinds of finishes. It can be used both for the interior or the exterior of a building, and as the exterior panels of SIPs.

Lighting

Lighting accounts for about 15 percent of the energy used in a home, so it is a primary focus in reducing energy consumption. Good lighting is also essential to the comfort of the occupants of a home and makes an important contribution to the way the home looks and feels. Lighting helps create ambience and a peaceful, relaxing atmosphere.

Green lighting design considers the needs of each occupant, as well as the purposes for which each room will be used and the times of day when it will be occupied. People feel better and work more efficiently in natural light. Maximizing natural light also reduces the need for electric lighting. At night, and in the darker areas of the house, lamps are strategically located to provide lighting exactly where it is needed and at appropriate intensities. In conventional homes, fixtures are often placed in the center of the ceiling or in places specified by building codes. This type of lighting can be harsh and impractical. Soft lighting that washes walls and ceilings, table lamps, and task lighting that illuminates specific work areas all make the home more comfortable and save on electricity. A lighting designer can help to identify lighting needs and choose appropriate lamps and fixtures for each room.

Sensors and dimmers

An effective way to save energy on lighting is to install sensors that prevent lights from being left on all day when no one is occupying a room.
Occupancy sensors turn lights on automatically when someone enters a

room and automatically turn lights off when they detect no movement in the room for an extended period of time. Sensors can be installed in a variety of common areas including kitchens, bathrooms, storage and utility closets, and garages.

Although lights on dimmers still use about half as much energy as when they are fully turned on, light dimmers reduce energy use. Dimmers allow the intensity of lighting to be adjusted to suit the activities in the room — for example, a bathroom light can be bright while someone is shaving or applying makeup, and very dim during the night.

Daylighting

Daylighting brings indirect natural light into the building using windows, skylights, and reflective surfaces. Daylighting has other benefits too: electric lights give off heat that raises the temperature in a building. Successful daylighting creates beautiful, appropriately lit spaces while saving energy. Because metrics for successful daylighting have yet to be established, good daylighting is a combination of art and science. It is achieved primarily through window placement. You can attach light shelves featuring glass partitions angled to reflect light further into the building to windows.

Skylights and roof monitors (cupolas with vertical glass windows) can be used to extend daylighting into deep spaces and closed areas, but their use is typically limited to one-story buildings. Solar tubes, which capture light with domes on the roof and channel it through reflective tunnels, can be used in some multi-story buildings. Light colored interior walls and furniture help to diffuse light throughout a room. External shading with trees and shrubs, shades, or architectural features prevent direct light and glare from causing discomfort.

Daylighting is often supplemented by electrical lighting that operates using sensors that turn it on when the natural light drops below a certain intensity. Climate and geographical region, building type and use, and building orientation determine the success of daylighting. Daylighting should be part of an integrated design process because the size and placement of the windows will affect heat gain or loss in the building.

Energy-efficient lighting

Only 10 percent of the energy used by and incandescent bulb produces light; the remaining 90 percent is given off as wasted heat energy. Compact fluorescent bulbs (CFLs), in contrast, give off the same amount of light using only one-fourth of the electricity. CFLs are narrow twisted glass tubes containing a mixture of three phosphors that give off light when exposed to ultraviolet light from mercury atoms. They are made to fit into standard light bulb sockets and are sometimes covered with globes to resemble incandescent bulbs.

CFL bulbs can cost $4 to $6 each, as opposed to as little as 50 cents for some incandescent bulbs, but the extra expense is recouped in energy savings by the time the bulb has been in use for 500 hours. Incandescent bulbs generally have to be

Compact Fluorescent Lighting (CFL) used in an exterior light fixture.

replaced after 500 to 2,000 hours of use, while CFLs are supposed to last 8,000 hours. The DOE is actively campaigning to encourage homeowners to switch to CFLs.

A CFL bulb in an outdoor uses little energy even if it is left on all night.

> **60 watt incandescent light globe x 8 hours a day = 480 watts**
> **15 watt CFL bulb x 8 hours a day = 120 watts**

A CFL qualifies for an ENERGY STAR rating if can save more than $40 in electricity costs over its lifetime, uses about 75 percent less energy and lasts up to 10 times longer than standard incandescent bulbs, and produces about 75 percent less heat to cut energy costs associated with home cooling. According to the DOE, if every American home replaced just one incandescent light bulb with a light bulb that has earned the ENERGY STAR, we would save enough energy to light 3 million homes for a year, save about $600 million in annual energy costs, and prevent 9 billion pounds of greenhouse gas emissions per year, equivalent to the emissions from about 800,000 cars.

The DOE recommends replacing the incandescent bulbs that are turned on in your home for the longest periods with similar CFLs. You can find an *ENERGY STAR Choose Your Light* guide on the ENERGY STAR website (**www.energystar.gov/index.cfm?c=cfls.cfls_choose_guide**).

CFLs contain mercury and must be disposed of properly.

Each CFL contains about 5 mg of mercury, a toxic heavy metal that can cause serious health problems if inhaled or ingested over a period of time or in large enough doses. This is less than the amount of mercury contained in a thermometer and presents no danger to occupants of the home, but old CFLs should be recycled at a hazardous waste facility to prevent them from going into landfills.

If you break a compact fluorescent lamp, open nearby windows immediately to disperse any escaping mercury vapor. Carefully sweep up the glass fragments, place them in a sealed plastic bag, and dispose of them with your other household trash. Remove any remaining fragments by wiping the area with a disposable paper towel. Do not try to pick up glass fragments with your hands, and do not use a vacuum.

Burning fossil fuels such as coal to produce electricity releases mercury into the air. Reducing the amount of electricity consumed by using CFLs prevents mercury from being released into the atmosphere.

Light emitting diode (LED) technology, also known as solid state lighting (SSL), is gaining popularity as energy-efficient lighting. According to the DOE, it has the potential to be ten times more energy efficient than traditional incandescent lighting. As part of the Recovery Act of 2009, the U.S. government allotted $37 million to help develop LED products. Europe, Japan, China, and South Korea have similar government initiatives. The current price of LEDs restricts their use in private residences, but as more products come to market, the manufacturing cost will go down.

LEDs are considered very energy efficient because the light they produce is directed only toward where it is being used. An incandescent or CFL bulb wastes energy because it radiates light in all directions. In a well-designed lighting fixture, the small amount of heat generated by an LED is absorbed into a heat sink instead of being emitted into the air. Incandescent and fluorescent lights contribute to the air conditioning load by giving off heat into a room. Only a limited number of LED products are ENERGY STAR rated, but the DOE expects that number to grow substantially by 2011. Some LEDs experience problems such as flickering, color shifting, dimness, uneven light, and consuming power when turned off after less than a year of use. The DOE recommends purchasing ENERGY STAR-rated LEDs that have met performance and efficiency standards and do not have these problems. A wide variety of LED products are available for use in the home, including under-cabinet kitchen lights, shelf-mounted lights, desk lamps, recessed lighting, cove lighting, outdoor step and pathway lights, and outdoor decorative lights. LEDs produce light of different qualities and colors and can be used to add ambience to outdoor areas.

ENERGY STAR performance standards for LEDs

- Brightness is equal to or greater than existing lighting technologies (incandescent or fluorescent) and light is well distributed over the area lighted by the fixture.
- Light output remains constant over time, only decreasing toward the end of the rated lifetime (at least 25,000 hours or 22 years based on use of 3 hours per day).
- Excellent color quality. The shade of white light appears clear and consistent over time.
- Efficiency is as good as or better than fluorescent lighting.
- Light comes on instantly when turned on.
- No flicker when dimmed
- No off-state power draw. The fixture does not use power when it is turned off, with the exception of external controls whose power should not exceed 0.5 watts in the off state.

Outdoor lighting

Low-voltage outdoor lamps that run on 12 volts have been used for more than 50 years and are safe around children and pets. They are powered by transformers plugged into standard outlets that reduce 120 volts to 12 volts. Low-voltage lamps come in a variety of brightness levels ranging from 4 watts up to 50 watts halogen. Outdoor lamps and lighting systems powered with solar cells store energy during the day when the sun is shining and turn on automatically when the sun goes down. Because they provide their own energy sources, they do not require installing wiring and electrical cords.

Motion sensors save energy by turning on driveway lights, spotlights, and security lights only when someone is approaching. Timers or light sensors can be used to automatically turn lights on at night and off in the morning. Instead of lighting up large areas of outdoor space with glaring lamps, green outdoor lighting is designed to provide illumination only where it is needed, such as over entryways and along pathways. This helps to eliminate light pollution and unwanted light shining in through windows at night.

Solar powered lights in a garden.

Universal Design

Universal design, also known as "design for all," "inclusive design," and "life-span design" is based on the idea that all environments and products should be usable by all people, regardless of their ages, sizes, or abilities. Areas of the home are designed to be both aesthetically pleasing and easily

Lever faucet handles in a bathroom.

accessible to children, the elderly, and those with disabilities. Universal design avoids the need to renovate to accommodate elderly or disabled occupants, or small children. Universal design features, such as large light switches and lever faucet handles, are convenient and easy to use.

The American Association of Retired Persons (**www.aarp.org/universal-home/solutions.html**) suggests the following universal design features to make a home safer and easier to live in for people of all ages. Even if the homeowners are active adults, implementing these features now ensures that future occupants and guests to the home will not experience inconveniences:

- Lever faucet handles or single lever faucets that are easy to turn.
- U-shaped drawer handles that are easier to grasp for cabinets and drawers.
- Decorative grab bars in the shower or by the toilet and tub.
- Rocker switches instead of standard light switches.
- Transition wedges at door thresholds to avoid tripping.
- Textured surfaces on sidewalks and driveways for traction and stability.
- Handrails on both sides of stairways.
- Appliances with large print keypads and control panels.
- Lighting near outside walkways, stairs, and entrances.
- Nightlights in hallways and bathrooms.
- Under-the-cabinet lights, or task lighting, over kitchen counter work areas.

Acoustics

Noise control is an often overlooked aspect of green building but has a significant impact on the comfort of building occupants. It is important to consider acoustics when choosing materials and designing both the envelope and the interior of your building. Outside noises include street traffic, the sound of pump motors and HVAC systems (both yours and your neighbors'), noise from nearby highways or construction sites, trains, and aircraft flying overhead. Green building emphasizes using less materials and creating more open spaces. With fewer materials such as ceiling tiles and carpeting to absorb sound, the noise level inside the house from conversation, children playing, music and television, and operating kitchen equipment may be higher in a green building than in a conventional one. Good design and selecting and properly installing building materials can help to control the noise level in the house.

Exterior walls can block 45 to 50 decibels of sound, but exterior noise often enters through the windows, air ducts, or doors. A dual pane or "superglass" window will block sound effectively. If the air seal around a door is weak, sound can enter wherever air comes in. Cellulose and foam insulations do a better job of blocking noise than fiberglass batt insulation. The effect of adding thicker insulation is only incremental. Doubling the amount of insulation in a wall only increases resistance to sound by 4 to 5 decibels.

If a house is located near a source of noise, the best solution is to build with SIPs, cementitious siding, and superglass windows. External noise can also be blocked with a barrier such as a mound of earth, a wall, or another building. To be effective, the barrier must obstruct the direct line of sight between the building and the source of noise.

Fabrics and Furnishings

The demand for furniture made from beautiful tropical woods such as teak and mahogany has been one of the causes behind the destruction of primary rainforests. Synthetic foams in upholstery cushions and dyes and fixatives in upholstery fabrics often contain reproductive or developmental toxins (such as the flame retardants containing PBDEs) and mutagens and endocrine disrupters (such as dioxins). Adhesives and particleboard used in furniture can offgas formaldehyde for years. The furniture and drapes that you bring into your home can seriously compromise both indoor air quality and your efforts to be environmentally responsible.

Purchasing furniture for your home should be guided by the same principles as selecting green building materials and products. Many specialty manufacturers produce eco-friendly furniture, but well-known furniture companies such as Crate & Barrel have also recognized the demand for healthy and sustainable products and have begun using certified woods and nontoxic materials in their furniture.

Look for furniture made with FSC-certified woods. Many companies manufacture furniture from reclaimed wood such as lumber salvaged from old barns and buildings, or from wood retrieved from river and lake bottoms or logged underwater from forests submerged by hydroelectric dams. The Rainforest Alliance certifies such wood as Rediscovered Wood and Underwater Salvage (**www.rainforest-alliance.org/forestry/certification/rediscovered-wood**). Furniture made from molded bamboo is beautiful and nontoxic.

Many designers refurbish and refinish old furniture and antiques. Second-hand furniture has already finished offgassing long ago and may increase in value over time. You can also make furniture by repurposing salvaged building materials; for example, an old door can become a desk or a tabletop. Be sure that low-VOC finishes have been used. Furniture made from recycled metals, plastics, and papers is also considered green because less energy is required to manufacture it.

An important aspect of green furniture is strength and durability and the ease with which it can be cleaned and repaired. A sofa should not have to be sent to a landfill just because a leg snapped off and could not be reattached. IKEA makes the fabric covers on many upholstered items removable and washable for easy cleaning.

Another consideration is whether the furniture can be disassembled and recycled when it is no longer usable. McDonough Braungart Design Chemistry (MBDC) (**www.mbdc.com**) offers a Cradle to Cradle® Certification that evaluates products and materials for human health, environmental health, and recyclability.

Look for cushions made with soy- and corn-based foam and fibers instead of petroleum-based foam, or padding made with cotton, hemp, or natural fibers. Low-impact fabric dyes usually do not contain toxic chemicals or mordants, and often have a high absorption rate into the fabric, generating less waste water during the dyeing process.

The Global Organic Textile Standard (GOTS) certifies organic only textile products that contain a minimum of 70 percent organic fibers. All chemical inputs such as dyestuffs and auxiliaries used must meet certain environmental and toxicological criteria. A functional wastewater treatment plant is mandatory for any wet-processing unit involved and all textile processors must comply with minimum criteria for social responsibility.

Conclusion

Many important elements of green building are not directly visible to the building occupants. However, aesthetic beauty is just as essential as energy efficiency and using natural, nontoxic materials. Green interior design means many things: convenience, privacy, noise reduction, good lighting, and a physical layout that allows social interaction and ease of movement.

A carpet or a living room sofa can undermine otherwise excellent indoor air quality by giving off VOCs, formaldehydes, and other chemicals. Principles of green building should not be overlooked when you are selecting furniture and other items to bring into your home.

Chapter 11

Green Renovation for Existing Homes

For every newly constructed building, there are more than 100 existing buildings.

Existing buildings are likely to have older, less energy-efficient fixtures and systems than new buildings, and they can be expected to remain in use for decades. It is obvious that renovating and retrofitting existing buildings would significantly reduce greenhouse gas emissions, water usage, and pollution.

A renovation may involve making structural changes, replacing old systems with new ones, removing toxic materials, and installing new fittings. A green retrofit is more simple and involves making changes to one or more building components, for example, replacing or updating the HVAC unit, adding a solar system to supply some of your electricity, or replacing windows or water fixtures.

A green renovation makes a home more comfortable, energy efficient, and healthy to live in. Green renovation can be as drastic as gutting an entire structure and re-constructing the interior and exterior using the existing frame or as simple as installing low-flow toilets and showerheads in the bathrooms. Many of the green materials used in building a new home can be installed, or ret-rofitted, in an existing home. A green makeover involves not only making changes to the physical structure of a house, but also changing the behavior of the people living in the house.

The primary goals for green home remodeling are the same as those for building a new green home — energy and water efficiency, sustainability, and an excellent indoor environment. The information in all the other chapters of this book applies to your choice of materials and selecting pro-fessionals to do the work — with some additional considerations:

Recycling and disposing of waste: Think about disposing of the old ma-terials being torn out to make way for new ones. Your only option may be to send those worn-out asphalt shingles or soggy drywall to a landfill, but do some research and find out what kind of recycling programs exist in your area. A green contractor should already know about them, but you can never be certain. The Building Materials Reuse Association (BMRA) website includes a directory listing recycling programs and businesses by state (**www.bmra.org**) and information on deconstructing rather than demolishing a building. Identify materials that could be refurbished and reused in your renovation, such as wood floorboards or doors. Take old tiles, sinks, light fixtures, doors, siding, and other reusable items to a local construction thrift store or salvage yard. Someone repairing an older home might use them as replacement parts.

Comfort and safety of the building occupants: If your family will be liv-ing in the home while the work is being done, arrange work schedules with the contractor to minimize disruption. Make sure living areas are sealed off from dust and fumes. Some materials such as spray-in foam insulation may offgas for hours or days after installation. Ductwork should be sealed to ensure that particles and dust from construction do not accumulate inside.

Toxic substances: Building materials in old homes may contain toxic sub-stances such as asbestos and lead. These materials must be handled cor-rectly so workers and building occupants are not exposed to harm.

Identifying Your Priorities

A successful renovation starts with good planning. Before you begin any renovation, identify your objectives and your priorities. Knowing exactly what you hope to accomplish will make it easier for you to negotiate with a contractor, evaluate costs, and make decisions about materials. Take some time to write down answers to the following questions. As the project progresses, you will be able to review your answers and see if your project is on track, or if your expectations have changed.

Why are you undertaking this renovation project?

Are you renovating because you have just bought the house and you want to make it totally green? Does someone in your household suffer from respiratory problems or allergies? Have you discovered your walls are infested with mold because of moisture in the insulation? Are ice dams causing your roof to leak in winter? Is it time to replace your water heater? Are your electricity bills costing you hundreds of dollars during the peak summer and winter months? Your reasons for undertaking a green project will become the primary objectives that will guide all future design and construction.

How much are you willing to spend?

Whether you are motivated by a deep personal commitment to sustainability or simply need to replace your old roof, green building makes economic sense: You will reduce your energy bills, your family will live in a healthier environment, and using durable materials means you will not have to spend more money to replace them in the near future. Some green retrofits, such as installing a solar system, involve a high initial cost, and some green materials and technologies are significantly more expensive than conventional ones. If you have the resources and a strong desire to demonstrate your commitment to protecting the environment, you might be willing to spare no expense. If your budget is tight however, you will want to stick to the technologies and materials that give you the greatest positive return on your investment.

How do you use your existing home?

Make a list of the tasks and activities you do in each room of your house. Do you have enough space? Is there some way to do tasks more conveniently? Are there areas or rooms that you do not use? Is the lighting adequate? Are there hazardous areas such as stairs, entryways, or kitchen and bathroom floors that might become slippery and cause falls?

What are your expectations?

What do you expect to accomplish with your renovation? How much do you hope to reduce your energy bills? How long do you expect the work to take and when do you want the project to be finished? You should communicate these expectations to your contractor, who will explain whether your expectations are reasonable and may adjust work schedules to finish by a specified date.

Make sure renovation work is done according to building codes.

Renovation work that does not conform to building codes may void your insurance policy. Be careful, especially when doing installations yourself, that the work is not done in a way that violates building codes. Building codes are created to ensure the safety and durability of buildings and equipment.

Make sure renovation work is done according to building codes.

Renovation work that does not conform to building codes may void your insurance policy. Be careful, especially when doing installations yourself, that the work is not done in a way that violates building codes. Building codes are created to ensure the safety and durability of buildings and equipment.

Calculating Your Returns

Before you launch into a major green renovation project, you should understand exactly how you can expect to benefit from the renovation and how much it will cost. A green renovation or retrofit can add to the resale value of your home, and the savings on energy bills will repay your investment over time. Not all the benefits are financial. If someone in your household suffers from asthma or allergies, you may be willing to spend extra money to have an allergen and toxin free indoor environment. Insulation against exterior noises and increased natural lighting make a home more peaceful and comfortable for the occupants. The satisfaction of knowing that you are being environmentally responsible and setting an example for others might be worth the extra expense.

Green homes are more popular in some parts of the country than in others. In Seattle, Washington, where green building is in demand, new homes with green certification sold for 8.5 percent more per square foot than comparable non-green homes, and sold 22 percent quicker. In other areas of the country, however, lenders are reluctant to provide mortgages for green homes because appraisers do not know how to appraise them accurately. Before you embark on your project, find out how green renovations have affected the prices of other homes in your area. Contact other homeowners who have done similar renovations and ask them how much they spent, how they feel about the results, and whether they have any recommendations based on their experiences.

ROI Tables on the website of green building consultancy, GreenandSave LLC, (**www.greenandsave.com/master_roi_table.html**) show the added cost of a variety of green renovation projects and technologies, and the estimated time it will take to recoup those costs through energy savings (payback time). Some green improvements cost little more than conventional renovations. An important consideration is how long you expect to live in the home after it is renovated. If you spend $15,000 to install a solar electricity system and then sell the house after two years, you may not be able to recoup the cost of the system.

Green Renovation Projects

Any home renovation becomes "green" if it is done using environmentally friendly materials and products. If you are planning to renovate or redecorate your home anyway, why not go a step further and actively implement green building practices? For little or no extra cost, you can achieve greater energy efficiency and better indoor air quality by upgrading insulation, sealing air leaks, and choosing low-VOC paints.

Below is a list of projects, small and large, that can make your home greener:

Energy and water efficiency

- Install a solar water heater or solar heating
- Install a PV or wind system to generate all or part of your electricity
- Caulk and weather-strip your home
- Insulate your foundation or slab
- Add insulation to walls, ceilings, and floors
- Replace old appliances with energy-efficient ones
- Switch to CFL bulbs or LEDs
- Upgrade your HVAC system and add an ERV
- Replace old windows with high-efficiency ones
- Install a whole-house fan
- Replace roof with energy-efficient roofing
- Replace showerheads and faucets with low-flow fixtures
- Replace old toilets

Indoor air quality

- Replace carpeting with tile, bamboo, cork, or polished concrete flooring
- Replace kitchen and bathroom cabinetry with formaldehyde-free cabinets
- Install an air filter
- Repaint with low-VOC paints
- Make sure the house has adequate ventilation

Exterior

- Replace lawn with native plants
- Plant trees for shelter and shade
- Remove invasive plants
- Install a rainwater collector

- Install drip irrigation
- Replace pavement with permeable pavement

Adding Passive Solar

Owners of existing homes can make minor changes to take advantage of passive solar energy. In most parts of the U.S., homeowners need to maximize solar heat in the winter and minimize it to keep their homes cool in the summer. Adding or enlarging south-facing windows will increase the amount

These homeowners installed a retractable awning. In the winter they keep it closed to maximize the sun exposure and in the summer they keep it open to help keep their home cool.

of solar energy entering the house. Skylights can also be installed in the south side of a home to let more sun in. Thermal mass can be added by covering a sunlit wall with a heat-absorbent material such as stone or brick.

If you do not want to undertake a major home improvement project, there are still small changes you can make to implement some principles of passive solar design. During the summer, a room facing south will probably be uncomfortably warm. To diminish the amount of sun and heat entering that room during the summer, glaze windows or hang awnings outside. Outdoor shades on south-facing windows are effective in blocking the sun's heat.

Home Energy Audit

A professional home energy audit will help you to identify areas in your home where energy is being wasted or lost every day. At the end of the audit, you will receive a list of recommended actions to reduce your energy consumption.

Who performs the audit?

Home energy auditors are trained in energy conservation. Several programs train and certify energy auditors, but a home energy audit does not need to be performed by a professional energy auditor. Contractors, energy inspectors, energy raters, and building analysts all perform energy audits. An **energy audit** is a building inspection that determines how to reduce energy consumption in a home and save the homeowners money. All energy auditors should be knowledgeable about energy, insulation, heating and cooling systems, water heating systems, and windows and doors.

There are two nationally recognized certifications for energy auditors: the Building Performance Institute (BPI) and the Residential Energy Services Network (RESNET) HERS (Home Energy Rating System) Rater. To become BPI certified, energy auditors must pass a written test and a field test. An HERS Rater must pass a written test and complete five ratings within a year of passing the test. HERS Raters must also take continuing education courses throughout the year. Currently, BPI focuses on older, existing homes, while RESNET focuses on new construction and newer homes.

Many utility companies conduct free or discounted home audits to encourage their customers to become more energy efficient. Some of these audits are visual inspections rather than extensive energy audits. Ask what the inspection encompasses. If it does not include blower door and thermography, the inspection might not uncover all of the energy inefficiencies in your home.

If your utility company does not offer a home energy audit, it may be able to recommend a company that does these audits. You can also find an energy auditor in the local yellow pages, on the Internet, or through the Better Business Bureau or Chamber of Commerce.

Some solar contractors also do home energy audits. Hiring a solar contractor to do an energy audit does not obligate you to hire them to install your PV system. Some companies may offer a discounted rate if you use them for both the audit and the installation.

Auditing your home

A professional energy auditor uses certain tools and procedures to search for energy inefficiencies in your home. A blower door measures air leaks in your building that allow cooled or heated air to escape. A powerful fan mounted into the frame of an exterior door pulls air out of the house and lowers the air pressure inside the house. Higher air pressure outside causes air to flow in through all your home's unsealed openings. You can detect where the air is flowing in by walking around your home and placing your hand over different areas in each room. For example, air will flow in through electrical sockets that are not insulated. The blower door test determines how drafty your house is and identifies where specific leaks are. Repairing these leaks will stop energy wastage by keeping heated or cooled air inside your home. Areas that commonly need repairs include electrical outlets, windows, and doors.

Another procedure home energy auditors use to detect air leakage is thermography, or infrared scanning. **Thermography** measures surface temperatures using infrared video and still cameras. Thermography done in cold weather will reveal variations in the temperature of your building's skin, or exterior walls, to show where your home might need additional insulation.

Thermal image of a house at night.

A thorough professional energy audit can take several hours and cost between $300 and $500, depending on the size of your home. It could cost as little as $125 if you get a special discounted rate from a solar contractor or utility company. Many auditors will provide a printed report with detailed recommendations for improving the energy efficiency of your home.

Recommendations for improving energy efficiency

An energy auditor may recommend a number of measures you should take to improve the energy efficiency of your home, including:

Exterior caulking

Caulking the exterior of your home will seal it off from outside air and moisture. Caulking involves using an impermeable substance to fill in cracks, holes, and seams and make them watertight. On the outside of the building, use a paintable acrylic latex caulk to seal vertical cracks around window and doorframes and corner boards. Pay special attention to holes around pipes, electrical outlets, and HVAC equipment.

The Home Star Energy Retrofit Act of 2010, informally known as the "cash for caulkers" bill and approved by the House of Representatives in June 2010, will give homeowners up to $3,000 in tax credits to pay for weatherization or insulation improvements.

Buying a quality thermostat

Programmable thermostats allow the temperature in a home to be set to four settings for when you are asleep, away, or at work, and also allow you to warm or cool the home before you return. These thermostats are easy to use and help you to control your heating and cooling costs.

A digital thermostat allows you to manage the temperature in your home when you are asleep or away.

If you have a manual thermostat, you can save by remembering to adjust the temperature when you will not be home for several hours or several days. This will prevent your thermostat from running your heating or cooling system on when no one is home.

Saving money with your thermostat

Excerpt from DOE Energy Savers: Thermostats and Control Systems (www.energy savers.gov/your_home/space_heating_cooling/index.cfm/mytopic=12720)

You can easily save energy in the winter by setting the thermostat to 68 degrees while you are awake and setting it lower while you're asleep or away from home. By turning your thermostat back 10 to 15 degrees for eight hours, you can save about 5 to 15 percent a year on your heating bill — a savings of as much as 1 percent for each degree if the setback period is eight hours long. The percentage of savings from setback is greater for buildings in milder climates than for those in more severe climates.

In the summer, you can follow the same strategy with central air conditioning by keeping your house warmer than normal when you are away, and lowering the thermostat setting to 78 degrees only when you are at home and need cooling. Although thermostats can be adjusted manually, programmable thermostats will avoid any discomfort by returning temperatures to normal as you wake or return home.

A common misconception associated with thermostats is that a furnace works harder than normal to warm the space back to a comfortable temperature after the thermostat has been set back, which results in little or no savings. This misconception has been dispelled by years of research and numerous studies. The fuel required to reheat a building to a comfortable temperature is roughly equal to the fuel saved as the building drops to the lower temperature. You save fuel between the time that the temperature stabilizes at the lower level and the next time heat is needed. So, the longer your house remains at the lower temperature, the more energy you save.

Programmable thermostats are generally not recommended for homes with heat pumps, electric resistance heating, steam heat, and radiant floor heating. Electric resistance systems, such as electric baseboard heating, require thermostats capable of directly controlling 120-volt or 240-volt circuits, which are manufactured by only a few companies. A programmable thermostat can cause a heat pump to operate inefficiently during heating mode. Steam heating and radiant floor heating systems take several hours to respond to a thermostat because they raise the temperature in a room very gradually. Recently, however, some companies have begun selling specially designed programmable thermostats that compensate for these limitations.

Installing dual pane windows

If you have single-pane windows, upgrading to dual pane windows can make a big difference in energy savings. Energy-efficient windows reduce condensation, reduce fading of draperies and furniture, and enhance the comfort of your home. They can also save you hundreds of dollars in heating and cooling bills each year. The current $1,500 federal tax credit for energy-efficient appliances and building components includes skylights and exterior windows.

The Efficient Windows Collaborative website (**www.efficientwindows. org**) has an interactive program to help you select the most energy-efficient windows for your home. It also provides a printable step-by-step fact sheet for selecting energy efficient windows in each state, and a state-by-state fact sheet for compliance with the International Energy Conservation Code (IECC), the most commonly adopted model energy code for residential buildings. Always follow manufacturers' guidelines for installing windows and use trained professionals. Proper installation ensures an airtight fit, avoids water leakage, and guarantees optimal window performance.

Properly insulating ducts

Houses with forced-air heating and cooling systems typically lose about 20 percent of the air moving through the duct system that distributes heated or cooled air throughout the house. Ducts that are concealed inside walls or between floors are difficult to repair. Exposed ductwork in attics, basements, crawl spaces, and garages can easily be inspected for leaks and poorly sealed connections. Leaks can be sealed with metal tape or duct sealant (also called duct mastic).

You can find more information about sealing and insulating ducts online in "An Introduction to Residential Duct Systems" (**http://ducts.lbl.gov**), a publication of the Ernest Orlando Lawrence Berkeley National Laboratory.

Weather stripping

Excerpt from U.S. Department of Energy - Energy Efficiency and Renewable Energy: Energy Savers (www.energysavers.gov/your_home/insulation_airsealing/index. cfm/mytopic=11280)

You can use weather stripping in your home to seal air leaks around movable joints, such as windows or doors. Before applying weather stripping in an existing home, you need to locate air leaks and assess your ventilation needs. Unless properly ventilated, an airtight home can seal in indoor air pollutants. Ventilation also helps control moisture, which can fuel the growth of mold and mildew.

- To determine how much weather stripping you will need, add the perimeters of all windows and doors to be weather-stripped, then add 5 to 10 percent to accommodate any waste. Also consider that weather stripping comes in varying depths and widths.

- Choose a type of weather stripping that will withstand the friction, weather, temperature changes, and wear and tear associated with its location. For example, when applied to a door bottom or threshold, weather stripping could drag on carpet or erode as a result of foot traffic. Weather stripping in a window sash must accommodate the sliding of panes — up and down, sideways, or out. The weather stripping you choose should seal well when the door or window is closed while allowing it to open freely.

- Choose a product for each specific location. Felt and open-cell foams tend to be inexpensive, susceptible to weather, visible, and inefficient at blocking airflow. However, the ease of applying these materials may make them valuable in low-traffic areas. Vinyl, which is slightly more expensive, holds up well and resists moisture. Metals (bronze, copper, stainless steel, and aluminum) last for years and are affordable. Metal weather stripping can also provide a nice touch to older homes where vinyl might seem out of place. Take durability into account when comparing costs.

- You can use more than one type of weather stripping to seal an irregularly shaped space.

Properly insulating walls and attics

According to the DOE, only 20 percent of homes built before 1980 are well insulated. A good insulating system includes a combination of products and construction techniques that protect a home from outside hot or cold temperatures, protect it against air leaks, and control moisture.

The higher the R-value of your insulation, the better your walls and roof will resist the transfer of heat, but excessive insulation is wasteful. *Consult the DOE map in Chapter 4 for the recommended R-values for your region.* Insulation must be correctly installed to be effective. Hire a professional or do careful research if you intend to do the installation yourself.

Insulating an attic should be done with care

Consult an expert when adding insulation to the walls and roof of an attic that has not previously been insulated. Insulating the attic makes it part of the building envelope, and the existing air conditioning system might not be sized to handle the extra cooling space. Changing to an unventilated attic may have unexpected consequences, such as voiding the warranty for the roof covering.

Do-it-yourself energy audit

You do not have to hire a professional to perform an energy audit for you. Going through your home looking for inefficiencies might make an interesting weekend project. The U.S. Department of Energy (DOE) (**www. energysavers.gov**) offers step-by-step instructions on its website for conducting your own energy audit. You might decide to call a professional energy auditor after you have performed your own audit.

Do-It-Yourself Home Energy Assessments

Excerpt from the U.S. Department of Energy - Energy Efficiency and Renewable Energy: Energy Savers (www.energysavers.gov/your_home/energy_audits/index.cfm/mytopic=11170)

You can easily conduct a do-it-yourself home energy audit. With a simple but diligent walk-through, you can spot many problems in any type of house. When assessing your home, keep a checklist of areas you have inspected and problems you found. This list will help you prioritize your energy efficiency upgrades.

Locating Air Leaks

- First, make a list of obvious air leaks (drafts). The potential energy savings from reducing drafts in a home may range from 5 to 30 percent per year, and the home is generally much more comfortable afterward. Check for indoor air leaks, such as gaps along the baseboard or edge of the flooring and at junctures of the walls and ceiling. Check to see if air can flow through these places:

  - Electrical outlets
  - Switch plates
  - Window frames
  - Baseboards
  - Weather stripping around doors
  - Fireplace dampers
  - Attic hatches
  - Wall- or window-mounted air conditioners.

- Also look for gaps around pipes and wires, electrical outlets, foundation seals, and mail slots. Check to see if the caulking and weather stripping are applied properly, leaving no gaps or cracks, and are in good condition.

- Inspect windows and doors for air leaks. See if you can rattle them, because movement means possible air leaks. If you can see daylight around a door or window frame, then the door or window leaks. You can usually seal these leaks by caulking or weather-stripping them. Check the storm windows to see if they fit and are not broken. You may also wish to consider replacing your old windows and doors with newer, high-performance ones. If new factory-made doors or windows are too costly, you can install low-cost plastic sheets over the windows.

- If you are having difficulty locating leaks, you may want to conduct a basic building pressurization test:

    1. First, close all exterior doors, windows, and fireplace flues.
    2. Turn off all combustion appliances such as gas burning furnaces and water heaters.
    3. Then turn on all exhaust fans (generally located in the kitchen and bathrooms) or use a large window fan to suck the air out of the rooms.

    This test increases infiltration through cracks and leaks, which makes them easier to detect. You can use incense sticks or your damp hand to locate these leaks. If you use incense sticks, moving air will cause the smoke to waver, and if you use your damp hand, any drafts will feel cool to your hand.

- On the outside of your house, inspect all areas where two different building materials meet, including all exterior corners, where siding and chimneys meet, and areas where the foundation and the bottom of exterior brick or siding meet.

- You should plug and caulk holes or penetrations for faucets, pipes, electric outlets, and wiring. Look for cracks and holes in the mortar, foundation, and siding, and seal them with the appropriate material. Check the exterior caulking around doors and windows, and see whether exterior storm doors and primary doors seal tightly.

- When sealing any home, you must always be aware of the danger of indoor air pollution and combustion appliance backdrafts. **Backdrafting** occurs when the various fuel-burning combustion appliances, such as space heaters, gas ranges, furnaces, fireplaces, water heaters, clothes dryers, and exhaust fans in the home compete for air. An exhaust fan may pull the combustion gases back into the living space. This can obviously create a very dangerous and unhealthy situation in the home.

- In homes where a fuel is burned (i.e., natural gas, fuel oil, propane, or wood) for heating, be certain the appliance has an adequate air supply. Generally, 1 square inch of vent opening is required for each 1,000 Btu of appliance input heat. When in doubt, contact your local utility company, energy professional, or ventilation contractor.

Insulation

Heat loss through the ceiling and walls in your home could be very large if the insulation levels are less than the recommended minimum. When your house was built, the builder likely installed the amount of insulation recommended at that time. Given today's energy prices (and future prices that will probably be higher), the level of insulation might be inadequate, especially if you have an older home.

- If the attic hatch is located above a conditioned space, check to see if it is at least as heavily insulated as the attic, is weather stripped, and closes tightly. In the attic, determine whether openings for items such as pipes, ductwork, and chimneys are sealed. Seal any gaps with an expanding foam caulk or some other permanent sealant.

- While you are inspecting the attic, check to see if there is a vapor barrier under the attic insulation. The vapor barrier might be tarpaper, kraft paper attached to fiberglass batts, or a plastic sheet. If there does not appear to be a vapor barrier, you might consider painting the interior ceilings with vapor barrier paint. This reduces the amount of water vapor that can pass through the ceiling. Large amounts of moisture can reduce the effectiveness of insulation and promote structural damage.

Make sure that the attic vents are not blocked by insulation. You also should seal any electrical boxes in the ceiling with flexible caulk (from the living room side or attic side) and cover the entire attic floor with at least the current recommended amount of insulation.

- Checking a wall's insulation level is more difficult. Select an exterior wall and turn off the circuit breaker or unscrew the fuse for any outlets in the wall. Be sure to test the outlets to make certain that they are not hot (conducting electricity).

- Check the outlet by plugging in a functioning lamp or portable radio. Once you are sure your outlets are not getting any electricity, remove the cover plate from one of the outlets and gently probe into the wall with a thin, long stick or screwdriver. If you encounter a slight resistance, you have some insulation there. You could also make a small hole in a closet, behind a couch, or in some other unobtrusive place to see what, if anything, the wall cavity is filled with. Ideally, the wall cavity should be totally filled with some form of insulation material. Unfortunately, this method cannot tell you if the entire wall is insulated, or if the insulation has settled. Only a thermographic inspection can do this.

- If your basement is unheated, determine whether there is insulation under the living area flooring. In most areas of the country, an R-value of 25 is the recommended minimum level of insulation. The insulation at the top of the foundation wall and first floor perimeter should have an R-value of 19 or greater. If the basement is heated, the foundation walls should be insulated to at least R-19. Your water heater, hot water pipes, and furnace ducts should all be insulated.

Heating/Cooling Equipment

- Inspect heating and cooling equipment annually, or as recommended by the manufacturer. If you have a forced-air furnace, check your filters and replace them as needed. Generally, you should change them about once every month or two, especially during periods of high usage.

- Have a professional check and clean your equipment once a year. If the unit is more than 15 years old, you should consider replacing your system with one of the newer, energy-efficient units. A new unit would greatly reduce your energy consumption, especially if the existing equipment is in poor condition.

- Check your ductwork for dirt streaks, especially near seams. These indicate air leaks, and they should be sealed with a duct mastic. Insulate any ducts or pipes that travel through unheated spaces. An insulation R-value of 6 is the recommended minimum.

Lighting

- Energy for lighting accounts for about 10 percent of your electric bill. Examine the wattage size of the light bulbs in your house. You may have 100-watt (or larger) bulbs where 60 or 75 watts would do.

- Consider compact fluorescent lamps for areas where lights are on for hours at a time. Your electric utility may offer rebates or other incentives for purchasing energy-efficient lamps.

Steps for Decreasing Energy Use

Even without performing a full-scale energy audit, there are steps you can take to make your house more energy efficient. Before beginning your building or renovation, make time for some home improvements that will reduce your energy consumption. If you do this several months ahead of time, you will have time to compare your utility bills to previous years and see if your energy requirements have been significantly lowered.

Your attic

Adequate insulation in your attic will keep your home warmer in winter and cooler in summer. The online DOE ZIP Code Insulation Calculator will give you recommended insulation levels tailored to your home.

Inadequate ventilation in your attic shortens the life of your roof, makes upstairs living spaces hot in the summer, and places heavier demands on your air conditioning system. Ventilation requirements are determined by factors such as roof color, the amount of insulation in the attic floor, the existence of a vapor barrier, whether openings in the attic are covered by screens, and the amount of shade protecting the roof. The basic standard is 1 square foot of cross-ventilation for every 300 feet of attic space. Static ventilators such as fixed gable louvers or roof ridge vents work best in combination with vents located around the base of the attic. For example, soffit vents in the eaves allow cooler air to enter from below and escape as hotter air through the gable or ridge openings in the roof above. In the winter, proper attic ventilation keeps the attic cold and protects your roof from structural damage from ice that forms when snow melts and refreezes on a warm roof. Make sure that vent openings are not obstructed by insulation.

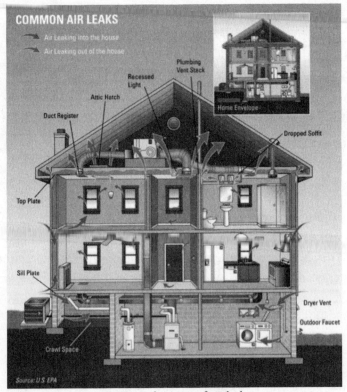

*Common locations of air leaks
in an existing home*

> **TIP: Adding insulation to your attic is one of the most cost-effective ways to make your home more comfortable year-round**
>
> Measure the thickness of the insulation in your attic. If it is less than R-30 (11 inches of fiberglass or rock wool or 8 inches of cellulose), you could probably benefit by adding more. According to the DOE, most U.S. homes should have between R-30 and R-60 insulation in the attic. Also add insulation to the attic trap or access door.

Windows, doors, and electrical outlets

Check your windows and doorframes for any small gaps or holes that allow air to escape from or enter your home. If, for instance, some of your windows have tiny gaps measuring 1/10 of an inch square, it would take ten of these gaps to make up a 1-inch hole. Thirty gaps 1/10 inch square equal a 3-inch hole in your wall. Visualize a 3-inch hole in your wall — how much of your air-conditioned or heated air can escape through that hole?

> **TIP: A candle can help you find leaks**
>
> Use a lighted candle or cigarette to check for air leaks around windows and electrical outlets. If the candle flame flickers or the smoke is disturbed, you will know that there is a leak in that area.

Install special insulators under the electrical outlets set in the perimeter walls of the home. Put new weather stripping along the bottom of all doors that lead outside. If this is difficult, you can lay long narrow cloth bags or tubes filled with sand along the bottom of doors to block drafts.

> **TIP: A Do-It-Yourself Guide to Sealing and Insulating with ENERGY STAR**
>
> The ENERGY STAR website offers a do-it-yourself guide for sealing and insulating your home (**www.energystar.gov/index.cfm?c=diy.diy_index**).
>
> ENERGY STAR estimates that a knowledgeable homeowner or skilled contractor can save up to 20 percent on heating and cooling costs (or up to 10 percent on their total annual energy bill) by sealing and insulating.

Energy Efficient Appliances

You can reduce your energy consumption by replacing old appliances with newer, more energy-efficient models. ENERGY STAR (**www.energystar. gov**), a joint program of the U.S. Environmental Protection Agency (EPA) and the DOE, gives an ENERGY STAR rating to appliances that meet certain standards for energy efficiency. To qualify, products must have the features and performance consumers demand in addition to increased energy efficiency. If a qualified product is more expensive than a conventional, less-efficient counterpart, those who purchase it must be able to recover their investment in increased energy efficiency through savings on their utility bills within a reasonable period of time. The product's energy consumption and performance must be measurable and verifiable with testing. Products must be clearly labeled with information on energy consumption.

When shopping for a new appliance, look for one with an ENERGY STAR rating. Each ENERGY STAR appliance has a label that outlines how much you can expect to save on your utility bill by switching to that energy-efficient model. For example, a refrigerator with new energy-saving features can save as much as 10 percent in annual consumption of electricity. To qualify for an ENERGY STAR rating, the refrigerator must use 20 percent less energy than a standard fridge. According to the DOE, replacing your old refrigerator from the 1980s with an ENERGY STAR model will save you more than $100 annually on your utility bills, and you can save $200 by replacing a refrigerator from the 1970s.

Dishwashers with an ENERGY STAR rating save on both water consumption and electricity. The DOE reports that dishwashers made before 1994 waste 10 gallons of water per cycle compared to new ENERGY STAR models. If you replace your old model with one that is ENERGY STAR-qualified, you can save an extra $40 a year on your utility bills.

According to the ENERGY STAR website, Americans saved enough energy to power 10 million homes in 2009 alone, helping reduce greenhouse gas emissions by an amount equivalent to the emissions of 12 million cars. In monetary terms, a savings of $6 billion was realized in 2009.

Incentives for energy-efficient appliances

The American Recovery and Reinvestment Act of 2009 included a "Cash for Appliances" rebate for the purchase of new ENERGY STAR-qualified appliances, including boilers, central air conditioners, washers, dryers, dishwashers, freezers, oil and gas furnaces, refrigerators, room air conditioners, and heat pumps. In 2010, $300 million in federal funds had been allocated to the program. Each state determined the amount consumers would be reimbursed under the plan, ranging from $50 to $250.

REGREEN Program

There is no official certification yet for a remodeled green home, but the REGREEN program, a partnership between the American Society of Interior Designers (ASID) Foundation and the U.S. Green Building Council (USGBC), has produced REGREEN Residential Remodeling Guidelines. The REGREEN guidelines address the major elements of any green renovation project, including the site of the home, water efficiency, material and resources, and indoor environmental quality. The guidelines combine product selection, building systems integration, and proven technologies to make a compilation of green strategies and case studies. Homeowners can use the guidelines for their own do-it-yourself projects or consult a professional who can apply REGREEN as a design guideline. Participants in the REGREEN certificate program have a demonstrated mastery of green building information. REGREEN guidelines can be found on the REGREEN website (**www.regreenprogram.org/docs/regreen_guidelines.pdf**).

Green Neighborhoods

An environmentally friendly home is good, but an environmentally friendly neighborhood is even better. A green neighborhood preserves native vegetation, makes it easy for residents to walk or bike to stores and restaurants, provides recreational areas and play spaces for children, and creates a social environment in which neighbors interact. Certain architectural features such as front porches encourage residents to spend time outdoors and form relationships with surrounding families. Beautiful landscaping gives pleasure to passers-by. Some developers specialize in creating green neighborhoods with sidewalks, bike paths, parks, nearby shopping areas, and homes with porches close to the street.

If you are doing a renovation or a green historical restoration to your home, look for opportunities to make your neighborhood greener too. Neighbors on adjoining sites might be interested in doing similar renovations and saving money by buying goods and services in bulk.

Conclusion

A green home renovation project can be as simple as switching out your incandescent light bulbs with CFLs or as complex as gutting your whole house, rearranging the interior, and replacing the roof. Green renovation not only saves on energy bills and increases your family's well-being, but it also benefits everyone by reducing the strain placed on the environment. Selecting green materials and technologies for your project also stimulates the demand for environmentally friendly products and services and will eventually help to bring manufacturing costs down.

Chapter 12

Certification and Financing

ny product or building can claim to be green, but as the movement for sustainable building began to expand during the 1980s, it became clear that official standards are needed to certify that a building is truly energy-efficient and environmentally sound. Someone buying a house that is advertised as green needs to know exactly what the green features are and how they compare to other green homes.

The first certification system, the Building Research Establishment's Environmental Assessment Method (BREEAM), was established in 1990 in the U.K. to measure the sustainability of new commercial buildings. The first program in the U.S. was Leadership in Energy and Environmental Design (LEED), introduced in 1994 by the U.S. Green Building Council (USGBC). The Green Globes® rating system for commercial buildings, an outgrowth of BREEAM, is administered in the U.S. by the Green Building Initiative (GBI) (**www.thegbi.org/green-globes**). The GBI works with local homebuilders associations to develop green building standards and practices. A directory of these homebuilders associations can be found on the GBI website (**www.thegbi.org/residential**).

Most green building assessment systems assign scores for a building's performance in different categories such as energy efficiency, waste management, water use, and land use. Green certification programs are constantly being re-evaluated and updated to reflect new information and an increasingly global view of environmental impact. Although there is no requirement that a building must be certified in order to be officially considered a green building, many developers and companies choose to seek certification because it adds a level of credibility to their claims of building green. Certification may be required in order to qualify for certain financial incentives, and lenders, investors, tenants, and prospective buyers are willing to pay more if a building is officially certified. Certification increases market demand for sustainable building, and fosters competition that will eventually result in the construction of more high-quality, high-performance homes.

The certification process adds to the cost of a green building project. Certain standards must be met when making decisions about design, building materials, and technologies. Additional work must be done to submit required documentation, conduct inspections and verify that the building is meeting green objectives, and certification fees must be paid. Some building owners choose not to have their buildings certified but still follow the certification guidelines to guarantee that they achieve the maximum in energy efficiency, water use reduction, and waste reduction.

Many state, city, and local governments sponsor green building programs and provide green building checklists as part of their energy-saving incentives. Examples are Seattle's Built Green program (**www.builtgreen.net**), New York State's Green Building Tax Credit (**www.dec.ny.gov/energy/218. html**), and California's CalRecycle (**www.calrecycle.ca.gov/Greenbuilding**). These checklists are specific to the climate and building codes of each region. Some of these programs include inspections by local authorities.

LEED Certification

The U.S. Green Building Council (USGBC) is a nonprofit organization dedicated to pursuing and supporting a more sustainable world through green, sustainable building. The organization was founded in 1993 and today has more than 15,000 members through dozens of local chapters. In 1994, the USGBC recognized the need for specific guidelines and national standards of green building and formed the Leadership in Energy and Environmental Design (LEED) program, led by scientist Robert Watson, who served on the National Resources Defense Council. LEED was established to provide builders and other professionals with a specific framework for building green.

In 1998, the USGBC launched a building assessment program for new construction, now known as LEED-NC, with Platinum, Gold, Silver, and Certified ratings based on the number of points a building scored in several categories. LEED for Homes was launched in 2008. Since the certification of the first 12 LEED buildings in 2000, more than 36,000 commercial projects and 38,000 single-family homes have participated in LEED. In November 2010, the USGBC announced that the total footprint of commercial projects certified under the LEED Green Building Rating System had surpassed 1 billion square feet, and that projects totaling another 6 billion square feet are currently registered and working towards LEED certification around the world.

U.S. Green Building Council (USGBC)

The USGBC website (www.usgbc.org) provides valuable information on green building, including how to get your building certified as a green building and how to join a local chapter of USGBC. The website offers extensive resources, from courses and study guides on green building to articles and research on every area of sustainable building. The USGBC also hosts an international conference on green building each year, bringing together builders, architects, corporations, manufacturers, designers, and other professionals in the industry that are focused on green building and sustainable living.

LEED certification serves as an official recognition that your home meets green building standards for energy efficiency, sustainability, and indoor air quality. LEED certification increases the market value of your home and attracts potential buyers. It may also qualify your for tax breaks and incentives, and speed up your permitting process by demonstrating that your home complies with building codes and standards.

Determine whether you are going to be seeking LEED certification before you begin building or remodeling your home. The certification process is lengthy and detailed, and points are earned for each recommendation that you implement, beginning with site selection and design. Correct documentation must be prepared and submitted at each stage. Thousands of architects, consultants, engineers, product marketers, environmentalists, Realtors, and other building industry professionals have a demonstrated knowledge of green building and rating systems and processes. These professionals can suggest ways to earn LEED credits without extra cost, identify means of offsetting certain expenses with savings in other areas, and find innovative ways to combine green technologies in your building project.

If you want your home to be LEED-certified, contact a LEED for Homes Provider at the beginning of the design process. A directory of LEED Providers can be found on the Green Building Council website. LEED Provider organizations administer a team of "Green Raters" who verify that homes are built to meet the rigorous requirements of the LEED for Homes Rating System. The LEED Provider will verify that your project is eligible for LEED certification and assist with your registration. LEED for Homes Green Raters come out to the project site and actually ensure that green measures are installed, that all performance testing is complete, and that the performance benchmark is met.

In order to receive LEED certification, a home must be a single-family home. Multi-family units such as condos can be certified only if all the units in the building are included in the certification process.

A building earns LEED points for meeting green building standards in six categories:

- Sustainable site
- Water conservation
- Energy and atmosphere
- Materials and resources
- Indoor environmental quality
- Green design innovations

The number of points a building earns determines its rating — Certified, Silver, Gold, or Platinum.

You can find a detailed list of LEED requirements on the USGBC website. USGBC also sponsors a Green Home Guide (**http://greenhomeguide. com**), a forum with news, articles, and advice on green building.

National Green Building Certification

National Green Building Certification is based on the ICC 700-2008 National Green Building Standard™, the first residential green building rating system to undergo the full consensus process and receive approval from the American National Standards Institute (ANSI). The Standard defines green building for single- and multifamily homes, residential remodeling projects, and site development projects, while allowing for regionally appropriate best green practices. Four green certification levels for homes are available — Bronze, Silver, Gold, and Emerald. Land Developments can earn One, Two, Three, or Four Stars — depending on how many green practices are incorporated.

Green certified homes incorporate green practices in six categories:

- Lot & Site Development
- Resource Efficiency
- Energy Efficiency
- Water Efficiency
- Indoor Environmental Quality
- Homeowner Education

To certify a home, a builder first prepares a report using the NAHB Green Scoring Tool (**www.nahbgreen.org/ScoringTool.aspx**) and hires an accredited verifier to do a preliminary inspection and submit the application. After the application process is complete and a final verification inspection is carried out, the NAHB Research Center reviews the report and issues a Certified Green Home certificate.

The National Green Building Standard™ is revised every three years; the next revision will be released in 2012.

Certification and Legal Issues

The decision to seek certification involves not only an additional financial commitment from the building owner, but also a commitment from the design team and the construction team to fulfill the requirements. Many things could go wrong during the construction process that could ultimately cost the building its certification. A design might prove to be less energy-efficient than expected, a contractor could decide to cut costs by using a toxic product instead of an approved one, or the construction crew could fail to observe proper procedures for waste disposal. Such mistakes translate into financial losses for the building owner who has invested money to seek certification, as well as failure to meet the stated objectives of the building project. Who is responsible when a building fails to receive certification, and who must pay for corrections, repairs and resubmissions? Some important legal issues to consider, particularly when seeking LEED certification, are:

Does the language in your contracts specify each professional's role in earning the desired level of certification?

Contracts should specify who will track, collect, assemble, and submit the supporting documentation for a certification program. Architects, contractors, and other professionals must make it clear that when they sign off on a document for submission to LEED or National Green Building Certification, it does not constitute any other kind of warranty or guarantee.

Do your design professionals and consultants have experience with sustainable design, green building rating systems, and the corresponding certification process, and have they participated in other green certification projects?

Experienced professionals are familiar with the challenges and requirements of seeking certification for a building. They are already aware of legal pitfalls and will be careful to avoid them.

Does your contract specify green materials, systems, and products whose green performance has already been verified?

New materials, products, and innovative technologies are constantly coming on the market, but their efficiency may be untested and undocumented. If you are seeking certification, it is safer to stick to acknowledged green products and materials.

Have you carefully reviewed all federal, state, and local green building requirements, and the requirements for any green building financial incentives?

Zoning laws, building codes, and requirements for financial incentives vary widely from one location to another. Failure to comply could cost you a valuable tax credit or discount.

Have you made allowances for the uncertainties and complexities of green building?

Most green building projects are covering new ground of one kind or another. Budget extra time and money wherever possible, and be especially conscious when negotiating costs and deadlines. Contracts should include provisions for resolving disparities and renegotiating budgets and schedules when necessary.

A USGBC decision not to award LEED certification or LEED points can be appealed, but the process is time-consuming. Critics of LEED have suggested that a third-party organization should review appeals instead of the USGBC, and that a standardized appeals process with time deadlines should be implemented.

Permits and Zoning Requirements

As in conventional building, permit requirements for green building vary significantly from one county, city, or town to another. Some municipalities have developed a building permit process specifically for green building projects and those seeking LEED certification. Contact your local municipal building department for information on permits and zoning requirements for your county.

Contact the Right Office

A municipal building department can be called a variety of names, including the Building and Zoning Division, the Office of Public Works, or the Office of Community Development. Call your local government headquarters and ask to be directed to the department that handles commercial building permits.

Financing Your Green Building Project

Funding for green home building and renovation projects can be obtained from financial institutions and banks, as well as private investment companies and the federal and local government. Some small community banks, such as Green Bank in Houston, Texas, specialize in sustainable community development. Green Bank offers mortgages and home improvement loans for green building projects.

Energy efficient mortgages (EEMs)

An Energy Efficient Mortgage (EEM) credits a home's energy efficiency in the mortgage itself. EEMs give green home loan applicants the opportunity to finance cost-effective, energy-saving measures as part of a single mortgage and stretch debt-to-income qualifying ratios on loans. EEMs allow green home loan applicants to qualify for a larger loan amount in order to build a better, more energy-efficient home. EEMs are typically used to purchase a new home that is already energy efficient such as an ENERGY STAR qualified home.

An Energy Improvement Mortgages (EIMs) is a form of EEM that allows a green home loan applicant to include the cost of energy-efficiency improvements to an existing home in the mortgage without increasing the down payment. EIMs allow the borrower to use the money saved in utility bills to finance energy improvements. The cost savings on energy bills and maintenance more than compensate for the slightly higher monthly mortgage payment. Lenders of both EEMs and EIMs typically require a home energy rating with the estimated monthly energy savings and the value of the energy efficiency measures — known as the Energy Savings Value.

EEMs (and EIMs) are sponsored by federally insured mortgage programs (FHA and VA) and the conventional secondary mortgage market (Fannie Mae and Freddie Mac). Lenders can offer conventional EEMs, FHA EEMs, or VA EEMs.

Conventional energy efficient mortgages

Conventional EEMs, offered by lenders who sell their loans to Fannie Mae and Freddie Mac, increase the borrower's purchasing power by increasing the borrower's stated income by a dollar amount equal to the estimated energy savings. The Fannie Mae loan also adjusts the value of the home to reflect the value of the energy efficiency measures.

Freddie Mac: Energy efficient mortgages

The rules for a Freddie Mac energy efficient mortgage are:

- Freddie Mac permits using higher housing expense to income and debt to income ratios if the home is energy efficient or contains energy efficient items.

- The lender may document the mortgage file with: Appraisal report indicating the energy efficiency of the home; Form 70A, energy addendum; An established home energy rating system (HERS)

- There is no maximum amount the income to expense ratios may be extended due to energy efficiency, however all mortgages are now subject to a maximum 45 percent Debt to Income ratio.

- Freddie Mac permits purchasing a property that is to be retro fitted, refurbished, or improved with energy efficient components. The purchase price may include the cost of the property plus the actual cost of energy efficient improvements. The cost of the energy efficient improvements may be included in the mortgage delivered to Freddie Mac prior to completion of the improvements. An escrow of up to 10 percent of value may be established to complete the upgrades.

- An appraisal of a new or existing property that already has energy efficient components should include them in the value of the property along with an explanatory note in the comments section.

FHA energy efficient mortgages

FHA EEMs allow lenders to add 100 percent of the additional cost of cost-effective energy efficiency improvements to an already approved mortgage loan (as long as the additional costs do not exceed $4,000 or 5 percent of the value of the home, up to a maximum of $8,000, whichever is greater). No additional down payment is required, and the FHA loan limits will not interfere with the process of obtaining the EEM. FHA EEMs are available for site-built as well as for manufactured homes. Applications for an FHA EEM may be submitted to the local HUD Field Office through an FHA-approved lending institution. Additional information is available from HUD's Office of Single Family Housing. (**www.hud.gov**).

VA energy efficient mortgages

The Veterans Administration (VA) EEM is available to qualified military personnel, reservists, and veterans for energy improvements when purchasing an existing home. The VA EEM caps energy improvements at $3,000–$6,000. Green home loan applicants should ask their lender about a VA EEM at the beginning of the lending process. More information about VA EEMs can be obtained from the website for the U.S. Department of Veteran's Affairs (**www.benefits.va.gov/homeloans/rlcweb.asp**).

Tax and Financial Incentives

Tax credits and rebates for green building are available at the local, state, and federal levels. These include property tax incentives, construction and design incentives, and rebates for increased energy efficiency of HVAC systems. Research the local, state, and federal programs that correspond to the objectives of your project to see whether it qualifies. The North Carolina Solar Center at North Carolina State University (NCSU) and the Interstate Renewable Energy Council (IREC) maintain an online database of federal, state, and local renewable energy incentives called Database of State Incentives for Renewables & Efficiency (DSIRE) (**www.dsireusa. org**). It is funded by the U.S. Department of Energy's Office of Energy Efficiency and Renewable Energy (EERE) and is regularly updated. DSIRE allows you to search by geographic region and type of incentive. Many states offer additional tax cuts for specific green building practices, and allocate funds for grants to support water conservation and using renewable energy. Check with your local building department for information on the incentives your state and municipality offer. Your local government website probably lists incentive programs on its website.

As green building becomes more prominent and the industry grows, more federal, state, and local governments will establish incentives to encourage the implementation of green building practices. Always check with your municipality and with your state and the federal government before beginning a green project to ensure you are up to date on all of the incentives available and their accompanying requirements and restrictions.

The Residential Renewable Energy Tax Credit

A tax credit reimburses part of the cost of an energy-efficient system by reducing the amount of personal income tax you must pay. It is different from a tax deduction, in which you subtract itemized amounts from your taxable income. A tax credit is subtracted from the tax you owe after all deductions have been taken. It increases your tax refund or decreases the amount of tax you owe. The Residential Renewable Energy Tax Credit reimburses homeowners for 30 percent of the cost of installing a solar electric or solar water heating system at their residences.

The federal Energy Policy Act of 2005 first established a 30 percent tax credit (up to $2,000) for purchasing and installing residential solar electric and solar water heating systems, and a 30 percent tax credit (up to $500 per 0.5 kilowatt) for fuel cells. These tax credits were scheduled to expire at the end of 2007 but were extended through December 31, 2008, by the Tax Relief and Health Care Act of 2006. They were extended again, until December 31, 2016 by The Energy Improvement and Extension Act of 2008, and a tax credit was added for small wind-energy systems and geothermal heat pump systems. In February 2009, The American Recovery and Reinvestment Act of 2009 (H.R. 1: Div. B, Sec. 1122, p. 46) removed the maximum credit amount limit for all eligible technologies (except fuel cells) placed in service after 2008. It also removed a previous limitation on using the credit for eligible projects that were also supported by "subsidized energy financing." This restriction does not apply to projects placed in service after December 31, 2008.

The Residential Renewable Energy Tax Credit is regulated by the Internal Revenue Service (IRS). Here are the rules:

- The PV system must serve a dwelling unit located in the United States that is used as a residence by the taxpayer. The home served by the system does not have to be the taxpayer's principal residence.

- Eligible expenditures include purchasing equipment, labor costs for onsite preparation, assembly or original system installation, and piping or wiring to interconnect a system to the home.

- Expenditures on equipment are treated as made when the installation is completed.

- Systems must be placed in service on or after January 1, 2006, and on or before December 31, 2016. If the installation is on a new home, the "placed in service" date is the date of occupancy by the homeowner.

- If the federal tax credit exceeds the homeowner's tax liability for that year, the excess amount may be carried forward to the succeeding taxable year. The excess credit can be carried forward until 2016 — after that, it is unclear whether the unused tax credit can be carried forward.

- There is no maximum credit for systems placed in service after 2008. The maximum credit is $2,000 for systems placed in service before January 1, 2009.

There are some additional requirements for solar water heaters and wind generators:

Solar water-heaters

- Equipment must be certified for performance by the Solar Rating Certification Corporation (SRCC) or a comparable entity endorsed by the government of the state in which the property is installed.

- At least half the energy used to heat the home's water must be from solar.

- The tax credit does not apply to solar water heating for swimming pools or hot tubs.

Small wind-energy property

- There is no maximum credit for systems placed in service after 2008. The maximum credit is $500 per half kilowatt, not to exceed $4,000, for systems placed in service in 2008.

To claim the tax credit, you must fill out *IRS Form 5695: Residential Energy Credits* (**www.irs.gov/pub/irs-pdf/f5695.pdf**) and include it in your income tax return. Keep your receipts for the equipment and labor, and copies of Manufacturer's Certification Statements for each component. A Manufacturer's Certification Statement is a signed statement from the manufacturer certifying that the product or component qualifies for the tax credit. These certifications should be available on manufacturers' websites. If not, call the manufacturer.

> **TIP: The Residential Renewable Energy Tax Credit is not limited by the AMT**
>
> The alternative minimum tax (or AMT) is an alternative set of rules for calculating your income tax that determine the minimum amount of tax that someone with your income should be required to pay. If your regular income tax falls below this minimum, you must pay the AMT instead. If you pay AMT, you can still receive the 30 percent tax credit for geothermal, solar, and wind installations.

A homeowner who receives a rebate from a local utility for a solar installation does not have to report the rebate as taxable income. The rebate should be subtracted from the cost of the solar system before calculating the 30 percent tax credit — the credit is for 30 percent of the net amount paid for the system. A commercial enterprise has to report rebates as taxable income and would calculate the commercial solar tax credit or Treasury cash grant based on the original cost of the system before the rebate.

The Residential Energy Efficient Property Credit

Until December 31, 2010, the Residential Energy Efficient Property Credit reimbursed you for 30 percent of the cost, up to $1,500, of products that make your home more energy efficient. Eligible products included water heaters, furnaces, boilers, heat pumps, central air conditioners, building insulation, windows, doors, roofs, circulating fans used in a qualifying furnace, and stoves that use qualified biomass fuel. The credit could not exceed $1,500 for 2009 and 2010 combined. On December 17, 2010, President Obama signed the Tax Relief, Unemployment Insurance Reauthorization, and Job Creation Act of 2010, extending the tax credits for energy efficiency into 2011, but reverting to the lower levels that were in effect in 2006 and 2007: 10 percent of the cost of the improvement, up to $500, with a $200 maximum for windows, and several other set maximums. Under the new law:

- You can get a tax credit of 10 percent, up to $500, of the cost of insulation, roofs, and doors.

- The tax credit for windows is capped at $200 for windows with the ENERGY STAR rating.

- The credit for furnaces and boilers is capped at $150, and all furnaces and boilers must meet 95 AFUE standards.

- A tax credit of $50 for and advanced main air circulating fan.

- A tax credit of $300 for air conditioners, air source heat pumps, water heaters, and biomass stoves.

- There is a $500 lifetime limit. If you already received over $500 in these tax credits from 2006 to 2010, you are not eligible for anything more.

The rules for this credit are:

- The home must be your primary residence.

- Equipment must be new and in compliance with all applicable performance and safety standards as described in tax code. Consult the federal ENERGY STAR website (**www.energystar. gov/index.cfm?c=tax_credits.tx_index**) for details.

- The tax credit does not cover labor or installation costs for insulation, doors, and roofs, only the cost of materials. Contractors should supply you with an itemized bill that separates the cost of labor and the cost of the products used.

TIP: Ask your contractor ahead of time for an itemized bill

Tell your contractor before the work is started that you wish to apply for the tax credit and need an itemized bill. This will ensure the contractor provides you with correct information and documentation.

Some of the items eligible for the tax credit are:

- Metal roofs with appropriate pigmented coatings and asphalt roofs with appropriate cooling granules that also meet ENERGY STAR requirements.
- Bulk insulation products such as batts, rolls, blow-in fibers, rigid boards, expanding spray, and pour-in-place.
- Products that reduce air leaks including weather stripping, spray foam air seal in a can, caulk designed to air seal, and house wrap.
- HVAC units that meet ENERGY STAR standards
- Advanced Main Air Circulating Fans for furnaces
- Heat pumps
- Gas, oil, or propane water heaters
- Biomass stoves

Not all products with an ENERGY STAR rating qualify for the tax credit.

The Residential Energy Efficient Property Credit is also claimed on *IRS Form 5695*. In 2010, unless Congress changes the law, you cannot receive this credit if you are paying AMT.

Rebates

A rebate is cash given back to you when you make a purchase. A variety of rebates are available to reduce the cost to a homeowner for installing an energy-saving system or device. Rebates are offered by state and local governments, local utility companies, and manufacturers of solar equipment and energy-efficient appliances. Rebate programs are intended to reduce the energy burden on local utilities and decrease the use of fossil fuels by encouraging local homeowners to install solar systems. State and local rebate programs might be funded by federal stimulus money, state taxes, or a small monthly surcharge on all utility customers.

Manufacturers sometimes offer rebates as an incentive to buy their product instead of a competitor's. Some manufacturer rebates are part of government incentive programs to encourage the development of solar industries. A manufacturer's rebate may be paid directly to the solar contractor who installs your system and the savings passed on to you as a lower bill. State and local programs may hand you a check to reimburse you for all or some of the cost of your PV system after you have paid in full. Utility company rebates may be in the form of reductions on your monthly energy bills.

Financing a Green Remodeling Project

Because your green retrofit or remodeling project will add to the value of your home, it makes economic sense to finance the project using the equity in your home. You can finance your project using your home as collateral for a home equity line of credit or a second mortgage, or by refinancing.

Home equity line of credit

A home equity line of credit is a form of revolving credit in which your home serves as collateral. The credit line is usually set at 75 to 80 percent of the appraised value of your home minus the balance of the first mortgage. Your credit history and ability to pay may also be considered in determining the amount of credit available. The interest on a home equity line of credit is usually a variable interest rate that is calculated by adding a margin to the current Prime Rate or some other index. Other costs associated with setting up a line of credit may also apply and will vary from lender to lender.

Second mortgage

A home equity loan, or second mortgage, is a fixed-rate, fixed-term loan based on the equity in your house that you pay back in equal monthly installments over a specific period of time.

Cash-out refinancing

If interest rates today are significantly lower than when you first purchased your house, you are a good candidate for refinancing your mortgage. Use the accumulated equity in your home to take out a new loan at a lower interest rate, pay off your existing mortgage, and then use the remaining funds for your remodeling project.

Keeping to Your Budget

Once you have obtained financing for your project, it is important to make sure that your expenses do not exceed your budget. Plan to spend only 80 percent of the available funds, and put the remainder aside to cover unexpected costs and changes to the original plans. When you get bids or projected costs from a contractor, look over the details carefully and make sure that everything is covered — labor, waste disposal, shipping costs, service agreements, and any other additional expenses — before you sign the contract. As much as possible, verify that the project plans are the way you want them before work begins, because any changes you make later will cost extra. Finally, resist the temptation to expand the project. Focus on achieving the original objectives, and evaluate any upgrades carefully to be sure they are worth the extra money.

Conclusion

Most people do not have cash on hand to finance a green building project or retrofit. Because green building adds value to your home and saves money on energy bills, it is a sound investment and lenders are willing to cooperate. Federal, state, and local tax incentives and rebates can help to lower the costs of your project — check with your local government to see what incentives are available.

Conclusion

uilding green is rewarding on many levels. You and your family can live in a comfortable and wholesome environment, free of allergens and environmental toxins, where the temperature and humidity are always adjusted, and the lighting and noise levels promote peace and relaxation. You will pay approximately 60 percent less for energy bills than your neighbors living in conventional homes. The components in your home will last for a long time with very little maintenance and you will not have to spend money replacing them every few years. Insects, birds, and wildlife will be attracted by the native plants in your garden. You will have the satisfaction of knowing that you have acted responsibly and reduced your impact on the environment. Best of all, you have learned to think in a new way.

The lessons you learn during a green renovation project about environmental impact, the harmful effects of toxic materials, and the importance of recycling and sustainability will stay with you and the other occupants of your home for the rest of your lives. Whether you move into a new green home, do a major renovation, install a solar system, or just implement simple energy- and water-saving measures in your home, you will never again use a resource without thinking about where it came from and where it is going. You will become more appreciative of the materials and technologies you use every day, will begin to ask more questions, and willl take fewer things for granted.

Making your home energy efficient also educates you about your use of energy. You will automatically begin to consume energy, water, and other resources more carefully. Your ideas will gradually influence your children, family members, friends, and neighbors. You will make new friends — the green professionals and tradesmen who generously share their knowledge and expertise while they work with you on your project.

Many aspects of green building that are voluntary and even innovative today will soon be incorporated as standards in local building codes. As builders and tradesmen become more familiar with the new green products appearing on the market, they will become more common. The world energy crisis and the rise in fossil fuel prices are compelling everyone to rethink the way houses are built.

This book is only an overview of green building. You can find in-depth information about any topics that have piqued your interest by researching on the Internet, consulting contractors and manufacturers, and reading magazines and publications. One of the defining characteristics of green building is that it is uniquely local. The first place to look is near home — you will be surprised at the resources and green businesses that already exist in your area. I hope this book will be the beginning of a long and fruitful exploration!

Appendix A

Load Analysis Worksheet for Solar or Wind Electricity System

1. **Appliance.** Using a spreadsheet or lined paper, make a chart like the one shown here. You can download an Excel spreadsheet with the formulas for calculations already included from Home Power Magazine's website (**http://homepower.com/webextras/** - *Load Calc. Spreadsheet*). Go through your house, room by room, listing each appliance that uses electricity. Do not forget the power tools in the garage or electric tools that you use for your hobbies.

2. **Quantity.** How many of each appliance do you operate? For light bulbs, assume that each member of the family turns lights on and off when he or she enters and leaves a room. Count one light bulb for each person in the household, and estimate how many hours those lights are in use. Lights that are left on all the time or for extended periods should be counted separately. Lights of different wattages should also be separate entries.

3. **Volts.** Most AC household appliances run on 110 V, but a few such as power tools and clothes driers run on 220 V. Battery-powered electronics like laptop computers, cameras, and shavers run on 12 V, 24 V, or 48 V and typically come with a charger or transformer that converts AC current to the right DC voltage. If you are building a new house or buying new appliances, you might find a refrigerator or TV that runs on 12 V DC.

You can find the voltage of your appliances in several ways:

- Read the label on the back of the appliance or on the power supply. The voltage may be listed as 120 volts, 120 V, 120 volts AC, or 120 VAC. This is the maximum voltage at which the appliance runs.
- Check the manual.
- Consult a list of typical power consumption for similar appliances. (See chart below.)
- Use a watt meter to measure the watts actually being used as the appliance operates. This is the most accurate measure, because many appliances have a range of power settings (such as volume settings or heat settings on a stove) or have motors that switch on and off.

4. **AC or DC.** Note whether the appliance runs on AC current from a utility or DC power from a battery or transformer. This information will be useful later if you are designing an off-grid system.

5. **Inverter Priority (IP).** Appliances that are automatically turned on and off by thermostats or timers, like refrigerators and air conditioners, take priority over appliances that you can turn on and off at will. This is because you cannot control when they might draw electricity from your system. Appliances like washing machines and hair dryers do not have priority because you can deliberately avoid using them at times when your system is already heavily loaded.

6. **Run Watts.** The watt rating shown on an appliance label typically represents the greatest amount of power the appliance uses when it is running at its top setting. You can safely reduce this number by 25 percent for appliances that you never use at their highest settings, such as your television or speaker system. Some appliance labels list only the current (amperage) and voltage. Amperage may be expressed as 0.5 amps, 0.5 A, or 500 mA. To calculate run wattage, simply multiply the volts and the amps.

$$W \text{ (power)} = V \times A$$

You can obtain the most accurate estimates by using a volt meter. When measuring the current drawn by an appliance using a motor, the meter will show about three times more current in the first second as the motor starts up than when the motor is running.

7. **Hours per Day.** Write down how many hours a day the appliance is used on the days when you use it. Appliances controlled by thermostats or timers have duty cycles when they are running and other times when they shut off. You will either need to observe when they are turning on and off during the day, or use a volt meter to find how much power they use. Remember that these appliances may run for longer hours in summer or winter.

8. **Days per Week.** Write down how many days per week the appliance is in use.

9. **Phantom Load.** Appliances that consume power when they are turned off are called **phantom loads.** Note whether the appliance has a phantom load. Phantom loads use small amounts of electricity 24 hours a day, and over time these small amounts add up. Examples of phantom loads are appliances with digital clocks or timers, appliances with remote controls, chargers, and appliances with wall cubes (the little boxes with power cords that plug into AC outlets). Wall cubes consume 20 to 50 percent of the appliance's total wattage when the appliance is turned off. To control phantom loads, unplug these appliances when not in use, or plug them into a power strip that can be turned off with a master switch.

10. **Watt Hours per Day.** Use the information from previous columns to calculate how much electricity each appliance uses on an average day.

Average Watt-hours per Day =
Quantity x Run Watts x Hours per Day x Days per Week ÷ 7 Days

Add up all these amounts. The total is the daily rate of electricity consumption that your off-grid PV system will have to support, which will determine the cost of your system.

11. **Percent of Total.** Using your figure for total daily consumption of electricity, calculate what percentage of the total is represented by each appliance.

Percentage of Average Daily Load =
Individual Average Watt-hours per Day ÷
Total Average Watt-hours per Day

Sample Load Analysis Worksheet

Appliance	Quan-tity	Volts	AC or DC	IP Y/N	Run Watts	Hours/ Day	Days/ Week	Ph-L Y/N	W-hours per day	Per-cent of Total
Refrig-erator (sample)										
TOTAL										

Average Wattage of Common Appliances

Appliance	Watts
Aquarium	50–1210
Clook radio	10
Coffee maker	900–1200
Clothes washer	350–500
Clothes dryer	1800–5000
Dishwasher (using the drying feature greatly increases energy consumption)	1200–2400
Dehumidifier	785
Electric blanket- Single/Double	60 / 100
Fans	
Ceiling	65–175

Window	55–250
Furnace	750
Whole house	240–750
Gas Dryer	300-400
Hair dryer	1200–1875
Heater (portable)	750–1500
Clothes iron	1000–1800
Microwave oven	750–1600
Personal computer	
CPU - awake/asleep	120 / 30 or less
Monitor - awake/asleep	150 / 30 or less
Laptop	50
Printer - Ink Jet	50
Printer - Laser	600
Radio (stereo)	70–400
Refrigerator (frost-free, 16 cubic feet)	725
Televisions (color)	
19"	65–110
27"	113
36"	133
53"-61" Projection	170
Flat screen	120
Toaster	800–1400
Toaster oven	1225
VCR/DVD	17–21 / 20–25
Vacuum cleaner	700–1440
Washing machine	200-900
Water heater (40 gallon)	4500–5500
Water pump 1/2 HP	500-900
Water pump - 1 HP	900-1500

Water pump (deep well)	250–1100
Water bed (with heater, no cover)	120–380

System inefficiencies

In addition to the electricity your appliances draw from your system, a certain amount of power is lost along the way due to inefficiencies in the batteries and inverter and resistance in the circuits. In order to ensure that your solar array will produce enough electricity for your needs, you will have to allow for this additional loss.

Batteries do not discharge 100 percent of the energy they store when they are charged. Charge Cycle Efficiency is a measure of the percentage of energy you can draw from the battery compared to the amount of energy used to charge it. Your battery manufacturer can supply you with the information, but the Charge Cycle Efficiency for standard industrial batteries is typically 95 percent. Whether you are designing an off-grid system or a grid tie system with battery backup, the energy from your solar panels is stored in batteries and then fed to your electrical circuits. You will need to compensate by adding another 5 percent of your total watt hours per day to your load analysis.

If your system is using an inverter to convert DC to AC, it typically loses about 10 percent of the energy flowing into it. You can get exact specifications from the manufacturer, but you would be safe adding another 10 percent of your total watt hours per day to your load analysis.

Low-voltage energy is also lost when it travels through cables for a distance. If you are installing a solar array on the ground or on a separate shed, you will also need to allow for loss due to resistance.

Completing a load analysis has given you the first specification for your PV system design — exactly how much energy it needs to produce. This is the final goal of your PV system design. The load analysis also shows which appliances use the most electricity and where you might be able to make changes that will improve the energy efficiency of your home.

Estimating the size of your solar or wind system

To estimate the size of the solar system you need to meet your energy requirements, take the total watt hours per day from Column 10 of your Load Analysis Worksheet and divide it by the lowest average irradiance for the year. This will give you the approximate size of the PV system you need. If the house will not be occupied during the winter months, you can exclude them and choose the month with the lowest irradiance during the period when the house will need electricity.

**Total Watt Hours per Day ÷ Lowest Average Irradiance =
Size of PV System**

For example, if you live near Orlando and you have calculated that your home uses an average of 800 kWh per day:

$$800 \div 3.08 = 259.74$$

You need a 260 watt solar array.

The output listed on the label of a solar panel is the amount of energy produced when that panel is exposed to full sunlight at solar noon in the middle of summer on a clear day. Depending on where you live, those conditions exist only for a short period of time, and not at all on cloudy and stormy days. The total amount of energy a solar panel can produce depends on the irradiance of its location. *The solar radiation maps in Chapter 3 show the average winter and summer irradiance for regions of the United States.* You need to know what the irradiance is for your specific location. NASA has been collecting data on solar irradiance for 22 years, and this data can be used to calculate the average monthly irradiation for your neighborhood. The National Renewable Energy Laboratory (NREL) PVWattsTM calculator (**www.nrel.gov/rredc/pvwatts**) determines the energy production and cost savings of grid-connected photovoltaic energy systems throughout the world. Solar Panels Plus LLC (SPP), a manufacturer, importer, and distributor solar power products, has a ZIP-Code Solar Insolation Calculator (**www.solarpanelsplus.com/solar-calculator**) that will give you the average monthly solar irradiance for your zip code. The Solar Electricity Handbook website (**http://solarelectricityhandbook.com/solar-irradiance.html**) has compiled solar irradiance data for cities and towns all over the world. Look up the solar irradiance in your area for each month of the year. Multiply the solar irradiance times the output wattage of a solar panel to calculate how much energy it can be expected to produce each month.

Below is the average monthly irradiance for Orlando, Florida, and Salt Lake City, Utah. You can see that though the yearly average irradiance is almost the same for both locations, there is a considerable difference between the estimated output in Florida and the estimated output in Utah during winter and summer months.

	Orlando, Florida Latitude: 28.4 Longitude: -81.4			Salt Lake City, Utah Latitude: 40.7 Longitude: -111	
Month	Irradiance in kWh/m^2*day	Estimated Output in Wh		Irradiance in kWh/m^2*day	Estimated Output in Wh
January	3.29	65.8		2.36	47.2
February	3.93	78.6		3.2	64
March	4.92	98.4		4.45	89
April	5.9	118		5.48	109.6
May	6.27	125.4		6.44	128.8
June	5.56	111.2		7.22	144.4
July	5.46	109.2		7.01	140.2
August	5.09	101.8		5.98	119.6
September	4.59	91.8		5.11	102.2
October	4.19	83.8		3.77	75.4
November	3.57	71.4		2.52	50.4
December	3.08	61.6		2.13	42.6
Yearly Average	4.65	93		4.64	92.8

Acronyms Used in the Book

AAC: Autoclaved Aerated Concrete

AIA: American Institute of Architects

ANSI: American National Standards Institute

APA: The Engineered Wood Association

ATFS: American Tree Farm System

BEE: Built environment efficiency

BIFMA: Business and Institutional Furniture Manufacturer's Association

BOMA: Building Owners and Manufacturers Association of Canada

BREEAM: Building Research Establishment's Environmental Assessment Method

BRE: Building Research Establishment

BRI: Building Related Illness

BTU: British Thermal Unit

CASBEE: Comprehensive Assessment System for Built Environment Efficiency

CBECS: Commercial Building Energy Consumption Survey

CCAEJ: Center for Community Action and Environmental Justice

CDM: Clean Development Mechanism

CFL: Compact Fluorescent Lamp

CLC: Closed loop cycle

CLMC: Closed loop material cycle

COTE: Committee on the Environment

CRI: Carpet and Rug Institute

DEP: Department of Environmental Protection

DfE: Design for the Environment

DIY: Do-it-yourself

DOE: U.S. Department of Energy

EEA: European Environmental Agency

EEM: Energy Efficient Measure

EERE: U.S. Office of Energy Efficiency and Renewable Energy

EIA: Energy Information Administration

EMS: Energy Management System

EPA: U.S. Environmental Protection Agency

EPDM: Ethylene Propylene Diene Monomer

EPS: Expanded polystyrene

ERA: EPDM Roofing Association

ERV: Energy Recovery Ventilator

EUI: Energy utilization index

EXPS: Extruded polystyrene

FEMP: Federal Energy Management Program

FPSP: Frost-Protected Shallow Foundations

FSC: Forest Stewardship Council

GBCI: Green Building Certification Institute

GBI: Green Building Initiative

GEM: Global Environmental Method

HBA: Home Builder Association

HEPA: High Efficiency Particulate Air

HFC: Hydroflourocarbon

HVAC: Heating, Ventilation and Air Conditioning

IGU: Insulated Glass Unit

GGA: Green Globe Assessor

GGP: Green Globe Professional

GWP: Global Warming Potential

I-BEAM: Indoor Air Quality Building Education and Assessment Model

IARC: International Agency for Research on Cancer

ICF: Insulated concrete form

IEQ: Indoor environmental quality

IFMA: International Facility Management Association

iiSBE: International Initiative for a Sustainable Built Environment

IPM: Integrated pest management

IUA: International Union of Architects

LCA: Life Cycle Assessment

LED: Light-emitting diode

LEED: Leadership in Energy and Environmental Design

LEED-AP: LEED-Accredited Professional

MDF: Medium Density Fiberboard

MIPS: Materials Intensity per Unit Service

MSDS: Material safety data sheet

NAHB: National Association of Home Builders

NAPCA: National Air Pollution Control Administration

NASA: National Aeronautics and Space Administration

NEM: Net Metering

NOAA: National Oceanic and Atmospheric Administration

NPDES: National Pollutant Discharge Elimination System

NRDC: National Resources Defense Council

O&M: Operation and Maintenance

OSB: Oriented Strand Board

OSHA: The U.S Occupational Safety and Health Administration

PCA: Property Condition Assessment

PCM: Phase change material

PEFC: Programme for the Endorsement of Forest Certification

PPE: Personal Protective Equipment

PV: Photovoltaic system

PVGFPD: PV ground-fault protection device

REC: Renewable Energy Credit

RFP: Request for Proposal

RFQ: Request for Qualifications

SBS: Sick Building Syndrome

SFI: Sustainable Forestry Initiative

SPF: Spray Polyurethane Foam

SPI: Sustainable Preservation Initiative

SRI: Solar Reflectance Index

TAB: Testing and Balancing

TIF: Tax increment financing

UFAD: Under Floor Air Distribution

UHI: Urban heat island

UL: Underwriters Laboratories

ULF: Ultra-low flush

UNEP: United Nations Environment Programme

USGBC: United States Green Building Council

VOC: Volatile organic compound

WTCA: Wood Truss Council of America

ZEB: Zero Energy Building

Helpful Websites

The Internet is a treasure trove of information on green building. The sites below provide detailed information on many aspects of green design and construction.

General Information

EPA: Green Building Statistics
(**www.epa.gov/greenbuilding/pubs/gbstats.pdf**)

Residential Building Codes, Construction Standards, Building Permit Information & Links (**www.b4ubuild.com/links/codes.shtml**)

Products and Materials

Reviews and Information

- Building Research Establishment Environmental Assessment Method (BREEAM) ECD and the Building Research Establishment (BRE). (**www.breeam.org**)

- DIY Flat Roofing (**www.flatroofsolutions.com**)

- Environmental Protection Agency (EPA) introduced its "Design for the Environment," or "DfE" label (**www.epa.gov/dfe/pubs/projects/ formulat/formpart.htm**)

- Formaldehyde (**www.cancer.gov/cancertopics/factsheet/risk/ formaldehyde**)

- Northwest Energy Efficiency Alliance (1998 – 2008) (**www.energyideas.org/products.aspx**)

- Reflective Insulation Manufacturers Association (RIMA) Radiant Barriers (**www.rimaintcrnational.org**)

- Strawboard panels (**www.toolbase.org/Technology-Inventory/Whole-House-Systems/strawboard-panels**)

- U.S. Consumer Product Safety Commission (CPSC) (**www.cpsc.gov**)

- Vegetated Roofs (**www.greenroofs.com**)

- *What Makes a Product Green?* BuildingGreen.com (**www.buildinggreen.com/auth/article.cfm/2000/1/1/Building-Materials-What-Makes-a-Product-Green**)

Sources and Manufacturers

- Dream Green Homes (**www.dreamgreenhomes.com/index.htm**)

- Durisol Wood Concrete Insulated Forms (**www.durisolbuild.com**)

- Sustainable Sources: Green Databases (**www.greenbuilder.com/general/greendbs.html**)

- Green Building Supply (**www.greenbuildingsupply.com//Public/Home/index.cfm**)

- Green Manufacturer (**www.greenmanufacturer.net/directory**)

- Nightscaping low voltage outdoor lighting (**www.nightscaping.com**)

- Truss Frame Construction (**www.truss-frame.com**)

- Information on structural insulated panels (**www.toolbase.org/pdf/techinv/sips_techspec.pdf**)

- Structural Insulated Panel Association (**www.sips.org**)

- Sustainable Sources: 17 years of online green building info (**http://insulation.sustainablesources.com**)

Indoor Air Quality

- Aerias AQS IAQ Resource Center, a resource offering information about indoor air quality (**www.aerias.org/DesktopDefault. aspx?tabindex=1&tabid=12**)

- EPA. *The Inside Story: A Guide to Indoor Air Quality* (**www.epa.gov/iaq/pubs/insidest.html**)

- Indoor air pressure an ventilation rate (**http://healthandenergy.com/ indoor_air_pressure.htm**)

- Indoor Air Quality Scientific Findings Resource Bank (**http://eetd.lbl.gov/ied/sfrb**)

- Indoor air quality in residential buildings (**www.aerias.org/desktopdefault.aspx?tabindex=3&tabid=79**)

- EPA information on radon in homes (**http://epa.gov/radon**)

- Facts about granite and radon (**www.radon.com/radon/granite.html**)

- *The Truth About Granite and Radon/Radiation.* Marble Institute of America (**www.marble-institute.com/industryresources/ consumerradonbrochure.pdf**)

- Washington Toxins Coalition (**http://watoxics.org**)

Insulation

- DOE Insulation Fact Sheet (**www.ornl.gov/sci/roofs+walls/insulation/ins_01.html**)

- Pros and Cons of Open and Closed Cell Spray Foam Insulation. (**http://sc.leadix.com/honeywell/files/LBM%20Journal%20OC%20 v%20CC%208-07.pdf**)

- *EcoHome Magazine* Product review: spray foam insulation (**www. ecohomemagazine.com/green-products/expanding-options.aspx**)

- Insulating Foundations (**www.espenergy.com/insulating_foundations.htm**)

- *Environmental Building News* "Insulation: Thermal Performance is Just the Beginning." (**www.toollending.com/UCBxweb/readings/EBN- insulation.pdf**)

- Insulation tips from the Natural Handyman (**www.naturalhandyman.com/iip/infxtra/infinsul2.html**)

- *Is Spray Foam Green Insulation?* (**www.sprayfoam.com/npps/story.cfm?nppage=187**)

- *Building Science Digests.* Understanding Vapor Barriers (**www.building science.com/documents/digests/bsd-106-understanding-vapor-barriers?topic=resources/more-topics/vapor_barrier_code_changes**)

- Radiant Barrier Attic Fact Sheet. Energy and Transportation Science Division. (**www.ornl.gov/sci/ees/etsd/btric/RadiantBarrier/index.shtml**)

- Spray polyuerthane foam health and safety (**www.spraypolyurethane.org/Main-Menu-Category/Consumers.aspx**)

- Spray insulation (**www.sky-side.com/Spray Insulation.html**)

- Spray foam roofing (**www.sprayfoam.com/newsarchives/archivedetails.cfm?id=192**)

- Super Therm® coatings: specs and uses (**www.spicoatings.com/products/supertherm/specs**)

- Ecologic spray foam insulation ask the experts (**www.ecologicinsulation.com/Questions.html**)

Interior Furnishings

- Carpet and Rug Institute (CRI) Green Label program (**www.carpet-rug.org/commercial-customers/green-building-and-the-environment/green-label-plus**)

- Flooring (**www.sierraclubgreenhome.com/go green/flooring/concrete-stone-terrazzo-and-tile-floors**)

- Richlite flooring (**www.richlite.com**)

Wood

- Bedford Technology manufactures recycled plastic decking and fencing (**www.plasticboards.com**)

- Columbia Forest Products (**www.columbiaforestproducts.com**)

- ES+Wood™ non-toxic pressure treated wood (**www.eswoodtreatment.com**)

- Mother Nature Network *How to Find Environmentally Friendly Wood.* (**www.mnn.com/your-home/green-building-remodeling/stories/how-to-find-environmentally-friendly-wood**)

- Renew Plastics (Trimax Structural Lumber) recycled plastic decking and fencing (**www.trimaxbp.com**).

- Roseburg SkyBlend particleboard (**http://roseburg.com**)

- SierraPine composite wood products (**www.sierrapine.com**)

- Smith & Fong Co. - Plyboo® bamboo plywood and bamboo flooring, and Durapalm® (**http://www.plyboo.com/products.html**)

- Sustainable Procurement of Wood and Paper-Based Products. (**www.sustainableforestprods.org**)

- Sustainable Woods Network (**www.sustainablewoods.com/index.php**)

- Wagner, John D. "SFI vs FSC: A wood certification battle with high stakes for dealers, builders and homeowners." *LBM Journal.* April, 2010. (**www.sfiprogram.org/files/pdf/LBMJournal_SFIvsFSC.pdf**)

- "Wood as a Building Material" (**http://cecontracosta.ucdavis.edu/files/28653.pdf**)

- Engineered Wood: Building Material: Practice Green, Renewable Construction with Beams, Framing, Siding (**www.suite101. com/content/engineered-wood-building-material-a61971#ixzz16cssYAnK**)

- TimberSil® wood (**www.timbersilwood.com**)

Green Professionals and Services

- American Institute of Architects (AIA) (**www.aia.org**)

- Austin Energy Green Building Professionals Directory (**www.austinenergy.com/energy%20Efficiency/Programs/Green%20 Building/Resources/usingDirectory.htm**)

- California's Build It Green (**www.builditgreen.org/en/directories/search.asp**)

- Green Building Certification Institute's (GBCI) LEED Professional Directory (**https://ssl27.cyzap.net/gbcicertonline/onlinedirectory**)

- "Find A Pro" directory on the USGBC's Green Home Guide website (**http://greenhomeguide.com/findapro**).

- Low Impact Living (**www.lowimpactliving.com/categories**)

- Rand Soellner Home Architects (**www.homearchitects.com/home-design-philosophy**)

- National Association of Home Builders' Directory of Professionals with Home Building Designations (**www.nahb.org/directory.aspx?directoryID=1415**).

- Northwest EcoBuilding Guild (**www.ecobuilding.org**)

- Sustainable Sources (**http://directory.greenbuilder.com/search.gbpro**)

- ZeroEnergy Design (**www.zeroenergy.com**)

Energy efficient roofing options

- The Cool Colors Project (**http://coolcolors.lbl.gov**)

- ENERGY STAR roofs (**www.energystar.gov/index.cfm?c=roof_prods.pr_crit_roof_products**)

- ENERGY STAR roof products (**www.energystar.gov/index.cfm?c=roof_prods.pr_other_roof_products**)

- Lexis reflective roof coatings (**www.lexiscoatings.com/reflective-coatings/solar-reflectance/**)

- Solar radiation control (**www.ornl.gov/sci/roofs+walls/facts/SolarRadiationControl.htm**)

- Cool Roof Rating Council (CRRC) online directory of cool roofing products (**www.coolroofs.org/products/search.php**)

- "Saving Energy with Reflective Roof Coatings." *Home Energy Magazine Online* May/June 1994 (**www.homeenergy.org/archive/hem.dis.anl.gov/eehem/94/940509.html**)

Design

- Institute for Human Centered Design (**http://www.adaptenv.org/universal**)

- Center for Universal Design at North Carolina State University: (**www.design.ncsu.edu/cud**)

- Built Green checklists for certification (**www.builtgreen.net/checklists.html**).

- Free Green house plans (**www.freegreen.com**)

- The Modern Cottage (**www.modcottage.org**)

- Decorated Shed (**www.decoratedshed.com**)

- Small House Society (**www.resourcesforlife.com/small-house-society**)

- *Small House Style* magazine (**www.smallhousestyle.com**)

- Sustainable renovation guides (**http://vancouver.ca/sustainability/RenovationGuides.htm**)

- "The Best of Green Design:Overview". *Popular Mechanics.* (**www.popularmechanics.com/science/environment/4212653**)

- Moss tiny houses (**http://tinyhouseblog.com/tiny-house-for-sale/ moss-tiny-houses/#more-15838**)

- The Passive House Institute (**www.passivehouse.us/passiveHouse/PassiveHouseInfo.html**)

Energy

- Carbon footprint calculator (**www.carbonfootprint.com/calculator.aspx**)

- Carbon footprint calculator (**www.nature.org/initiatives/climate change/calculator/?gclid=CImTnI_er6UCFU1m7Aodn0bEbQ**)

- ENERGY STAR Target Finder (**www.energystar.gov/index. cfm?c=new_bldg_design.bus_target_finder**)

- EnergySavvy.com (**www.energysavvy.com**)

- EPA household emissions calculator (**www.epa.gov/climatechange/emissions/ind_calculator.html**)

Financing

- *The Borrower's Guide to Financing Solar Energy Systems: A Federal Overview* (**www.nrel.gov/docs/fy99osti/26242.pdf**)

- ENERGY STAR new homes partner location (**www.energystar.gov/index.cfm?fuseaction=new_homes_partners.locator**)

- GreenandSave.com ROI Tables (**www.greenandsave.com/master_roi_table.html**)

- U.S. Department of Housing and Urban Development (**www.hud.gov**).

- Green Home Building questions about financing (**www.greenhomebuilding.com/QandA/financial/cost.htm**)

Foundations

- Precast Concrete Foundation Walls. (**www.askthebuilder.com/266_Precast_Concrete_Foundation_Walls_-_Oh_Yeah_.shtml**)

- Frost-protected shallow foundations (**www.toolbase.org/Technology-Inventory/Foundations/frost-protected-shallow-foundations**)

- Fly ash concrete (**www.toolbase.org/Technology-Inventory/Foundations/fly-ash-concrete**)

Landscaping

- Native plant database (**www.wildflower.org/plants**)

- NC State's guide to creating a native landscape (**www.ncsu.edu/goingnative/create/index.html**)

- Irrigation water conservation (**www.irrigationtutorials.com/faq/save-water.htm**)

- Trees and clean air (**http://ecology.com/features/trees-air-quality/trees-clean-air.html**)

- Environmental Health Perspective's *Why the Grass Isn't Always Greener* (**http://ehp.niehs.nih.gov/docs/1998/106-8/focus.html**)

Certification

- BIFMA (Business and Institutional Furniture Manufacturers' Association) (**www.bifma.org**)

- Cradle to Cradle® certification -McDonough Braungart Design Chemistry (MBDC) (**www.mbdc.com**)

- Getting Started on Your LEED Home (**http://greenhomeguide.com/ getting-started-on-your-leed-home**)

- Green Home Building Rating Systems – A Sample Comparison. NAHB. (**www.nahbgreen.org/Content/pdf/ GreenHomeRatingComparison.pdf**)

- ISEAL Alliance (**www.isealalliance.org**)

- U.S. Green Building Council (**www.usgbc.org**)

- NAHB's Voluntary Mdoel Green Home Building Guidelines (**www. scribd.com/doc/2363067/NAHBs-Voluntary-Model-Green-Home-Building-Guidelines**)

- NAHB National Green Certification Program (**www.nahbgreen.org/Certification/default.aspx**)

- Rainforest Alliance - Rediscovered Wood and Underwater Salvage (**www. rainforest-alliance.org/forestry/certification/rediscovered-wood**)

- REGREEN Residential Remodeling Guidelines (**www.regreenprogram.org/docs/regreen_guidelines.pdf**).

Walls

- Dynamic Thermal Performance and Energy Benefits of Using Massive Walls in Residential Buildings (**www.ornl.gov/sci/roofs+walls/ research/detailed_papers/dyn_perf/thermal.html**)

- Straw-bale construction (**www.greenhomebuilding.com/pdf/ buildingstandards_strawbale.pdf**)

- Wrapping the House: Do's and Don'ts (**www.boardwalkbuilders.com/ pages/art/art8.htm**)

Water

- ENERGY STAR Summary of Residential Water Heater Programs. (**www.energystar.gov/ia/partners/downloads/ SummaryResidentialWaterHeaterPrograms.pdf**)

- EPA – Water Efficiency (**www.epa.gov/ow/water_efficiency.html**)

- How to use grey water (**http://greenhomeguide.com/know-how/article/easy-as-1-2-3-how-to-use-greywater-to-save-water-at-home**)

Wind Energy

- American Wind Energy Association (**www.awea.org**)

- DOE Wind & Water Program (**www.windpoweringamerica.gov/wind_maps.asp**)

- *Home Power* Magazine (**www.homepower.com**)

- National Climatic Data Center (**www.ncdc.noaa.gov**)

- Wind Energy Resource Atlas of United States, U.S. Department of Energy (DOE). (**www.nrel.gov/wind**)

Publications and Newsletters

- USGBC's Green Home Guide (**http://greenhomeguide.com**)

- Home Energy magazine (**www.homeenergy.org**)

- Living Green magazine (**www.livinggreenmag.com**)

- ProudGreenHome.com (**www.proudgreenhome.com**)

Appendix D

Green Building Glossary

Acoustics – The science of managing noise levels in a building.

Action threshold – The point at which a situation requires action.

Active living wall – A vegetative wall incorporated into a building's air conditioning and filtration system and used to clean and de-pollute the indoor air.

Active solar heating – A solar heating system that collects heat from solar radiation and uses a system of mechanical pumps and fluids to transfer it to the interior of a building.

Aerator – A low-flow fixture that mixes air with water to slow down the water without affecting the pressure.

Air exchange rate – The rate at which outdoor air replaces indoor air.

Air-based system – A system that collects solar energy as heat and heats air in an air collector.

Ambient lighting – Lighting systems that provide illumination for an entire space. A typical example of ambient lighting is a florescent overhead lighting in an office space.

American Institute of Architects – A professional association of architects in the U.S.

Amphorous solar panels – The cheapest form of solar panel to manufacture but only have 6 percent conversion efficiency.

AP – LEED Accredited Professional.

Asbestosis – A lung disease that involves scarring of lung tissue caused by inhaling asbestos fibers.

ASHRAE – American Society of Heating, Refrigerating, and Air Conditioning Engineer.

Avoided cost – The utility's whole-sale cost to produce electricity, which is usually about one-fourth the retail price.

Backdrafting – When fuel-burning combustion appliances, such as space heaters, gas ranges, furnaces, fireplaces, water heaters, clothes dryers, and exhause fans in the home compete for air.

Backfilling – Filling in the earth around the outside of the foundation.

Baseline usage – The electricity consumption during the months when a homeowner is not running an air conditioner or a heater.

Batch collectors – A solar collector that heats water in dark tubes in an insulated box.

Below-grade drain – An underground drainage system that collects water and directs it away from the foundation of a building.

BIFMA – Business and Institutional Furniture Manufacturer's Association.

BIM (Building Information Modeling) – A three-dimensional building software that enables designers to manage the building design process.

Biodiversity – The diversity of life forms and ecosystems and species that exist in the world.

Biomass – Fuels derived from timber scrap, agriculture and food processing wastes, sewage sludge, and animal.

Biophilia Hypothesis – The concept that human beings have a genetically based need to interact with nature.

Blackwater – The excess waste water generated by toilets, showers, faucets, and other water systems.

BOMA – Building Owners and Managers Association.

BPA – Bisphenol, the most common building block of plastic and a known toxin.

Breezeway – A hallway that runs through the center of the house from the front door to the back door.

British Thermal Unit (BTU) – The amount of heat energy needed to raise the temperature of one pound of water by one degree Fahrenheit.

Brownfield sites – Abandoned industrial and commercial facilities and plots of land that can be cleaned up and reused for a new building.

Building commissioning – The verification by a third party that all the systems of a building are operating as designed.

Building envelope – The space between the interior and exterior of a building, which determines how well a building retains heat and cool air and how much energy is needed for forced air systems.

Building Information Modeling (BIM) – Three-dimensional building software that enables designers to manage the building design process.

Building related illnesses (BRIs) – Advanced forms of SBS that are diagnosed when the air quality of a building and its contaminants can be directly linked to specific illnesses.

By-products – Secondary products created as a result of manufacturing.

Carbon offsetting – The practice of investing in renewable energy in order to compensate for using energy generated from fossil fuels.

Carbon payback – The amount of time a solar panel must operate to compensate for its carbon footprint.

Cast-in-place concrete – A system where concrete is made and poured on-site into its final form.

Certificate of insurance – A legal document verifying that an insurance policy has been taken out on a property.

CFL – Compact Fluorescent Lamp, a lamp that uses a spiral fluorescent tube.

Charette – A brainstorming session that starts the green design process.

Clean Development Mechanism (CDM) – A program established by the United Nations as part of the Kyoto Protocol that certifies green projects in developing countries.

Closed-loop material cycle (CLMC) – A construction project that employs materials and building elements that can later be recovered and infinitely recycled through natural or industrial processes.

Color rendering index (CRI) – A way of measuring lighting levels in light bulbs that can be equated to different levels of natural sunlight.

Commercial Building Energy Consumption Survey (CBECS) – An assessment of the energy consumed in a commercial building.

Committee on the Environment (COTE) – A committee of the American Institute of Architects that advocate for buildings that are environmentally responsible.

Construction delivery system – The procedure for designing and constructing a building.

Controller – A device that manages the power going into and coming out of your batteries.

Conversion efficiency – The percentage of solar radiation that is converted into electricity.

Cool colors – Colored roofing materials with special reflective pigments or colors that have higher SRIs than similar dark-colored materials.

Cool roof – A roof material that strongly reflects solar radiation and efficiently emits the heat that it absorbs.

Cordwood – An ancient form of construction that utilizes short, round pieces of wood, stacked and set in mortar.

Corporate social responsibility (CSR) – The commitment by a corporation to positive and ethical business practices.

Cradle-to-cradle – A method for evaluating the impact of a product on both human life and the environment by assessing every synthetic and natural material and process associated with the product from inception through the manufacturing process, use, demolition, recycling, and ultimately to its non-use.

Daylighting – The process of using natural sunlight to illuminate space.

Deconstructability – Construction of a building using components that can be removed and re-used when the product becomes broken or obsolete.

Desiccant dehumidification – Removing moisture through absorption.

Dimensional planning – Creating a design that minimizes the amount of materials needed to achieve the objectives of a building.

Dioxins – Environmental toxins produced when organic materials are burned in the presence of chlorine.

Direct circulation system – A system where water is pumped through the collectors and into homes.

Direct exchange system – A heat transfer system that in which the liquid absorbing the heat is circulated directly to where the heat is transferred.

Drainage board – A board that is porous on the outside and contains channels to carry water.

Dual plumbing system – A plumbing system that provides clean water for drinking and washing, and recycles water from sinks and showers (gray water) for purposes like flushing a toilet or irrigating landscape.

Earth berming – Burying the lower parts of a house's walls, typically with 3 or 4 feet of earth.

Earth sheltering – Burying a house under soil that is then seeded with grass or plants.

Eaves – Projecting roof edges.

Eco-friendly – Causes little or no harm to the environment, minimally interfering with natural ecosystems

Eco-roof – Vegetative roof.

Ecological design – Using systems compatible with nature and modeled after natural systems to synergize with the surrounding environment and minimizing damage to the landscape.

Ecological footprint – The amount of land needed to provide the resources that support a specific population or a human activity.

Ecological rucksack – The total quantity of natural material (in pounds of kilos) that must be physically displaced to produce a particular product.

Embodied energy (Embedded energy) – An assessment of the amount of energy consumed during the manufacture, transportation and installation of all of a building's components and materials.

Energy audit – A building inspection that determines how to reduce energy consumption in a home and save the homeowners money.

Energy Information Administration (EIA) – A federal agency responsible for independent statistics and analysis.

Energy utilization index (EUI) – A measure of the energy consumption over time for each source of energy in a building.

Engineered wood – Wood products made by gluing together layers or wood fibers.

Environmentally friendly – Causes little or no harm to the envi-

ronment, minimally interfering with natural ecosystems.

Evacuated tube solar collector – One of the most efficient types of solar collectors that contains glass tubes. Inside each tube is a pipe with heat-transferring fluid, covered with material that collects heat from the sun.

Evapotranspiration – The plant process of transferring water from a surface to the atmosphere.

Federal Water Quality Administration (FWQA) – A division of the U.S. Department of Labor, replaced in 1970.

FEMP – Federal Energy Management Program.

Flat-plate collectors – A form of solar collector that has copper tubes fitted to absorber plates and are typically big enough to heat 40 gallons of water.

Footing drain – A perforated 4-inch pipe filled with gravel and covered with geotextile fabric to prevent clogging that carries the water away from the structure.

Footprint – The area of land required to sustain a human activity or an individual human's lifestyle.

Forced air system – A heating, cooling or ventilation system that uses pumps to move air through a building.

Formaldehyde – A toxic chemical used in many wood products and adhesives.

Free cooling – The process of cooling water and air by using the natural cooler external air temperatures.

Friable – Easily crumbled material.

Frost heaving – When accumulations of water in the ground expand as they freeze, forming ice lenses that push up the soil and displace the structures on top.

Frost-protected shallow foundation (FPSF) – Foundations that provide protection agains frost damage without excavating below the frost line.

Gallons per minute (gpm) – The rate at which water flows from a water faucet or through a plumbing system.

Geotextile – A fabric that allows water to soak through while blocking soil.

Geothermal energy – Heat stored in the earth from the decaying or organic matter, absorption of solar energy, and heat from the interior of the earth.

Geothermal heat pump system – A system that extracts and transfers heat and cool air from the earth to a building.

Geothermal systems – Cooling systems that circulate water through pipes burined in the cool earth.

Global warming – The slow rise of the Earth's average surface, air, and water temperatures.

Grade – The ground level of a building site.

Gray water – Wastewater collected from sinks and showers.

Green Building Certification Institute (GBCI) – An independent third-party organization that administers LEED certification.

Green power – The electricity represented by Renewable Energy Certifications

Green renovation – A complete makeover that may involve reconstructing some or all of an existing home's architectural features; replacing old equipment, appliances, furnishings, and flooring; installing energy efficient windows and doors; repairing walls, foundation, and roof and adding insulation; adding alternative energy sources; or changing the landscaping.

Green roof – Vegetative roof.

Greenfield sites – Building sites that have not been previously occupied by an industrial building and are used for new construction are called.

Greenhouse gases – Gases that retain solar energy in the Earth's atmosphere.

Greenwashing – The false advertisement of products, services or companies as environmentally friendly when they are not.

Grid fallback system – The power a solar array generates is storied in a bank of batteries.

Ground-source heat pump system – A system that extracts and transfers heat and cool air from the earth to a building.

Groundwater – The water that flows and seeps through the soil and rock underground.

Growing media – Plants, shrubbery, and greenery incorporated into a green roof.

Guyed towers – A wind power system tower that consists of lattice sections, pipe, tubing, and supporting guy wires.

GWP – A measure of how much a given mass of greenhouse gas is estimated to contribute to global warming.

Hard costs – Costs that can be clearly quantified and calculated.

Heat islands – Areas where the temperature is several degrees higher than surrounding rural lands.

Heat-loss analysis – This measure calculates room-by-room air conditioning loads for duct design purposes, and whole house loads for equipment selection purposes.

Heating climates – Cold climates where heating is required during part of the year.

Heating degree day – A measure of how often outdoor daily dry-buld temperatures fall below an assumed base, normally 65 degrees.

High Efficiency Particulate Air (HEPA) filter – A high-performance filtration device.

High Global Warming Potential gases (High GWP gases) – Synthetic gases such as hydrofluorocarbons, perfluorocarbons, and sulfur hexafluoride that are powerful greenhouse gases.

Housewrap – A material that keeps water from coming into contact with the structural sheathing and framing.

Hybrid heating systems – Passive solar heating systems assisted by mechanical fans and blowers.

Hydroelectric power – The generation of electricity through water movement; it is one of the most used forms of alternative energy production.

Hydrostatic pressure – Pressure created by the weight of water.

Inactive living walls – Vegetative walls that do not contribute to air filtration and are typically not hooked up to the building's air filtration system.

Indirect circulation systems – A circulation system them pumps a non-freezing, heat-transferring fluid through solar collectors. The liquid absorbs solar heat and passes through a heat exchanger where the heat is transferred to the home's water supply.

Indirect gain passive solar heating system – A passive solar heating system that uses a south-facing wall to absorb heat from radiation and gradually transfer it to the interior of a building.

Indirect heat exchange – A system that uses a transfer medium to carry heat.

Infiltration – When uncontrolled outdoor air flows into the house through openings, joints, and cracks in walls, floors, ceilings, and around windows and doors.

Insulated concrete forms (ICFs) – Blocks of expanded polystyrene — a form of recyclable plastic — that incorporate bars of reinforced steel.

Integrated pest management (IPM) – A pest control technique using knowledge of the biological cycles of insects and a minimum of pesticides.

Intensive vegetated roof – An integrated system of soil, plants, trees, and other shrubbery and greens that becomes a part of the outdoor environment.

Inverters – Increase the DC voltage coming from solar panels or batteries to the 120v AC voltage used for most household appliances.

Isolated gain solar heating system – A system that collects solar heat energy in a designated space, then circulates it out into the rest of the building.

Kraft paper – A high-strength paper made of softwood pulp processed with a sulfur solution.

Latent cooling – Using forced air cooling systems to control the humidity.

Lateral framing: Horizontal framing that provides resistance to wind and can be comprised of a number of different systems or materials, depending on the building type.

LEED – Leadership in Energy and Environmental Design, a set of official guidelines for designing and building a green building.

LEED-AP (LEED-Accredited Professional) – A professional who has passed the LEED-AP examination, demonstrating his or her knowledge of green building and LEED requirements.

Life cycle – A cycle that encompasses every phase of a building, product, or material's existence from its initial creation to its destruction.

Light emitting diode (LED) – A lamp that emits light when electricity passes through a semi-conductor.

Liquid-based system – A system that collects solar energy as heat and heats either water or an anti-freeze solution in a liquid-based collector.

Living roof – A vegetated roof.

Living wall – A vertical system of living plants that helps clean storm water or filter air in the interior of a building.

Loft – The depth or thickness of a batt insulating material.

Low emissivity (low-E) glass – Window glass with a very thin coating of metal that reflects heat and lowers the condensation levels on the glass

Low-flow orifice – A control at the bottom of a detention pond that regulates the egress of water.

Material efficiency – A measure of how efficiently a material fulfills its function.

Material safety data sheet (MSDS) – An information sheet required by the government that provides information on chemicals contained in a product.

McMansion – Large, showy homes built of inexpensive materials.

Mechanical ventilation – Devices that include both outdoor-vented exhausted fans like those used in kitchens and bathrooms, and whole-house air handling systems that remove indoor air and distribute filtered and conditioned outdoor air throughout the house.

Mesothelioma – A form of cancer directly linked to asbestos exposure, found most often in the lining of the lungs, abdomen, and heart.

MIPS (Materials Intensity per Unit Service) – A measure of the amount of service delivered by a product.

Modular block vegetated roofs – A garden of plants placed in smaller sections around the roof of a building.

Mudroom – A small entryway sealed off from the rest of the house by a closed door.

Natural building – Using natural materials for a building structure.

Natural ventilation – A process that allows the air to move through opened windows and doors.

Net metering – An arrangement that subtracts the amount of electricity supplied to a power grid by a building's solar system from the amount of electricity supplied to the building when the solar system is not operating.

Noise travel – A situation in which noise is audible at a distance from its source.

Occupancy sensors – Motion detectors that turn lights on automatically when someone enters the room and turn them off when the room is empty.

Off-gassing – The release of chemicals into the air from building materials, paints, flooring and carpet.

On-demand hot water systems – Systems that heat water only as it is being used.

Orientation – The position of the building on a plot of land and its position in relation to roadways, sidewalks, and landscaping.

OSHA – The U.S Occupational Safety and Health Administration.

Particulate – Indoor air pollution that consists of various types of particles suspended in the air, such as bacteria, viruses, dust mite feces, cockroach body parts, pet dander, fungal spores, pollen, particles and asbestos fibers.

Passive house – A house that aims to reduce energy consumption by 90 percent by using passive solar heating and natural cooling.

Passive solar heating – Heat radiated from surfaces that absorb solar radiation.

Payback period – The number of months or years it will take for the savings realized by the product to pay for its initial cost.

Permeable pavement – A method of paving roads, walkways, driveways, and other outdoor spaces to enable storm water to drain properly.

Pervious paving – A specialty pavement that enables water absorption and prevents runoff.

Phase change material – A material that is capable of storing and releasing large amounts of energy as it freezes and melts.

Phenolic resin – A binder used in engineered wood products.

Photovoltaic effect – When sunlight produces electricity when it strikes certain types of materials.

Photovoltaic system (PV) – The system that obtains, processes, and transfers power from the sun to usable energy within a building or home.

Point-of-use hot water system – Water heaters installed at faucets that heat water as it flows out.

Post-and-beam framing – A timber frame consisting of heavy posts (vertical members) and beams (horizontal members) held together by metal fasteners.

Post-consumer waste – Waste that is discarded after the consumer is done with it.

Powered attic ventilators (PAVs) – Fans mounted on the rooftop or a sidewall of the attic to move hot air out of attic spaces and lower the temperature under the roof.

Pre-consumer waste –Waste that is created during the product's manufacturing period before it reaches the consumer.

Primary energy – Raw fuel such as natural gas or fuel oil that is burned to generate heat and electricity on a building site.

R-value – A measure of a material's resistance to heat transmission.

Racking strength – The resistance of wall to wind loads.

Radiant heat systems – Systems that give off heat from a masonry stove, radiator, or a system of pipe.

Radon – A tasteless, colorless, odorless, radioactive gas that can cause serious health problems, including lung cancer and other respiratory diseases, if inhaled in large amounts.

Raised-heel trusses – Trusses that have the edges raised a few inches to allow the insulation to expand to its full thickness all the way to the edges of the walls.

Reclaimed materials – Materials that can be re-used in their original form for a new purpose.

Recyclable materials – Materials that can be recycled and used to manufacture new products.

Renewable resources – A resource that can be replenished naturally at a rate that is greater than the rate at which it is consumed.

Retention pond – A pond built to hold excess storm water runoff.

Retrofit – Upgrading some of a home's features or systems with a greener alternative, such as a solar power system or an energy efficient air conditioner.

Right sizing – Designing infrastructure and mechanical systems to accommodate future plans so that future modifications can be done with little additional cost.

Secondary energy – Heat or electricity created from a raw fuel and purchased by a building site.

Sensible cooling – Using forced air cooling systems to control the temperature.

Set points – The voltage level at which the controller switches on or off, or changes the charge rate.

Sick building syndrome – An illness that can be directed correlated to working in a specific building, but generally cannot be attributed to specific sources.

Site energy – The amount of heat and electricity consumed by a building as reflected in utility bills.

Slag wool – Insulation made from mineral fibers.

Soffit vents – Perforated panels or screens that allow air to flow in under the eaves.

Soft costs – Costs associated with benefits that are not easily measured, such as the cost of improving productivity or reducing absenteeism.

Solar collector – A box with glass sides that concentrates the sun's light into heat energy.

Solar gain – The heat that accumulates inside the house when the sun's radiation passes through the windows.

Solar power – Radiation from the sun converted into electricity through photovoltaics.

Solar reflective index (SRI) – A measure of the solar reflectance and infrared emittance of a roofing material.

Solar tracker – A mechanical device that changes the angle of the solar panels to follow the path of the sun so your solar array is always at the optimum angle.

Sone – A measure of the noise level produced by a fan.

Source-site ratios – The factors used to restate primary and secondary energy in terms of the total equivalent source energy units.

Stack effect – When temperature differences at the top and bottom of a house cause columns of air to travel upward or downward.

Stackwall – An ancient form of construction that utilizes short, round pieces of wood, stacked and held in place with mortar.

Stakeholder – Anyone who is involved in the planning, design and construction of a building, or who is affected by it in any way.

Storm water management – The science of controlling excess water runoff from storms.

Storm water runoff – Water from rain and melted snow that carries pollution from parking lots, fertilizers and pesticides into the water table.

Structural building components – Prefabricated framing elements such as roof trusses, floor trusses, and wall panels.

Structural insulated panels – High-performance building panels used in floors, walls, and roofs.

Sub-floor air distribution system – A heating and cooling system that is installed beneath the flooring.

Sump pump – A pump that removes water from a low-lying pool or reservoir.

Sun tempering – Solar heating by means of enlarged south-facing windows and other simple measures.

Superwindows – Windows that combine the best technologies and materials to produce a window that has an R-vale similar to a wall.

Surface water – Water that runs across the ground when it rains or when snow melts.

Surface water – The water that runs across the ground when it rains or when snow melts.

Sustainability – Using available resources in a way that does not deplete them for future generations and allows their use to continue indefinitely

Swale – A v-shaped trench with a layer of gravel or crushed rock in the bottom.

Swept area – The quantity of wind intercepted by the turbine.

Task lighting – Lighting that can be used for specific tasks. An example of task lighting includes lamps and small light fixtures at an employee's desk that can be turned on and off only when needed.

Tax increment financing (TIF) – A public funding method that uses future income from taxes to fund development projects.

Testing and Balancing (TAB) – The traditional procedure for verifying that a building's HVAC system is operating as it was designed to.

The Natural Step – A framework developed by Swedish oncologist Karl Henrik Robert for evaluating the health effects of materials selected for a building.

Thermal bridging – The process of heat loss or gain through a material.

Thermal storage wall – Trombe wall.

Thermography – Measuring surface temperature using infrared video and still cameras.

Tight envelope – A foundation and walls that seal out radon gases.

Tilt-down towers – Wind power towers that can be tilted and lowered to the ground during rough weather.

Timber framing construction – An ancient craft where the frame of a house is built of precisely shaped wooden posts and beams carefully fashioned to fit together and joined together with traditional mortise and tenon and dovetail joints and pegs.

Trombe wall – An exterior wall that collects solar heat energy and transfers it to the interior of a building.

U-value – The inverse of an R-value. The lower the U-value, the less heat transfers through a window.

Under Floor Air Distribution (UFAD) – A heating and cooling system that is installed beneath the flooring.

Urban heat islands (UHIs) – An area that has a higher temperature than areas around it. Heat islands are the result of solar radiation that becomes absorbed by all the buildings, sidewalks, and rooftops in a particular area, contributing to elevated temperatures in that area.

Urea-formaldehyde – An adhesive used for particleboard and medium density fiberboard (MDF) that offgasses formaldehyde and lowers IAQ.

USGBC – United States Green Building Council.

Vapor diffusion retarder – A membrane, coating, or sheet of solid material that impedes vapor diffusion in basements, ceilings, crawl spaces, floors, foundations, and walls.

Vegetated roof – A roof covered with plants growing in specially designed plastic trays that absorb rainwater and help insulate the building.

Volatile organic compounds (VOCs) – Harmful carbon-based toxins found in paints and plastics that cause long-term damage to the health of humans and animals.

Whole-house system – Viewing the building envelope as a single insulated unit and aims to prevent heat transfer through any part of the structure.

Xeriscaping – Landscaping with plants that thrive naturally without irrigation or fertilization.

Zero landfill policy – A commitment to recycling all waste products from a building so that nothing is disposed of in a landfill.

Zero-energy building (ZEB) – A passive home that uses solar energy, wind turbines or some other form of renewable energy to supply its electricity.

Bibliography

About NAHBGreen. National Association of Home Builders. (**www.nahbgreen.org/AboutNAHBGreen/default.aspx**)

"Advanced Framing Techniques: Optimum Value Engineering (OVE)." NAHB Research Center. Toolbase.org. (**www.toolbase.org/Technology-Inventory/Whole-House-Systems/advance-framing-techniques**)

"Below Grade Residential: Drainage Boards & Footing Drains." *Waterproof! Magazine.* November 2007. (**www.waterproofmag.com/back_issues/200711/drainage.php**)

Carter, Tim. Precast Concrete Foundation Walls. *Ask the Builder.* (**www.askthebuilder.com/266_Precast_Concrete_Foundation_Walls_-_Oh_Yeah_.shtml**)

Cooper, Arnie. "The Nature of Design." *August 2008 Environment News and Options Science & Environment.* Miller-McCune. July 14, 2008 (**www.miller-mccune.com/science-environment/the-nature-of-design-4430**)

"Cordwood." Greenbuilding.com. (**www.greenhomebuilding.com/cordwood.htm**)

Hurst, Timothy B. "Despite Recession, Green Building Soars in U.S.". *Earth and Industry.* November 15, 2010. (**http://earthandindustry.com/2010/11/despite-recession-u-s-green-building-sector-soars**)

Johnston, David and Scott Gibson. *Green From the Ground Up.* The Taunton Press. Newton, CT. 2008.

King, Bruce. "Straw-bale Construction." *Building Standards.* September-October 1998. Albuquerque, NM. (**www.greenhomebuilding.com/pdf/buildingstandards_strawbale.pdf**)

Lstiburek, Joseph. BSD-102: Understanding Attic Ventilation. Building Science Digests. October 27, 2006. (**www.buildingscience.com/documents/digests/bsd-102-understanding-attic-ventilation/view?searchterm**)

Marshal, Chris. "Close-up on Alternative Roofing: New materials make durable shingles." *Handy.* March – April 2002. (**http://namgnewsletter.com/dy/ROOFING.pdf**)

McHenry, Paul Jr., "Adobe: A Present from the Past." *Building Standards.* September-October 1998. Albuquerque, NM. (**www.greenhomebuilding.com/pdf/buildingstandards_adobe.pdf**)

Parkinson, Chris and Lauren Fleer. "Cabinetry 101." *GreenBuilder.* December 2007. (**www.neilkelly.com/files/Documents/News/Green_cabinets.pdf**)

"Radiant Barrier Fact Sheet." Oak Ridge National Library. (**http://www.ornl.gov/sci/ees/etsd/btric/RadiantBarrier/index.shtml**)

"Rammed Earth." Greenhomebuilding.com. (**www.greenhomebuilding.com/rammedearth.htm**)

Small Wind Electrical Systems: A North Carolina Consumer's Guide. U.S. Department of Energy. (**www.windpoweringamerica.gov/pdfs/small_wind/small_wind_nc.pdf**)

Wagner, John D. "SFI vs. FSC: A wood certification battle with high stakes for dealers, builders and homeowners." LBM Journal. April 2010. (**www.sfiprogram.org/files/pdf/LBM Journal_SFIvsFSC.pdf**)

Martha Maeda has lived and worked in Australia, Japan, Latin America, and several African countries, where she experienced firsthand how environmentally friendly buildings and construction techniques contribute to the well-being of people on every economic level. She currently resides in Orlando, Florida, and is an advocate for preservation and restoration of the natural environment.

Index